BUYING A HOME ABROAD

by

David Hampshire

SURVIVAL BOOKS • LONDON • ENGLAND

First published 1996
Second Edition 1998
Reprinted 1999
Third Edition 2002

Survival Books Limited, 1st Floor, 60 St James's Street
London SW1A 1ZN, United Kingdom
☎ +44 (0)20-7493 4244, ▤ +44 (0)20-7491 0605
✉ info@survivalbooks.net
💻 www.survivalbooks.net

British Library Cataloguing in Publication Data.
A CIP record for this book is available from the British Library.
ISBN 1 901130 46 0

Printed and bound in Italy by LegoPrint

ACKNOWLEDGEMENTS

My sincere thanks to all those who contributed to the successful publication of this book, in particular the many people who provided information and took the time and trouble to read and comment on the many draft versions. I would especially like to thank Joanna Styles (research for Country Profiles and Appendices), Joe and Kerry Laredo (proof-reading and formatting), Charles King, Louise Stapleton, Pam Miller, Veronica Orchard, Ron and Pat Scarborough, Adèle Kelham, Erik Gottschalk and Jean and Owen Bullock for their help, and everyone else who contributed in any way whom I have omitted to mention. Also a special thank-you to Jim Watson (☎ UK 01788-813609) for the excellent cartoons, illustrations and cover.

By the same publisher:

The Alien's Guide to Britain
The Alien's Guide to France
Buying a Home in Britain
Buying a Home in Florida
Buying a Home in France
Buying a Home in Greece & Cyprus
Buying a Home in Ireland
Buying a Home in Italy
Buying a Home in Portugal
Buying a Home in Spain
Living and Working Abroad
Living and Working in America
Living and Working in Australia
Living and Working in Britain
Living and Working in Canada
Living and Working in France
Living and Working in Germany
Living and Working in Holland, Belgium
& Luxembourg
Living and Working in Ireland
Living and Working in Italy
Living and Working in London
Living and Working in New Zealand
Living and Working in Spain
Living and Working in Switzerland
Rioja and its Wines
The Wines of Spain

What Readers and Reviewers

When you buy a model plane for your child, a video recorder, or some new computer gizmo, you get with it a leaflet or booklet pleading 'Read Me First', or bearing large friendly letters or bold type saying 'IMPORTANT – follow the instructions carefully'. This book should be similarly supplied to all those entering France with anything more durable than a 5-day return ticket. It is worth reading even if you are just visiting briefly, or if you have lived here for years and feel totally knowledgeable and secure. But if you need to find out how France works then it is indispensable. Native French people probably have a less thorough understanding of how their country functions. – Where it is most essential, the book is most up to the minute.

Living France

We would like to congratulate you on this work: it is really super! We hand it out to our expatriates and they read it with great interest and pleasure.

ICI (Switzerland) AG

Rarely has a 'survival guide' contained such useful advice This book dispels doubts for first-time travellers, yet is also useful for seasoned globetrotters – In a word, if you're planning to move to the USA or go there for a long-term stay, then buy this book both for general reading and as a ready-reference.

American Citizens Abroad

It is everything you always wanted to ask but didn't for fear of the contemptuous put down – The best English-language guide – Its pages are stuffed with practical information on everyday subjects and are designed to complement the traditional guidebook.

Swiss News

A complete revelation to me – I found it both enlightening and interesting, not to mention amusing.

Carole Clark

Let's say it at once. David Hampshire's *Living and Working in France* is the best handbook ever produced for visitors and foreign residents in this country; indeed, my discussion with locals showed that it has much to teach even those born and bred in *l'Hexagone*. – It is Hampshire's meticulous detail which lifts his work way beyond the range of other books with similar titles. Often you think of a supplementary question and search for the answer in vain. With Hampshire this is rarely the case. – He writes with great clarity (and gives French equivalents of all key terms), a touch of humour and a ready eye for the odd (and often illuminating) fact. – This book is absolutely indispensable.

The Riviera Reporter

The ultimate reference book – Every conceivable subject imaginable is exhaustively explained in simple terms – An excellent introduction to fully enjoy all that this fine country has to offer and save time and money in the process.

American Club of Zurich

Have Said About Survival Books

What a great work, wealth of useful information, well-balanced wording and accuracy in details. My compliments!

Thomas Müller

This handbook has all the practical information one needs to set up home in the UK – The sheer volume of information is almost daunting – Highly recommended for anyone moving to the UK.

American Citizens Abroad

A very good book which has answered so many questions and even some I hadn't thought of – I would certainly recommend it.

Brian Fairman

A mine of information – I may have avoided some embarrassments and frights if I had read it prior to my first Swiss encounters – Deserves an honoured place on any newcomer's bookshelf.

English Teachers Association, Switzerland

Covers just about all the things you want to know on the subject – In answer to the desert island question about the one how-to book on France, this book would be it – Almost 500 pages of solid accurate reading – This book is about enjoyment as much as survival.

The Recorder

It's so funny – I love it and definitely need a copy of my own – Thanks very much for having written such a humorous and helpful book.

Heidi Guiliani

A must for all foreigners coming to Switzerland.

Antoinette O'Donoghue

A comprehensive guide to all things French, written in a highly readable and amusing style, for anyone planning to live, work or retire in France.

The Times

A concise, thorough account of the DOs and DON'Ts for a foreigner in Switzerland – Crammed with useful information and lightened with humorous quips which make the facts more readable.

American Citizens Abroad

Covers every conceivable question that may be asked concerning everyday life – I know of no other book that could take the place of this one.

France in Print

Hats off to Living and Working in Switzerland!

Ronnie Almeida

CONTENTS

APPENDICES   235

INDEX   249

ORDER FORMS   253

IMPORTANT NOTE

Readers should note that the rules and regulations for buying property can vary considerably from country to country, and in some countries they even vary by region or are open to local interpretation! **I cannot recommend too strongly that you always check with an official and reliable source (not always the same) and take expert legal advice before paying any money or signing any legal documents. Don't, however, believe everything you're told or read, even, dare I say it, herein!**

To help you obtain further information and verify data with official sources, useful addresses and references to other sources of information have been included in all chapters and in **Appendices A** and **B**. Important points have been emphasised throughout the book **in bold print**, some of which it would be expensive and foolish to disregard. **Ignore them at your peril or cost.** Unless specifically stated, the reference to any company, organisation, product or publication in this book *doesn't* constitute an endorsement or recommendation. Any reference to any place or person (living or dead) is purely coincidental.

AUTHOR'S NOTES

- Frequent references are made in this book to the European Union (EU), which comprises Austria, Belgium, Denmark, Finland, France, Germany, Greece, Ireland, Italy, Luxembourg, the Netherlands, Portugal, Spain, Sweden and the United Kingdom.

- **Property prices quoted should be taken as estimates only**, although they were largely correct when going to print. Prices vary considerably depending on the local property market and the world economy, and have increased considerably in recent years in most countries.

- Times are shown using am (latin: ante meridiem) for before noon and pm (post meridiem) for after noon.

- His/he/him also means her/she/her (please forgive me ladies). This is done to make life easier for both the reader and (in particular) the author, and isn't intended to be sexist.

- All spelling is (or should be) English and not American.

- Warnings and important points are shown in bold type.

- The following symbols are used in this book: ☎ (telephone), 🖷 (fax), ✉ (e-mail) and 💻 (Internet).

- Lists of **Useful Addresses, Further Reading** and **Useful Websites** are contained in **Appendices A, B** and **C** respectively.

- For those unfamiliar with the metric system of weights and measures, imperial conversion tables are included in **Appendix D**.

- A **Service Directory** containing the names, addresses and contact numbers of companies and organisations doing business in the countries featured in this book is contained in **Appendix E**.

INTRODUCTION

If you're planning to buy a home abroad or even just thinking about it, this is **THE BOOK** for you! Whether you want a cottage in France, an apartment in Spain or a villa in Florida, this book will help make your dreams come true. The main aim of *Buying a Home Abroad* is to provide you with the information necessary to help you choose the most suitable country, the most favourable location, and the most appropriate home **to satisfy your individual requirements.** Most important of all, this book will help you avoid the risks and pitfalls often associated with buying a home abroad, which for most people is one of the largest financial transactions they will undertake during their lifetime.

You may already own a home in your home country; however, buying a home abroad is a different matter altogether. One of the most common (and sometimes disastrous) mistakes people make when buying a home abroad is to assume that the laws and purchase procedure are the same as in their home country. **This is certainly not true!** The system for buying property can vary considerably from country to country and in some countries even varies depending on the region or state. As many people have discovered to their cost, buying property in a foreign country can range from very safe through moderately risky to disastrous.

Before buying a home abroad you need to ask yourself numerous questions, not least *exactly* why you want to buy a home abroad. Is your primary concern a good long-term investment or do you plan to work or retire abroad? Where and what can you afford to buy? What about property taxes, capital gains tax and inheritance tax? *Buying a Home Abroad* will help you answer these and many other questions. It won't, however, tell you where to live and what to buy, or whether having made your decision you will be happy – that part is up to you!

For many people, buying a home abroad has previously been a case of pot luck. However, with a copy of *Buying a Home Abroad* you'll have a wealth of priceless information at your fingertips. Information derived from a variety of sources, both official and unofficial, not least the hard won personal experiences of the author, his friends, colleagues and acquaintances. This book doesn't, however, contain all the answers (most of us don't even know the right questions to ask). What it *will* do is reduce the risk of making an expensive mistake that you will bitterly regret later, and help you make informed decisions and calculated judgements, instead of costly mistakes and uneducated guesses (forewarned is forearmed!). **Most importantly of all, it will help you save money and will repay your investment many times over.**

The world-wide recession in the early '90s caused an upheaval in world property markets, during which many 'gilt-edged' property investments went to the wall, although prices have long since recovered. Property remains one of the best long-term investments and it's certainly one of the most pleasurable. Buying a home abroad is a wonderful way to make new friends, broaden your horizons and revitalise your life – and it provides a welcome bolt-hole to recuperate from the stresses and strains of modern living. I trust this book will help you avoid the pitfalls and smooth your way to many happy years in your new home abroad, secure in the knowledge that you have made the right decision.

Good luck!

David Hampshire
November 2001

1.

CHOOSING THE COUNTRY

Before deciding where, when, or indeed whether to buy a home abroad, it's important to do your homework thoroughly and investigate all the possibilities. It may be that you already know the country where you wish to buy a home and have a good idea exactly what you want – but have you thought about the alternatives? It isn't uncommon for buyers to regret their decision after some time and wish they had purchased a different type of property in a different region – or even in a different country. Unless you know exactly what you're looking for and where, you should rent a property for a period until you're more familiar with a country or region.

As when making all major financial decisions, you should never be in too much of a hurry. Many people make expensive (even catastrophic) errors when buying a home abroad, often because they don't do sufficient research and are simply in too much of a hurry, often setting themselves ridiculous deadlines such as buying a home during a long weekend break or a week's holiday. Not surprisingly, most people wouldn't dream of acting so rashly when buying a property in their home country!

This chapter will help you decide on a country and includes important considerations such as permits, retirement, working, communications, getting there (including motoring abroad) and getting around.

WHY DO YOU WANT TO BUY A HOME ABROAD ?

The first question to ask yourself is *exactly* why you want to buy a home abroad? For example, are you seeking a holiday or retirement home? Do you want a summer or winter holiday home, or both? Are you primarily looking for a sound investment or do you plan to work or start a business abroad? Perhaps you've been transferred abroad by your employer or offered a job abroad for a limited period (in which case it's usually better to rent than buy). Often there are a combination of reasons for buying a home abroad, for example many people buy a holiday home with a view to living abroad permanently (or semi-permanently) when they retire. If this is the case, there are many more factors to take into account than if you're 'simply' buying a holiday home. On the other hand, if you plan to work or start a business abroad you will be faced with a whole set of different criteria.

Can you really afford to buy a home abroad? What of the future? Is your income secure and protected against inflation? In the '80s many people purchased homes abroad by taking out second mortgages on their family homes and stretching their financial resources to the limits. Not surprisingly, when the recession struck in the early '90s many people lost their homes abroad when they were unable to keep up the mortgage payments. Buying a home abroad can be an excellent long-term investment, although in recent years many people have had their fingers burnt in the volatile property market, particularly in European countries such as France and Spain. In many countries, local people don't buy domestic property as an investment, but as a home for life. **You shouldn't expect to make a quick profit when buying property abroad (although it's possible), but should look upon it as an investment in your family's future happiness, rather than merely in financial terms.**

In most countries, property values increase at around 4 or 5 per cent a year (or in line with inflation), which means that you must usually own a home for at least three years simply to recover the costs associated with buying. House prices rise faster than average in some fashionable areas, but the stable property market in most countries acts as a discouragement to speculators wishing to make a quick profit, particularly when in many countries capital gains tax (see page 63) can wipe out much of the profit on the sale of a second home.

WHICH COUNTRY?

Having decided exactly why you want to buy a home abroad, the next thing you need to do is choose the country. If you're looking for a holiday or retirement home or 'simply' wish to make a long-term investment, you will be faced with a wealth of choices. There is, of course, no perfect country for everybody, although most people manage to find *their* particular dream home in *their* ideal country. Many retirees, particularly northern Europeans, spend the winter abroad and return to their home countries in the spring or summer. This allows them to take advantage of the milder winter weather abroad, e.g. in southern Europe, Florida or South Africa, and spend summer with their families in their home countries.

When choosing a country there are numerous considerations to be made. For example, do you want to enjoy year-round sunshine or are you only interested in a summer home? Do you want to live inland or close to the sea? Do you wish to ski, sail or play golf? Do you need or wish to be close (in driving or flying time) to your home country or another country? Do you fancy living on an island? City, town, village or country? Can you speak the language or are you willing to learn? Will you be able to sell (at a realistic price) should the need arise?

You may already have some preferences, possibly influenced by where you've spent a number of enjoyable holidays or where your family and friends already own homes. Whether you're looking for a permanent or holiday home, you should choose a country that suits your personality and tastes, as this will be a key factor in your future enjoyment. For most people the primary consideration is the climate, particularly if they're buying a holiday home. If you're buying a home that will be used between spring and autumn only, you won't be too concerned if it's deluged or buried in snow during the winter. On the other hand, if you're seeking a winter holiday home you will want somewhere with a reliable snow record.

Many winter sports enthusiasts dream of buying an apartment or a chalet in a ski resort, which can be an excellent long-term investment. The values of homes in winter resorts held up well during the property slump in the early '90s and are often a better long-term investment than homes in summer resorts. As an added bonus, homes in winter resorts also make attractive summer homes (particularly if you enjoy hiking or climbing) and offer the best of both worlds for sports and outdoor enthusiasts. Those in the market for a home in a ski resort can choose from many countries, including Andorra, Austria, Canada, France, Germany, Italy, Spain, Switzerland and the USA.

Before deciding on a country, you should do as much research as possible and read books especially written for those planning to live or work abroad (particularly those published by Survival Books – see page 253). It will also help to read property magazines such as **World of Property** and **International Homes**, and visit overseas property exhibitions such as those organised by Outbound Publishing. **Bear in mind that the cost of investing in a few books or magazines (and other research) is tiny compared to the expense of making a mistake!**

DO YOU NEED A PERMIT OR VISA?

Before making any plans to buy a home abroad, you must ensure that you will be permitted to use the property for whatever purpose you have in mind and (if applicable) obtain a residence or work permit. For example, a national of a European Union (EU) country can live and work in any other EU country, although retirees must meet minimum income levels. Non-resident foreigners are permitted to buy property in the USA, but most aren't permitted to remain longer than six months a year without an appropriate permit (green card) or visa.

If there's a possibility that you or a family member may wish to work or live permanently in a country where you're planning to buy a home, you should enquire whether it will be possible before making any plans. In some countries the rules and regulations governing permits and visas change frequently, therefore it's important to obtain up-to-date information from an embassy or consulate in your home country. **Permit infringements are taken seriously by the authorities in all countries and there are penalties for breaches of regulations, including fines and even deportation for flagrant abuses.**

RETIREMENT ABROAD

If you wish to buy a retirement home abroad or are planning to buy a holiday home with a view to living abroad permanently when you retire, you must ensure that this is (or will be) possible *and* that you will be able to afford to live abroad permanently. Note that if you don't qualify to live in a country by birthright or as a national of a country that's a member of a treaty zone such as the EU, it may be impossible to obtain a residence permit. Americans may find it difficult to retire in a European country and the USA doesn't permit foreigners without a green card to retire in America, irrespective of their income or whether they own a home there.

However, despite the bureaucracy and red tape encountered in some countries, an increasing number of people are retiring abroad and the number is expected to rise sharply in the future as more people choose early retirement. Many retirees seeking a home abroad are northern Europeans who can often buy a retirement home abroad for much less than the value of their family homes. The difference between the money raised on the sale of your family home and the cost of a home abroad can be invested to supplement your pension, allowing you to live comfortably in retirement, particularly when the often lower cost of living abroad is taken into consideration.

However, before planning to live abroad permanently you must take into account many factors including the cost of living, pension payments (some countries such as Britain automatically freeze state pensions when retirees move to certain countries), investment income and local taxes. In most countries, it's necessary for retirees to have a minimum income to qualify for a residence permit, and in some countries residents must also own a property (a long-term lease on a property may be insufficient). There are both advantages and disadvantages to retiring abroad, although for most people the benefits far outweigh the drawbacks.

Advantages: The advantages of retiring abroad may include a more favourable climate; lower taxation, lower cost of living, increased standard of living, and the availability of a wider range of leisure and sports activities at an affordable cost. For most people, one of the principal benefits is the improved health that results from living in a warmer climate and a more relaxing environment (provided you don't expect things to be done the same way as at 'home'). Those who suffer from arthritis and other illnesses exacerbated by cold and damp weather may enjoy longer and more agreeable lives in a warm climate, while those who suffer from stress are often advised to live in a country with a more relaxed way of life. However, if you're planning to retire abroad for health reasons, you should ask your doctor for his advice regarding suitable countries and locations. For retirees (and many others) the advantages of living abroad add up to an improved quality of life and an increased life expectancy.

Disadvantages: The main disadvantages of retiring abroad include separation from family and loved ones, language problems, boredom (what are you going to do all day?), the dangers imposed by too much sun and alcohol, overeating and too little exercise, poor social services, e.g. less state support for the elderly and infirm, dangers of disease and infection and inferior health facilities (in some countries), financial problems (e.g. high cost of living, high taxation, exchange rate fluctuations and poor investments), possible loss of pension indexation, homesickness (e.g. sadness or depression from missing friends and family), and culture shock. Before buying a retirement home abroad, you should also consider how you would cope if your mobility was restricted.

WORKING ABROAD

If there's a possibility that you or your family may wish to work in a country where you're planning to buy a home abroad, you *must* ensure that it will be possible before making any commitments. If you don't qualify to live and work in a country by birthright or as a national of a country that's a member of a treaty (such as the European Union), obtaining a work permit may be impossible. Americans and others without the automatic right to work in the EU must have their employment approved by a country's Ministry of Labour and obtain an employment visa before arriving in an EU country. Most Europeans find it equally difficult to obtain a permit to work in the USA or Canada (unless they buy a business).

Even when you don't require a permit, you shouldn't plan on obtaining employment in a particular country unless you have a firm job offer, special qualifications and/or experience for which there's a strong demand. If you want a good job, you must usually be well qualified and speak the local language fluently. If you plan to arrive without a job (assuming it's permitted), you should have a detailed plan for finding employment and try to make some contacts before you arrive. Being attracted to a country by its weather, cuisine and lifestyle is understandable, but doesn't rate highly as an employment qualification. It's extremely difficult to find work in most Mediterranean countries, particularly in rural and resort areas, and it's becoming increasingly difficult in most cities and large towns.

Prospects: Before moving abroad to find employment, you should dispassionately examine your motives and credentials. What kind of work can you realistically expect to do? What are your qualifications and experience? Are they recognised abroad? How good is your local language ability? Unless you're fluent, you won't be competing on equal terms with the locals (you won't anyway, but that's a different matter!). Most employers aren't interested in hiring anyone without, at the very least, an adequate working knowledge of the local language. Are there any jobs in your profession or trade in the country and area where you plan to live? Could you work in a self-employed capacity or start your own business? The answers to these and many other questions can be quite disheartening, but it's better to ask them *before* moving abroad rather than afterwards.

Self-Employment: Many people turn to self-employment or starting a business to make a living, although this path is strewn with pitfalls for the unwary. **Most people don't do sufficient homework before moving abroad.** While hoping for the best, you should plan for the worst case scenario and have a contingency plan and sufficient funds to last until you're established. Note that in many countries, anyone planning to start a business must do battle with notoriously obstructive local bureaucracies.

Research: BEWARE! For many foreigners, starting a business in a foreign country is one of the quickest routes to bankruptcy known to mankind! In fact, many foreigners who start a business abroad would be better off investing in lottery tickets - at least they would then have a chance of getting a return on their investment. Many would-be entrepreneurs return home with literally only their shirts on their backs, having learnt the facts of life the hard way. **If you aren't prepared to thoroughly research the market and obtain expert business and legal advice, then you shouldn't even think about starting a business abroad.**

Generally speaking you shouldn't consider running a business in a field in which you don't have previous experience. It's often wise to work for someone else in the same line of business to gain experience, rather than jump in at the deep end. Always thoroughly investigate an existing or proposed business before investing any money. **As any expert (and many failed entrepreneurs) will tell you, starting a business abroad isn't for amateurs, particularly those who don't speak the local language.**

Many small businesses exist on a shoestring, with owners literally living from hand to mouth, and they certainly aren't what could be considered thriving enterprises. Self-employed people usually work extremely long hours, particularly those running bars or restaurants (days off are almost impossible in the high season), often for little financial reward. In most countries, many people choose to be self-employed for the lifestyle and freedom it affords (no clocks or bosses), rather than the money. It's important to keep your plans small and manageable and work well within your budget, rather than undertake a grandiose scheme.

If you're planning to buy or start a mainly seasonal business based on tourism, check whether the potential income will be sufficient to provide you with a living wage. This applies particularly to bars, restaurants and shops in resort areas, especially those run by foreigners relying on the tourist trade, hundreds of which open and close within a short space of time. Don't overestimate the length of the season or the potential income and, most importantly, don't believe everything a person selling a business tells you (although every word may be true). Nobody sells a good business for a bargain price, least of all one making huge profits. In most areas trade falls off dramatically out of the main holiday season, e.g. June to September, and many businesses must survive for a whole year on the income earned in the summer months. The rest of the year you could be lucky to cover your costs.

Legal Advice: Before establishing a business or undertaking any business transactions in a foreign country, it's important to obtain expert legal advice from an experienced lawyer and accountant (who speaks English or a language you speak fluently) to ensure that you will be operating within the law. There are severe penalties for anyone who ignores the regulations and legal requirements. Expert legal advice is also necessary to take advantage of any favourable tax breaks and to make sense of the myriad rules and regulations. It's imperative to ensure that contracts are clearly defined and water-tight before making an investment, because if you become involved in a legal dispute it can take years to resolve.

Further Information: Most international firms of accountants, e.g. Arthur Anderson, Ernst & Young and Price Waterhouse, have offices in many countries and are an invaluable source of information (in English and other languages) on subjects such as forming a company, company law, taxation and social security. Most also publish free booklets about doing business in all major countries.

Wealth Warning: Don't be seduced by the apparent relaxed way of life in many countries – if you want to be a success in business you cannot play at it. In most countries there are many failures for every success story, although many foreigners *do* run successful businesses abroad. However, those who make it do so as a result of extensive market research, wise investments, excellent customer relations, and most important of all, a lot of hard work.

KEEPING IN TOUCH

The availability, quality and cost of local services such as mail, telephone (including mobile phones) and fax may be an important consideration when buying a home abroad, particularly if you wish to keep in close touch with family, friends, or your business or office abroad. The range of services and the reliability and speed of mail deliveries varies considerably with the country. In some countries airmail letters can take weeks to be delivered, even to neighbouring countries, and thousands of items of mail go astray each year.

Most western countries provide an excellent telephone service, although there's a long wait to have a telephone line installed in some countries (you can sometimes pay a surcharge to have a phone installed quicker). If you're buying a holiday home or will be absent from a home abroad for long periods, you should pay your telephone bill (and all other regular bills) by direct debit from a local bank or post office account. If you fail to pay a bill on time your service could be cut and it can take weeks to get it reconnected.

International Calls: The cost of international telephone calls varies considerably with the country and can be *very* expensive. However, competition in most countries has increased considerably in recent years and it's now possible to make international calls at a fraction of the cost of a even just a few years ago. For example, in most European countries the old public-owned monoliths have now been privatised and much-needed competition has been introduced, particularly in the area of international calls. Shop around and compare call rates from a number of companies. Tariffs are constantly being reduced and you should consult individual companies to find the cheapest rate for particular countries. There are telephone call boxes in many countries from where you can make inexpensive international calls and even pay by credit card.

Mobile Phones: Most countries provide a mobile phone service in densely populated areas or nationally in many countries. A mobile phone is particularly useful in countries where there's a long wait for the installation of a fixed phone line. Note, however, that in some countries mobile phones are expensive to buy and operate, and have high connection fees, standing charges and call rates. **International tariffs can vary by hundreds of per cent according to your network provider and your contract.** Digital mobile phones that subscribe to the Global System for Mobile (GSM) communications system can be used to make and receive calls in over 160 countries (called international roaming). For information about individual countries, contact the GSM Association, 6–8 Old Bond Street, London, UK (☎ 020-7518 0530, 🖳 www.gsmworld.com/gsminfo/gsminfo.htm).

Before using a GSM phone abroad, you must contact your service provider to make sure that your tariff allows this. You must also ensure that your phone will operate in the country you're planning to visit, e.g. in North America you normally need a tri-band phone that operates across three frequencies. Note that when you take a GSM phone abroad, all calls made to your phone will go via the country where the phone is registered and you must pay for the call from that country to the country where you're located. For example, if your GSM phone is registered in Britain, a caller in Britain pays the standard call charge for calls to mobile phones and you pay for the call from Britain to where you are abroad. This is because callers have no way of knowing that you've taken your phone abroad (unless you tell them!). You can, however, divert all incoming calls to voicemail when abroad. Calls made from abroad are routed automatically via a local GSM service provider.

Internet 'Telephone' Services: The success of the Internet is built on the ability to gather information from computers around the world by connecting to a nearby service provider for the cost of a local telephone call. If you have correspondents or friends who are connected to the Internet, you can make international 'calls' for the price of a local telephone call (which is free in some countries) to an Internet provider. Once on the Internet there are no other charges, no matter how much distance is covered or time is spent on-line. Internet users can buy inexpensive software that effectively turns their personal computer into a voice-based telephone (both parties must have compatible computer software). You also need a sound card, speakers, a microphone and a modem, and access to a local Internet provider. While the quality of communication isn't as good as using a telephone (it's similar to a CB radio) and you need to arrange call times in advance, making international 'calls' costs virtually nothing. **The Internet can also be used to send electronic mail (e-mail), which has become the standard way of sending text (letters, etc.), illustrations and photographs almost instantaneously throughout the world.**

Fax Services: Fax machines are available in all countries, although the cost varies considerably. It may be possible to take a fax machine abroad, but you must check that it's compatible or that it can be modified at a reasonable cost. Most fax machines made for use in a European country will operate in most other European countries, although getting a fax machine repaired abroad may be difficult unless the same model is sold locally. Public fax services are provided by main post offices in many countries, although they may only send faxes, not receive them. Telexes can also be sent via post offices, and telexes and faxes can be sent and received via major hotels, business services offices and newsagents in many countries.

Business Services: In major towns and tourist areas in most countries there are companies (such as Mail Boxes Etc.) offering a range of communications services which may include telephone, fax, PO box, mail-hold, mail forwarding, call-in service and 24-hour access, stamps, envelopes, postcards, packing supplies, air shipping/receiving, postal metering, money orders and transfers, telegrams, voicemail, e-mail, Internet, telex, copying and message taking.

GETTING THERE

Although it isn't so important if you're buying a permanent home and planning to stay put, one of the major considerations when buying a home abroad is communications (road, rail, air and sea links) with your home country. How long will it take to get there, e.g. by air, taking into account journeys to and from airports? Is it possible to drive? One of the main advantages of being able to drive to a holiday home abroad is that you can take much more luggage with you (including provisions unavailable locally) and the cost for a family may be significantly lower than using public transport.

Could you travel by bus or rail, e.g. via Le Shuttle from Britain? What does it cost? How frequent are buses, flights or trains at the time(s) of year when you plan to travel. Is it feasible to visit a holiday home abroad for a long weekend, given the cost and travelling time involved? Note that some charter flight companies can be unreliable, and over-booking is often a problem in the high season. If you intend to make frequent trips to a home abroad, it obviously makes sense to choose somewhere that involves a relatively short journey *and* isn't too expensive. If a long journey is involved, you should bear in mind that it takes most people a day or two to fully recover from a long journey, particularly when a long flight (and possibly jet-lag) is involved.

Those travelling between Britain and the continent by ferry can make savings (around one-third) by joining a 'Property Owners Club' such as those operated by Brittany Ferries for homeowners in France and Spain. P&O shareholders owning a certain amount of stock receive discounts of up to 50 per cent on most routes. Many airlines offer discounts for shareholders and special deals for frequent fliers. However, if flying is your only alternative, you should bear in mind that if you need to take a flight at short notice it can be prohibitively expensive as you may be unable to get a inexpensive charter or APEX flight. However, it's possible to insure against emergency travel (see page 38) in some countries.

Always shop around for the lowest fares available. For some destinations it may be cheaper to fly via another country than to take a direct flight from your home country. British readers should compare the fares listed in newspapers such as *The Sunday Times*, the *Observer* and London's *Time Out* entertainment magazine.

GETTING AROUND

For many people, an important aspect of owning a home abroad is being able to get around easily and relatively cheaply while they're there. Bear in mind that driving is a nerve-wracking and even dangerous experience in some countries, and most people are more accident-prone when driving abroad, particularly when the traffic drives on the 'wrong' side of the road. A car can be a liability in towns if you don't have private parking and you will save a lot of money if you can manage without one (which is why many retirees on a limited budget live in towns).

If you don't drive or aren't planning to own a car abroad, you will usually need to buy a home in a city or large town where there's adequate public transport. In some countries, public transport is poor and there's no rail service and only an infrequent and unreliable local bus service. In rural areas, it's usually essential to have your own transport. Note that if you don't have a car you will need to carry all your shopping home or have it delivered.

Having your own transport will also allow you a much wider choice of where you can buy a home abroad. However, if you own a holiday home abroad, it isn't necessary to drive there in order to enjoy the convenience of your own transport. Many people buy an inexpensive car (locally or in their home country) and leave it at their home abroad. Before planning to do this, you should check whether it's permitted and the costs involved (insurance, road tax, etc.), and compare them with the cost of renting a car.

If you're buying a permanent home abroad, you can usually import a new or second-hand car duty-free. Check the regulations in any country you must pass through to reach your destination (you may need a *Carnet de Passage* for travel outside western Europe). When buying a car for use in continental Europe, you will often find it pays to buy a diesel-engined car with air-conditioning (which is a blessing in a hot country).

EU nationals with a holiday home in another EU country can use a vehicle registered in their home country abroad without time limits or paying local taxes. However, the period of use is determined by the time that a non-resident is permitted to remain in another EU country without becoming a resident, which is a maximum of six months (182 days) in a calendar year. A vehicle must be insured, inspected (for roadworthiness) and taxed in its country of registration.

Renting a car is prohibitively expensive in some countries, particularly during the high season or for long periods. **There are inexpensive car rental companies in some countries, but you must be *very* careful who you rent from, as many cars are unroadworthy or even dangerous.** One way to reduce the cost is to rent a car through the American office of an international car rental company such as Alamo, Avis, Budget and Hertz and pay by credit card. This is a legitimate practice and can save 50 per cent or more on local European rates. The US freephone (800) numbers of other international rental companies can be obtained from international directory enquiries. Note that when dialling freephone numbers from abroad, you're charged at international rates.

Car Insurance

When driving abroad, always ensure that you have valid insurance. Motorists insured in an EU country, the Czech Republic, Hungary, Liechtenstein, Norway, Slovakia and Switzerland are automatically covered for basic third-party liability in all those countries. In Europe an international insurance certificate (green card) is compulsory when driving in certain countries and it's mandatory to buy car insurance at the border to enter some countries. A green card is available at no extra cost when you're insured in most western European countries and extends your normal insurance (e.g. fully comprehensive) to other countries covered by the green card agreement. However, you must check whether there are any restrictions.

This doesn't, however, apply to cars insured in Britain, where insurance companies charge a fee or provide a free green card for a limited period of 30 or 45 days a year, and usually cover motorists for a maximum period of around three months a year. However, British drivers should shop around, as some companies allow motorists a green card for up to six months a year or longer. If you're British and have fully comprehensive insurance in Britain, it's wise to have a green card when driving in Europe. If you drive a British-registered car and spend over six months a year on the continent, you may need to take out a special (i.e. expensive) European insurance policy or obtain insurance with a foreign insurance company. Some foreign insurance companies will insure foreign-registered cars, although there may be a limit on the period.

Breakdown Insurance: When driving abroad it's important to have motor breakdown insurance (which may include holiday and travel insurance), including repatriation for your family and your car in the event of an accident or breakdown. If you're a member of a European motoring organisation, you may be covered when travelling elsewhere in Europe by a reciprocal agreement with national breakdown services, although cover is usually fairly basic. When motoring in some countries it's also wise to take out special legal protection insurance such as bail bond insurance, without which the local authorities may lock you up and throw away the key if you're involved in an accident. In some European countries motor breakdown insurance is provided by local car insurance companies.

Many companies providing European breakdown insurance operate multi-lingual, 24-hour, emergency centres where assistance is available for motoring, medical, legal and travel problems. Some organisations also provide economical annual motoring policies for those who travel abroad frequently, e.g. owners of holiday homes.

Car Security

Most countries have a problem with car theft and theft from cars, particularly in major cities and resort areas. In many countries, foreign-registered vehicles, especially camper vans and mobile homes, are targeted by thieves. If you drive anything other than a worthless wreck, you should have theft insurance that includes your car stereo and belongings (although this may be prohibitively expensive). If you drive a new or valuable car, it's wise to have it fitted with an alarm, an engine immobiliser (the best system) or other anti-theft device, and to also use a visible deterrent such as a steering or gear stick lock. It's particularly important to protect your car if you own a model that's desirable to professional car thieves, e.g. most new sports and executive models, which are often stolen by crooks to order.

Most cars can be broken into in seconds by a competent thief. Even a good security system won't usually prevent someone from breaking into your car or stealing it, but it will make his task more difficult and may persuade him to look for an easier target. Thieves often smash windows (in some countries BMW is short for 'break my window') to steal stereo systems and other items from cars, even articles of little value such as sunglasses or cigarettes. When leaving your car unattended, remove all belongings, including clothes, or stow them in the boot (trunk). Note, however, that it isn't always safe to keep valuables in the boot, particularly if it can be opened from inside the car. You should never leave your original car papers in your car (which may help a thief dispose of it). When parking overnight or after dark, you should park in a secure car park or garage, or at least in a well-lit area.

If your car is stolen or anything is stolen from it, report it as soon as possible to the police in the area where it was stolen. You can usually report it by telephone but must go to the station to complete a report. Don't, however, expect the police to find you car or belongings (or even take any interest in your loss). Report a theft to your insurance company as soon as possible.

Driving Abroad

You may be unfamiliar with the road rules and regulations in the country where you're planning to buy a home, which may differ considerably from those in your home country. The following tips are designed to help you survive driving abroad:

- Don't forget your car registration and insurance papers, passports, identity cards, visas, children, and vaccination certificates (also for pets). Make sure you have sufficient local currency (for petrol, tolls, food, fines, etc.) for the countries you will pass through.

- Note that the procedure following an accident isn't the same in all European countries, although most western European countries use a standard accident report form provided by insurance companies. As a general rule, you should call the police to the scene of anything other than a minor accident.

- Drivers of foreign-registered cars must have the appropriate nationality plate or sticker affixed to the rear of their car when motoring abroad. (If your nationality plate has been incorporated into the registration plate, a separate nationality plate isn't required.) In many countries you can be fined on the spot for not displaying it, although this seldom happens. Cars must show the correct nationality plate only and not an assortment.

- Ensure that your car complies with local laws and that you have the necessary equipment. For example, spare tyre, spare bulbs and fuses, warning triangle (in some countries, e.g. Spain, you need two), first-aid kit, fire extinguisher, petrol can (note that carrying cans of petrol or keeping petrol in plastic containers is forbidden in some countries) and headlight beam deflectors. Check the latest regulations with a motoring organisation in your home country.

- Make sure that you have sufficient spares, particularly if you're driving a rare or exotic car (i.e. any car that isn't sold locally). A good map will come in handy, particularly when you're lost. If your car runs on diesel or LPG, make sure that it's freely available locally and in *all* the countries you intend to visit or pass through.

- Seat belts must be worn in all European countries and in North America. In some countries dipped headlights (low beam) must be used at all times.

- If you're planning a long journey, a mechanical check-up for your car is recommended, particularly if it's a while since your car's last service or inspection.

- The legal blood alcohol level when driving varies with the country and is 80mg per 100ml of blood in most European countries. Some countries have lower levels, e.g. Portugal (50mg), France (40mg), Sweden (20mg) and Turkey (0 mg). A level of 50mg has been recommended by the EU Commission for EU countries, although its implementation has been resisted by many countries. Alcohol is estimated to be a major factor in at least a third of all road accidents and in countries with a 'drink-drive culture' it's much higher. Note that the strength of alcoholic beverages (and the size of drinks) varies considerably from country to country.

- An international driving licence or a translation of your foreign driving licence is necessary in some countries (check with a motoring organisation). In most countries foreign residents can exchange their foreign driving licence for a local licence without taking a test (although a test is necessary in some countries, depending on your nationality). If you have a driving licence issued by an EU country, it's no longer necessary to exchange it for a local licence when you're resident in another EU country, but you may be required to register with the local motor licensing authorities.

- If you're buying a home in a country where traffic drives on a different side of the road from your home country, take extra care until you're accustomed to it. Be particularly alert when leaving lay-bys, T-junctions, one-way streets and petrol stations, as it's easy to lapse into driving on your usual side of the road. It's helpful to display a notice, e.g. 'keep right!' or 'keep left!', as a constant reminder on your car's dashboard.

- In continental Europe, where all traffic drives on the right, most main roads are designated priority roads, as indicated by a sign, the most common of which is a yellow diamond on a white background (the end of priority is shown by the same sign with a black diagonal line through it). On roads *without* priority signs and in built-up areas, you must give way to all vehicles coming from your RIGHT. **Failure to observe this rule is the cause of many accidents.** If you're ever in doubt about who has priority, always give way to trams, buses and all traffic coming from your RIGHT (particularly large trucks!). Emergency (ambulance, fire, police) and public utility (electricity, gas, telephone, water) vehicles attending an emergency also have priority on all roads in most countries. Note that at roundabouts (traffic circles) vehicles on the roundabout normally have priority and not those entering it, usually indicated by a 'give way' sign.

- **Never carry anything across an international border unless you're absolutely sure what it contains, as it could contain drugs or other prohibited goods. The same applies to any passengers (and their baggage) that you pick up on your journey.**

When driving anywhere **NEVER** assume that you know what another motorist is going to do next. Just because a motorist is indicating left, it doesn't mean he's *actually* going to turn left – in some countries he's just as likely to be turning right, stopping or about to reverse. Don't be misled by any semblance of road discipline or marked lanes. Try to be courteous, if only in self-defence, but don't expect others to reciprocate. The most dangerous countries in which to drive vary according to the newspapers and magazines you read and whose statistics they use. What is certain is that the likelihood of having an accident is much higher in some countries. Take extra care in winter, when ice and snow can make driving particularly hazardous.

2.

FURTHER CONSIDERATIONS

This chapter contains important further considerations for anyone planning to buy a home abroad, particularly those planning to live abroad permanently, whether in the near or distant future. It contains information about health, insurance, shopping, pets, learning the language, and television and radio.

HEALTH

One of the most important aspects of living abroad – or anywhere for that matter – is maintaining good health. The quality of health care and health care facilities varies considerably from country to country, although most countries provide good to excellent health care for those who can afford to pay for private treatment (although many Americans may not agree). However, nursing care and post-hospital assistance in many southern European and Mediterranean countries are well below what northern Europeans and North Americans take for granted, and spending on preventive medicine is low.

Public Health Services: Many countries have a public health service providing free or low cost health care for those who contribute to social security, including their families. Retirees from a European Union (EU) member country enjoy free public health services in other EU countries. If you don't qualify for health care under a public health service, it's essential to have private health insurance (see page 32). In fact it may be impossible to obtain a residence permit without it. Private health insurance is often recommended in any case, because of the shortcomings of public health services and long waiting lists in some countries. Visitors should have holiday insurance (see page 38) if they aren't covered by a reciprocal health care agreement (see page 34).

Health Problems Abroad: Common health problems experienced by expatriates include sunburn and sunstroke, stomach and bowel problems (due to the change of diet and more often, water, but they can also be caused by poor hygiene), and various problems related to excess alcohol, including a high incidence of alcoholism in some countries. The dangers of disease and infection are considerably greater in some countries. Other health problems are caused by the high level of airborne pollen in spring in many countries, which affects asthma and hay fever sufferers, and noise and traffic pollution (particularly in major cities).

Climate: If you aren't used to the hot sun, you should limit your exposure and avoid it altogether during the hottest part of the day, wear protective clothing (including a hat) and use a sun block. Too much sun and too little protection will dry your skin and cause premature ageing, to say nothing of the dangers of skin cancer. Care should also be taken to replace the natural oils lost from too many hours in the sun, and the elderly should take particular care not to exert themselves during hot weather. The warm climate in many countries is therapeutic, particularly for sufferers of rheumatism and arthritis, and those prone to bronchitis, colds and pneumonia. The generally slower pace of life in most southern hemisphere countries is also beneficial for those prone to stress (it's difficult to remain uptight while lying in the sun), although it takes some people a while to adjust. The climate and lifestyle in any country has a noticeable effect on your mental health, and those who live in hot climates are generally happier and more relaxed than people living in cold, wet climates (such as North America and northern Europe).

Retirees: Health (and health insurance) is an important issue for those retiring abroad, many of whom are ill prepared for old age and the possibility of health problems. There's a dearth of welfare and home nursing services for the elderly in most popular 'retirement' countries, either state or private, and many foreigners who can no longer care for themselves are forced to return to their home countries. In most countries there are few state residential nursing homes or hospices for the terminally ill, although there are private sheltered homes and developments for those who can afford them in most countries. Provision for handicapped travellers and wheelchair access to buildings and public transport is also poor in many countries.

Pre-Departure Check: It's wise to have a full health check before going to live abroad, particularly if you have a record of poor health or are elderly. The only immunisation that's mandatory is yellow fever for parts of Africa and South America, although a number of others are recommended for some countries, as are anti-malaria tablets. If you're already taking regular medication, you should note that the brand names of drugs and medicines vary from country to country, and you should ask your doctor for the generic name. If you wish to match medication prescribed abroad, you need a current prescription with the medication's trade name, the manufacturer's name, the chemical name and the dosage. Most drugs have an equivalent in other countries, although particular brands may be difficult or impossible to obtain.

It's possible to have medication sent from abroad and no import duty or tax is usually payable. If you're visiting a home abroad for a limited period, you should take sufficient drugs to cover your stay. In an emergency a local doctor will write a prescription that can be filled at a local pharmacy or a hospital may refill a prescription from its own pharmacy. It's wise to take some of your favourite non-prescription drugs, e.g. aspirins, cold and flu remedies, ointments, etc, with you, as they may be difficult or impossible to obtain abroad or may be much more expensive. If applicable, take a spare pair of glasses, contact lenses, dentures or a hearing aid with you.

INSURANCE

An important aspect of owning a home abroad is insurance, not only for your home and its contents, but also for your family when visiting your home abroad. If you live abroad permanently you will require additional insurance, which may in certain cases be compulsory. It's unnecessary to spend half your income insuring yourself against every eventuality from the common cold to being sued for your last penny, but it's important to insure against any event that could precipitate a major financial disaster, such as a serious accident or your house falling down.

As with anything connected with finance, it's important to shop around when buying insurance. Just collecting a few brochures from insurance agents or making a few phone calls, could save you a lot of money. Note, however, that not all insurance companies are equally reliable or have the same financial stability, and it may be better to insure with a large international insurance company with a solid reputation than with a small local company, even if this means paying a higher premium. International insurance companies have offices and representatives in many countries.

Read all insurance contracts before signing them. If a policy is written in a language that you don't understand, get someone to check it and don't sign it unless you understand the terms and the cover provided. Some insurance companies will do almost anything to avoid paying out in the event of a claim and will use any available legal loophole, so it pays to deal only with reputable companies – not that this provides a guarantee! Policies often contain traps in the small print, and you should obtain professional advice and have contracts checked before signing them.

In all matters regarding insurance, you're responsible for ensuring that you and your family are legally insured abroad. Regrettably you cannot insure yourself against being uninsured or sue your insurance agent for giving you bad advice! Bear in mind that if you wish to make a claim on an insurance policy, you may be required to report an incident to the police within 24 hours (this may also be a legal requirement). You should obtain legal advice for anything other than a minor claim, as the law abroad may differ considerably from that in your home country or your previous country of residence – so *never* assume that it's the same.

This section contains information about health insurance, building & household insurance, third party liability insurance and travel insurance. See also **Car Insurance** on page 24.

Health Insurance

The majority of residents in European countries are covered for health treatment under a national health service or a compulsory health insurance schemes. This often includes foreign retirees over the age of 65 who are members of the public health scheme in their home countries. Many countries provide emergency treatment for visitors under reciprocal agreements (see page 34), although these don't apply to citizens of some countries, e.g. the USA. Visitors spending short periods abroad should have travel health insurance (see page 38) if they aren't covered by a reciprocal agreement or an international health policy.

If you're living abroad permanently and don't qualify for 'free' medical treatment under a public health service, it's usually *imperative* that you have private health insurance (unless you have a *very* large bank balance), which is compulsory in some countries. In many countries with a public health service, those who can afford it often take out private health insurance, which provides a wider choice of medical practitioners and hospitals, and frees you from inadequate public health services, waiting lists and other restrictions. Private insurance may also allow you to choose an English-speaking doctor or a hospital where staff speak English or other languages.

A health insurance policy should, if possible, cover you for *all* essential health care whatever the reason, including accidents, e.g. sports accidents, and injuries, whether they occur at your home, your place of work or while travelling. Note that policies offered in different countries vary considerably in the extent of cover, limitations and restrictions, premiums, and the free choice of doctors, specialists and hospitals. **Don't take anything for granted, but check in advance.**

Note that some insurance companies can (and will) cancel a policy at the end of the insurance period if you contract a serious illness with constant high expenses, and some companies automatically cancel a policy when you reach a certain age, e.g. 65. You should avoid such a policy at all costs, as to take out a new policy at the age of 65 at a reasonable premium is difficult or impossible in most countries.

International Policies: If you do a lot of travelling, it's best to have an international health policy. These generally offer wider cover than local policies, although if local medical facilities are adequate and you rarely travel abroad, they can be a waste of money. Most international health policies include repatriation or evacuation (although it may be optional), which can be an important consideration if you need treatment that's unavailable locally, but is available in your home (or another) country. Repatriation may also include repatriation (by air) of the body of someone who dies abroad to their home country for burial. Some companies offer policies for different areas, e.g. Europe, world-wide excluding North America, and world-wide including North America. A policy may offer full cover anywhere within Europe and limited cover in North America and certain other countries, e.g. Japan. Some policies offer the same cover world-wide for a fixed premium, which may be an important consideration for globetrotters. Note that an international policy allows you to choose to have non-urgent medical treatment in another country. Most companies offer different levels of cover, for example basic, standard, comprehensive and prestige.

There's always a limit on the total annual medical costs, which should be at least £250,000 ($375,000), and some companies limit costs for specific treatment or costs such as specialist's fees, surgery and hospital accommodation. Some policies also include permanent disability cover, e.g. £100,000 ($150,000), for those in full-time employment. A medical isn't usually required for health policies, although existing health problems are excluded for a period, e.g. one or two years. Claims are usually settled in all major currencies and large claims are usually settled directly by insurance companies (although your choice of hospitals may be limited). Always check whether an insurance company will settle large medical bills directly. If you're required to pay bills and claim reimbursement from the insurance company, it may take you several months to receive your money (some companies are slow to pay). It isn't usually necessary to translate bills into English or another language, although you should check a company's policy. Most international health insurance companies provide 24-hour emergency telephone assistance.

The cost of international heath insurance varies considerably according to your age and the extent of cover. Note that with most international insurance policies, you must enrol before you reach a certain age, e.g. between 60 and 80, to be guaranteed continuous cover in your old age. Premiums can sometimes be paid monthly, quarterly or annually, although some companies insist on payment annually in advance. When comparing policies, always carefully check the extent of cover and exactly what's included *and* excluded from a policy (which may be noted only in the *very* small print), in addition to premiums and excess charges. In some countries, premium increases are limited by law, although this may apply only to residents in the country where a company is registered, and not to overseas policy holders. Although there may be significant differences in premiums, generally you get what you pay for and can tailor your premiums to your requirements. The most important questions to ask yourself are does the policy provide the cover required and is it good value for money? If you're in good health and are able to pay for your own out-patient treatment, such as visits to your family doctor and prescriptions, then the best value for money policy is usually one limited to specialist visits and hospital treatment.

Make sure you're fully covered abroad before you receive a large bill. It's foolhardy for anyone living abroad (or even visiting) not to have comprehensive health insurance. If your family isn't adequately insured, you could be faced with some *very* high medical bills. When changing employers or moving abroad, you should ensure that you have uninterrupted health insurance. If you're planning to change your health insurance company, make sure that important benefits aren't lost.

Reciprocal Health Agreements

If you're entitled to social security health benefits in a European country, you can take advantage of reciprocal health care agreements in most other European countries. For example, anyone insured under social security in a European Union (EU) country is covered for medical expenses while travelling in other EU countries, provided certain steps are taken in advance. You must usually obtain a form (E111) from your social security office before leaving home.

Full payment (possibly in cash) must usually be made in advance for treatment received abroad, although you will be reimbursed on your return home. **Note, however, that you can still receive a large bill, as your local health authority assumes only a percentage of the cost.** This applies to all EU countries except Britain, where everyone receives free health care, including visitors. You're also reimbursed for essential treatment in non-EU countries, although you must obtain detailed receipts. Note that reimbursement is based on the cost of comparable treatment in your home country. In certain countries there are no reciprocal agreements, e.g. Canada, Japan, Switzerland and the USA, and medical treatment can be *very* expensive. You're advised to have travel or holiday insurance (see page 38) when visiting these countries. In fact this is recommended wherever you're travelling, as insurance provides more comprehensive medical cover than reciprocal health care agreements (and usually includes other services such as repatriation). If you do a lot of travelling abroad it's usually worthwhile taking out an annual international health insurance policy (see above).

British visitors planning to travel abroad can obtain information about reciprocal health treatment from the Department of Social Security, Overseas Branch, Newcastle-upon-Tyne, NE98 1YX, UK.

Household Insurance

In most countries, insurance for a private dwelling includes third-party liability, building and contents insurance, all of which are usually contained in a multi-risk household or homeowner's insurance policy (although in some countries these risks must be insured separately). When buying a home abroad you're usually responsible for insuring it from the moment you become the owner, e.g. for third-party risks. In some countries, many homeowners don't have household insurance, and of those that do, the vast majority have insufficient insurance for their homes and possessions. **This is extremely unwise, particularly regarding building insurance, as it isn't unusual for buildings to be severely damaged by floods and storms in some countries.**

Third-Party Liability: In many countries, e.g. France and Spain, all property must be insured for third-party liability at all times or when building work starts on a new home. The existing third-party liability insurance of the previous owner may automatically transfer to a new owner unless he takes out his own insurance. If you take over the existing insurance, you should ensure that it provides adequate cover and that it isn't too expensive. Third-party liability insurance covers you against financial responsibility for injuries to third parties on your property or accidents directly attributed to something connected with your property. Note that if you own a home that's part of a development or community property (see page 84), such as an apartment or a town house, you must usually be insured for third-party risks in the event that you cause damage to neighbouring properties, e.g. through flood or fire.

Building Insurance: Although it isn't usually compulsory for owners, it's wise to take out building insurance, which generally covers damage caused by fire, lightning, water, explosion, storm, smoke, freezing, snow, theft, riot or civil commotion, vandalism or malicious damage, acts of terrorism, impact (e.g. by aircraft or vehicles), broken glass (constituting part of the building), and natural catastrophes (such as falling trees). Insurance should include glass, external buildings, aerials and satellite dishes, and gardens and garden ornaments. Note that if a claim is made as a result of a defect in the building or design, e.g. the roof is too heavy and collapses, the insurance company won't pay up (yet another reason to have a survey before buying).

The amount for which you should insure your home isn't the current market value, but its replacement value, i.e. the cost of rebuilding a property should it be totally destroyed. This should be increased each year in line with inflation. **Make sure that you insure your property for the true cost of rebuilding.** If you have a mortgage, your lender will usually insist that your home, including most permanent structures on your land, has building insurance. It may be mandatory to take out buildings insurance with a lender for the whole of the mortgage term, with the premium being paid in a single lump sum.

In some countries, e.g. the USA, many people lose their homes each year as a result of natural disasters such as earthquakes, fires, floods, hurricanes and tornadoes. In high risk areas, owners must usually pay an extra premium to cover risks such as subsidence, e.g. where homes are built on clay, floods or earthquakes, although the cost may be extremely high (only some 15 per cent of Californians have earthquake insurance, as it's simply too expensive). Read the small print carefully, e.g. some policies don't include water coming in from ground level, e.g. flood water, and provide cover only for water seeping through the roof. **You should investigate the occurrence of natural disasters in an area where you're planning to buy and the cost of insurance before committing yourself, as the cost can be prohibitive.** Note that in certain cases, claims for damage caused by storms aren't considered by insurance companies unless the situation is declared a natural catastrophe or an Act of God by the government.

If you own an apartment or a town house that's part of a communal property (see page 84), building insurance should be included in your service charges, although you should check exactly what is covered. You must, however, still be insured for third-party risks in the event that you cause damage to neighbouring properties, e.g. through flood or fire. New buildings should be covered by a builder's warranty (see page 79), although unless a warranty is guaranteed by an independent national organisation it may not be worth the paper on which it's printed.

Contents Insurance: Your home contents are usually insured for the same risks as a building (see above) and in most countries are insured for their replacement value (new for old), with a reduction for wear and tear for clothes and linen. However, in some countries, e.g. the USA, possessions are insured for their 'actual cash value' (cost minus depreciation). You can, however, buy replacement value insurance, although policies often include limits and are more expensive. Valuable items are covered for their authenticated value. Most policies include automatic indexation of the insured sum in line with inflation.

Optional Cover: Contents insurance may include accidental damage to sanitary installations, cash, replacement of locks following damage or loss of keys, alternative accommodation cover, and property belonging to third parties stored in your home, although these may all be optional. Optional items usually also include credit cards (and their fraudulent use), frozen foods, emergency assistance, e.g. plumber, glazier, electrician, redecoration, garaged cars, replacement pipes, loss of rent, and the cost of emergency travel to a home abroad (for holiday homeowners). Many policies offer third-party liability as an option. A basic policy may exclude items such as musical instruments, jewellery, valuables, sports equipment and bicycles, for which you may need to take out extra cover. A basic policy also *doesn't* usually include accidental damage caused by your family to your own property, e.g. 'accidentally' putting your foot through the TV during a political broadcast!

Valuables: High-value possessions such as works of antiques, art, furs and jewellery aren't usually covered (or fully covered) by a standard policy and must be insured separately for their full value. They must usually be itemised, and photographs and documentation such as a professional appraiser's report provided. Some companies even recommend or insist on a video film of belongings. When making a claim you should always produce the original bills if possible (always keep bills for expensive items) and bear in mind that replacing imported items locally may be more expensive than their original cost. Contents policies always contain security clauses and if you don't adhere to them a claim won't be considered. If you're planning to let a property, you may need to inform your insurer.

Security: Note that in some countries a building must have iron bars on the ground-floor windows and patio doors, window shutters and secure locks. In countries and areas with a high risk of theft, e.g. major cities and resort areas, an insurance company may insist on extra security measures, e.g. two locks on all external doors (one of a mortise type) and shutters or security gratings on windows. A policy may specify that all forms of protection on doors must be employed whenever a property is unoccupied and that all other forms (e.g. shutters) must also be used at night (e.g. after 10pm) and when a property is left empty for more than a few days. It's unwise to leave valuable or irreplaceable items in a holiday home or in a property that's vacant for long periods.

Some companies offer a discount if properties have steel reinforced doors, security locks and alarms (particularly alarms connected to a 24-hour security centre). An insurance company may send someone to inspect your property and to advise on security measures. Policies usually pay out for theft only when there are signs of forced entry and don't include thefts by a tenant (but may include thefts by domestic staff). All-risks cover is available from some insurance companies, offering a world-wide extension to a household policy and including items such as jewellery and cameras.

Inventory: When insuring your possessions, don't buy more insurance than you need. Unless they're particularly valuable, insurance may cost more than replacing your possessions, and you may be better off insuring just a few valuable items. To calculate the amount of insurance you need, make a complete list of your possessions containing a description, purchase price and date, and their location in your home.

Some insurance companies use a formula based on your building insurance value (i.e. the value of your home), although this is no more than a 'guesstimate'. Keep the list and all receipts in a safe place (such as a safety deposit box), and add new purchases and make adjustments to your insurance cover when necessary.

Under-insurance: Take care that you don't under-insure your house contents, that you include anything rented, such as a TV or video recorder, and that you periodically reassess their value and adjust your insurance premium accordingly. Your contents should include everything that isn't a fixture or fitting and which you could take with you if you were moving house. In many countries, if you under-insure your contents, a claim will be reduced by the percentage by which you're under-insured. For example, if you make a claim for £1,000 ($1,500) and you're found to be under-insured by 50 per cent, you will receive only £500 ($750).

Premiums: The cost of household insurance varies considerably according to the country, the type of property, its location, and the local crime rate. Premiums are usually calculated on the size of the property, either the habitable (constructed) area in m^2 or the number of rooms, rather than its value. The sum insured may be unlimited, provided the property doesn't exceed a certain size and is under a certain age, e.g. 200 years, although some companies restrict home insurance to properties with a maximum number of rooms or a maximum value of contents. In general, detached, older and more remote properties cost more to insure than apartments and new properties (particularly when located in towns), because of the higher risk of theft. Premiums are also higher in certain high risk areas and some policies impose a small excess (deductible) for each claim.

Holiday Homes: In some countries premiums are higher for holiday homes, because of their high vulnerability, particularly to theft. Premiums are usually based on the number of days a property is inhabited each year and the interval between periods of occupancy. Cover for theft, storm, flood and malicious damage may be suspended when a property is left empty for more than three weeks at a time (or if there's no evidence of forced entry in the event of theft). It's possible to negotiate cover for periods of absence for a hefty surcharge, although valuable items are usually excluded. If you're absent from your property for long periods, e.g. over 30 days at a time, you may also be required to pay an excess on a claim arising from an occurrence that takes place during your absence (and theft may be excluded). Some companies refuse to insure holiday homes in high risk areas. **You should read all small print in policies.** Note that if you let a home abroad, even for short periods, you may be required to notify your household insurance company.

European Union (EU) residents with a home in another EU country must be insured by an insurance company licensed to underwrite insurance in the country where the property is located, and any taxes or charges that apply in that country must be paid. However, this ruling doesn't prevent EU residents from buying insurance abroad, e.g. in their home country, and there are policies available which meet the criteria in most EU countries. The advantage of buying household insurance in your home country is that you have a policy you can understand (apart from all the legal jargon) and can make claims in your own language, which is an important factor. However, you should bear in mind that insuring with a foreign insurance company may be more expensive than insuring with a local company, some of which provide policies in English and other languages for foreigners.

Claims: If you wish to make a claim, you must usually inform your insurance company in writing (by registered letter) within two to seven days of the incident or 24 hours in the case of theft. Thefts should also be reported to the local police within 24 hours, as the police statement (of which you receive a copy for your insurance company) constitutes 'irrefutable' evidence of a theft. Check whether you're covered for damage or thefts that occur when you're away from the property and are therefore unable to inform the insurance company (or the local police) immediately.

Settlement of Claims: Bear in mind that if you make a claim you may need to wait months for it to be settled. Generally the larger the claim, the longer you will have to wait for your money, although in an emergency some companies will make an interim payment. If you aren't satisfied with the amount offered, don't accept it, but try to negotiate a higher figure. If you still cannot reach agreement on the amount or the time taken to settle a claim, you may be able to take your claim to an ombudsman or an independent industry organisation for arbitration. **Note that some insurance companies will do their utmost to find a loophole which makes you negligent and relieves them of liability.**

Third-Party Liability Insurance

It's common practice in many countries to have third-party liability insurance. Third-party liability insurance covers all members of a family and includes damage caused by your children and pets, for example, if your dog or child bites someone. Where damage is due to negligence, compensation may be reduced. In some countries, if your children attend school they're automatically covered by third-party liability insurance. Third-party liability insurance also protects you against claims from anyone who injures himself or suffers loss while on your property. Check whether third-party liability insurance covers you against accidental damage to your home's fixtures and fittings (which may be covered by your household insurance).

Third-party liability insurance is often combined with household insurance (see above). If it isn't included in your household insurance, third-party liability insurance is usually inexpensive and costs around costs £10 to £20 ($15 to $30) a year for each £50,000 ($75,000) of cover, although you may be required to pay the first £50 or £100 ($75 to $150) of a claim.

Holiday & Travel Insurance

Holiday and travel insurance is recommended for all who don't wish to risk having their holiday or travel spoilt by financial problems or to arrive home broke. As you probably know, anything can and often does go wrong with a holiday, sometimes before you even reach the airport or port (particularly when you *don't* have insurance). Travel insurance is available from many sources, including travel and insurance agents, motoring organisations, transport companies and direct from insurance companies. Package holiday companies also offer insurance polices, most of which are compulsory, expensive **and don't provide adequate cover.**

Before taking out travel insurance, carefully consider the level of cover you require and compare policies. Most policies include cover for loss of deposit or holiday cancellation, missed flights, departure delay at both the start *and* end of a holiday (a common occurrence), delayed baggage, personal effects and lost baggage, medical expenses and accidents (including repatriation if necessary), money, personal liability, legal expenses, and protection against a tour operator or airline going bust.

Medical expenses are an important aspect of travel insurance and you shouldn't rely on reciprocal health care agreements (see page 34). It also isn't wise to depend on travel insurance provided by charge and credit card companies, household policies or private medical insurance, none of which usually provide adequate cover abroad (although you should take advantage of what they offer). The minimum medical insurance recommended by most experts is £250,000 ($400,000) in Europe and £500,000 to £1 million ($750,000 to $1.5 million) in North America and some other countries, e.g. Japan. If applicable, check whether pregnancy related claims are covered and whether there are any restrictions for those over a certain age, e.g. 65 or 70. Third-party liability cover should be £500,000 to £1 million ($750,000 to $1.5 million) in Europe and £1 to £2 million ($1.5 to $3 million) in North America.

Always check any exclusion clauses in contracts by obtaining a copy of the full policy document (all relevant information *won't* be included in the insurance leaflet). Skiing and other high risk sports and pursuits should be specifically covered and *listed* in a policy. Special winter sports policies are available and are usually more expensive than normal holiday insurance. The cost of travel insurance varies considerably according to your destination and the duration required. Usually the longer the period, the cheaper the daily or weekly cost, although the maximum period is usually six months. In Europe you should expect to pay from around £10 to £20 ($15 to $30) for a week's insurance, £15 to £25 ($25 to $40) for two weeks and £30 to £40 ($45 to $60) for a month. Premiums are around double these amounts for travel to North America, where medical treatment costs an arm and a leg (although they also accept dollars!). Premiums may be higher for those aged over 65 or 70.

Annual Policies: For people who travel abroad frequently or spend long periods abroad, an annual travel policy usually provides the best value, but always carefully check exactly what it includes. Many insurance companies offer annual travel policies for a premium of around £100 to £150 ($150 to $250) for an individual (the equivalent of around three months' insurance with a standard travel insurance policy), which are excellent value for frequent travellers. Some insurance companies also offer an 'emergency travel policy' for holiday homeowners who need to travel abroad at short notice to inspect a property, e.g. after a severe storm. The cost of an annual policy may depend on the area covered, e.g. Europe, the whole world excluding North America, and the whole world including North America, although it doesn't usually cover travel within your country of residence. There's also a limit on the number of trips per year and the duration of each trip, e.g. 90 or 120 days. **Always check exactly what is covered (or omitted), as an annual policy may not provide adequate cover.**

Claims: Although travel insurance companies gladly take your money, they aren't always so keen to honour claims and you may have to persevere before they pay up. Always be persistent and make a claim *irrespective* of any small print, as this may be unreasonable and therefore invalid in law. Insurance companies usually require you to report a loss (or any incident for which you intend to make a claim) to the local police or carriers within 24 hours and obtain a written report. Failure to do this may mean that a claim won't be considered. Many policies have an excess (deductible) of £25 to £50 ($40 to $75).

SHOPPING

After buying a home abroad, you will probably need to buy furniture, furnishings and assorted household items. Where you decide to buy these items can make a considerable difference to the cost of establishing a home abroad. If you decide to purchase goods in your home country or another country (other than where a property is situated), you should check whether there are any import restrictions and the cost of shipping them to your home abroad. However, before shopping abroad check the prices in local markets and cut-price stores, which may offer better value for money. Those living close to an international border can sometimes reduce their cost of living considerably by shopping abroad, although you generally need to be selective. In most countries a wide range of imported foreign foods are available in specialist food shops, and most supermarkets in major cities and resort areas offer a selection of foreign foods, although these are usually expensive.

Furniture & Furnishings

In most countries there's a huge choice of traditional and contemporary furniture in every price range, although (as with most things) the quality is usually reflected in the price. The kind of furniture you buy will depend on a number of factors, including the style and size of your property, whether it's a permanent or holiday home, your budget, the local climate, and not least, your taste. If you intend to furnish a holiday home with antiques or expensive modern furniture, bear in mind that you will need adequate security and insurance.

If you plan to live abroad permanently in the near future and already have a house full of good furniture in your home country, there's little point in buying expensive furniture abroad. However, many people moving abroad permanently prefer to sell their existing furniture, rather than take it abroad. In any case, foreign furniture often isn't suitable for the climate, e.g. antique furniture usually doesn't stand the heat well, and house styles abroad.

You should compare the cost of furniture locally and in your home country (or other countries). Furniture and home furnishings are a competitive business in most countries and you can usually reduce the price by some judicious haggling, particularly when spending a large amount. The best time to buy furniture and furnishings is during sales (particularly in winter), when prices are often slashed. If you cannot wait for the sales and don't want or cannot afford to pay cash, you may be able to find an interest-free credit deal. Some stores offer 'rooms-to-go' deals, where you can buy furnishings for a complete room in one go, and most offer special packages when you're furnishing a whole house or apartment. Many stores have designers and decorators whose services may be provided free of charge to customers spending over a certain amount. You should reckon on spending £2,000 to £4,000 ($3,000 to $6,000) to furnish a two-bedroom home and £3,000 to £5,000 ($5,000 to $7,500) for a three-bedroom home, depending on the quality of furniture and furnishings required.

In many countries, furniture manufacturers sell direct to the public, although you shouldn't assume that this will result in large savings and should compare prices *and* quality before buying (the least expensive furniture may be poor value if you want something that will last). If you want reasonably priced, good quality, modern furniture, there are a number of companies selling furniture for home assembly which helps reduce the cost. However, beware of buying poor quality, complicated, home-assembled furniture with foreign instructions (and too few screws). In many countries, low cost furniture can also be purchased from hypermarkets. Pine and cane furniture is particularly inexpensive and popular in most hot countries. Most large furniture retailers publish free catalogues.

In some countries, e.g. Spain, many holiday homes are sold furnished, particularly apartments, although furniture may be of poor quality and not to your taste. However, buying a furnished property can represent a real bargain (some vendors even include the TV, VCR and stereo system). If you're buying a property as an investment for letting, most developers or agents will arrange to furnish it for you. Many offer furnishing packages which include everything from furniture to a corkscrew and teaspoons, although deals may not offer huge (or indeed any) savings over the selective purchase of individual items. Check other homes that developers have furnished and local shop prices before committing yourself.

If you're looking for antique furniture at affordable prices, you may find a few bargains at markets in rural areas. However, you must usually drive a hard bargain, as the asking prices can be ridiculous. If you need carpets at reasonable prices, many carpet shops and stores sell remnants at bargain prices. There's an active market for second-hand furniture in most countries and many private sellers and dealers advertise in the local press, particularly in expatriate publications. Second-hand furniture can also be purchased from charity shops and yard, garage and estate sales, when people are having a clear out of their 'old' furniture and furnishings. This is usually the cheapest way to furnish a home. Furniture rental for both home and office is common in some countries, although it isn't cost-effective in the long term. There are DIY hypermarkets in most countries offering everything for the home, including furniture, bathrooms, kitchens, decorating and lighting, tool rental and wood cutting.

Household Goods

The choice, cost, design and quality of household goods varies considerably with the country. The cheapest places to buy household goods are usually supermarkets and hypermarkets, although supermarkets may have little choice and hypermarkets are few and far between in some countries. There are specialist hardware stores in most towns, although prices at stores in tourist areas can be high. In smaller countries, prices can be very high, as almost everything must be imported, in which case it's best to import household goods from your home country. Note, however, that many household goods can be purchased at markets at bargain prices, although you must be selective, as the quality isn't always the best.

You should bear in mind when importing goods that aren't sold locally, that it may be difficult or impossible to get them repaired or serviced. If you bring appliances with you or buy them abroad, don't forget to bring a supply of spares and consumables such as bulbs for a refrigerator or sewing machine, and spare bags for a vacuum cleaner. Note that the standard size of kitchen appliances and cupboard units in different countries *isn't* usually the same and it may be difficult to fit an imported dishwasher or washing machine into a kitchen in some countries. However, if you can tailor your kitchen to accommodate foreign appliances, you may save a lot of money by buying them abroad. Check the size *and* the latest safety regulations before shipping these items or buying them abroad, as they may need expensive modifications. Washing machines in many countries take in cold water (only) and heat it in the machine, which makes machines that require a hot water intake useless.

If you already own small household appliances, it's worth taking them abroad, as usually all that's required is a change of plug or an adapter. However, if you're coming from a country with a 110/115V electricity supply (such as the USA), you'll need a lot of expensive transformers (see page 110) and it's usually better to buy new appliances locally. Appliances such as vacuum cleaners, grills, toasters and electric irons aren't expensive in most of Europe and in North America, and are generally of good quality. Don't take a TV or a video cassette recorder (VCR) abroad without checking its compatibility first, as TVs sold in many countries won't work abroad without expensive modifications (see page 48).

If your need is only temporary, many electrical and other household items (such as TVs, beds, cots/highchairs, electric fans, refrigerators, heaters and air-conditioners), can be rented by the day, week or month. Tools and do-it-yourself equipment can also be rented in most countries. There are DIY hypermarkets in most countries, although DIY equipment and supplies may be expensive, particularly in countries where most items are imported. If you need kitchen measuring equipment and cannot cope with decimal measures, you will need to take your own measuring scales, jugs, cups and thermometers with you. Note that bed and pillow sizes are often different abroad and you may have to buy new bed linen, which can be expensive in some countries.

Shopping Abroad

Shopping abroad includes day trips to neighbouring countries as well as shopping excursions further afield. A day trip abroad makes an interesting day out for the family and can save you a substantial sum, depending on what and where you buy. Don't forget your passports or identity cards, car papers, dog's vaccination papers and foreign currency. Most shops in border towns gladly accept foreign currency, but usually offer a lower exchange rate than a bank. Whatever you're looking for, compare prices and quality before buying. Bear in mind that if you buy goods that are faulty or need to be repaired, you may need to return them to the place of purchase.

Within the European Union: From 1993 there have been no cross-border shopping restrictions within the European Union (EU) for goods purchased duty and tax paid, provided all goods are for your own consumption or use and not for resale. However, although there are no restrictions, there are 'indicative levels' for certain items, above which goods may be classified as for commercial use. The following amounts of alcohol and tobacco can usually be exported from one EU country to another by anyone aged 17 or over:

- 10 litres of spirits (over 22° proof);
- 20 litres of sherry or fortified wine (under 22° proof);
- 90 litres of wine (or 120 x 0.75 litre bottles/10 cases) of which a maximum of 60 litres may be sparkling wine;

- 110 litres of beer;
- 800 cigarettes *or* 400 cigarillos *or* 200 cigars *or* 1kg of smoking tobacco.

There's no limit on perfume or toilet water. If you exceed the above amounts, you may need to convince the customs authorities that you aren't planning to sell the goods. There are large fines (and possible confiscation of a vehicle) for anyone suspected of planning to sell duty-paid alcohol and tobacco, which is classed as smuggling.

Mail-order: It's also possible to shop abroad by mail or telephone, when almost anything can be purchased using an international credit or charge card. Many foreign companies publish catalogues and will send goods anywhere in the world, and many also provide account facilities. If you're an avid mail-order shopper, you should contact Shop The World by Mail (PO Box 1599, Sarasota, FL 34230-1599, USA, 🖹 941-365 2419), who supply catalogues from around the world. If you purchase goods from abroad you may be required to pay local sales or value added tax (VAT), although this doesn't apply if the goods were purchased tax paid in an EU country and are being shipped to another EU country. When shipping goods from abroad, particularly by air freight, make sure that they're fully insured.

Internet Shopping: Retailers and manufacturers in most countries offer Internet shopping, but the real benefit comes when shopping abroad, when savings can be made on a wide range of products, including CDs, clothes, sports equipment, electronic gadgets, jewellery, books, CDs, wine and computer software, and services such as insurance, pensions and mortgages. Savings can also be made on holidays and travel. Small high-price, high-tech items, e.g. cameras, watches and portable and hand-held computers, can usually be purchased cheaper somewhere abroad, particularly in the USA, with delivery by courier world-wide within a few days. However, when comparing prices, take into account shipping costs, insurance, duty and VAT.

Shopping on the Internet is very secure (secure servers, with addresses beginning https:// rather than http://, are almost impossible to crack) and in most cases safer than shopping by phone or mail-order. **However, it isn't infallible and credit card fraud is a growing problem.** To find companies or products via the Internet, simply use a search engine such as Altavista, Google or Yahoo.

Duty-free Allowances: Most countries allow the import of limited quantities of goods purchased duty-free by travellers. Duty-free shopping within the EU ended on 30th June 1999, although it's still valid for trips to non-EU countries, when EU residents aged 17 or over are entitled to import the following goods duty-free:

- 1 litre of spirits (over 22° proof) *or* 2 litres of fortified wine, sparkling wine or other liqueurs (under 22° proof);
- 2 litres of still table wine;
- 200 cigarettes *or* 100 cigarillos *or* 50 cigars *or* 250g of tobacco;
- 60 ml of perfume;
- 250 ml of toilet water;
- other goods (including gifts and souvenirs) up to a certain value.

Duty-free allowances apply on both outward and return journeys, even if both are made on the same day, and the combined total (i.e. double the above limits) can be imported into your 'home' country.

Reclaiming Local Taxes: Most countries allow non-residents to reclaim local VAT or purchase tax on goods above a certain value. For example, if you live outside the EU you can reclaim VAT on purchases above a certain value made in an EU country, although you may be required to pay iport duty when importing them into your home country. An export sale invoice is provided by retailers and must be validated by a customs officer when returning home, so keep in in your hand luggage. Your refund will be posted to you later or credited to a credit card account. With certain purchases, particularly large items, it's best to have them sent directly abroad, when local tax won't be charged. Department stores in many countries have a special office where foreign shoppers can arrange for the shipment of goods abroad.

Never attempt to import illegal goods into any country and don't agree to deliver goods or parcels in another country without knowing exactly what they contain. A common ploy is to ask someone to post a parcel abroad (usually to a *poste restante* address) or to leave a parcel at a railway station or restaurant abroad. THE PARCEL USUALLY CONTAINS DRUGS! Many truck drivers are languishing in foreign jails having been the unwitting victims of drug traffickers (who conceal drugs in shipments of goods).

PETS

If you plan to take a pet abroad, it's important to check the latest regulations. Make sure that you have the correct papers, not only for your country of destination, but for all the countries you will pass through to reach it, e.g. when travelling overland. Particular consideration must be given before exporting a pet from a country with strict quarantine regulations, such as the UK. If you need to return prematurely, even after a few hours or days abroad, your pet may need to go into quarantine, e.g. for six months in Britain (see **British Pet Owners** below).

Many countries in addition to Britain, e.g. Australia, require a quarantine period, which may be in the owner's own home, and some (such as Britain and Sweden) have a pet passport scheme. Note that there's no quarantine period (or only a token one) in many countries when pets are exported from countries without rabies. Most countries require pets to have a health certificate issued by an approved veterinary surgeon and vaccination certificates for rabies and possibly other diseases. A rabies vaccination must usually be given not less than 20 days or more than 11 months prior to the date of issue of the health certificate. Pets aged under 12 weeks are usually exempt but must have a health certificate, you must provide evidence that no cases of rabies have occurred for at least six months in the local area.

If you're transporting a pet by ship or ferry, you should notify the shipping company. Some companies insist that pets are left in vehicles (if applicable), while others allow pets to be kept in cabins. If your pet is of a nervous disposition or unused to travelling, it's best to tranquillise it on a long sea crossing. Pets can also be transported by air. Contact airlines for information. Animals may be examined at the port of entry by a veterinary officer in the country of destination.

In many countries, pets must be registered and may be issued with a disc to be worn on a collar around their neck, while others require dogs to be tattooed on their body or in an ear as a means of registration. In recent years, some countries have introduced a microchip identification system for dogs (which has replaced tattooing), whereby a microchip is inserted under the skin. Registration can be expensive, particularly if you have more than one dog. Irrespective of whether your dog is tattooed or microchipped, you should have it fitted with a collar and tag with your name and telephone number on it and the magic word 'reward'. Most countries have rules regarding the keeping of dogs, which may require a health card if they're older than three months. In public areas, a dog may need to be kept on a lead (and muzzled if it's dangerous) and wear a health disc on its collar. Dogs are usually prohibited from entering places where food is manufactured, stored or sold, and may also be barred from sports and cultural events and from beaches.

In areas where there are poisonous snakes, some owners keep anti-venom in their refrigerator (which must be changed annually). Note that in some countries the keeping of dogs may be restricted or banned from long-term rental or holiday accommodation (so check when renting an apartment). Some countries also have strict laws regarding cleaning up after pets in public places (so called 'poop-scoop' laws) and you can be heavily fined for not doing so.

If you intend to live abroad permanently, dogs should also be vaccinated against certain other diseases in addition to rabies, which may include hepatitis, distemper and kennel cough. Cats should be immunised against feline gastro-enteritis and typhus. Pets should also be checked frequently for fleas and tapeworm. Note that there are a number of diseases and dangers for pets in some countries, e.g. Spain, that aren't found in North America and northern Europe. These include the fatal leishmaniasis (also called Mediterranean or sandfly disease), which can be prevented by using a spray such as DefendDog, processionary caterpillars, leeches, heartworm, ticks (a tick collar can prevent these), feline leukaemia and feline enteritis. Obtain advice about these and other diseases from a veterinary surgeon in your home country or on arrival abroad. Take extra care when walking your dog in country areas, as hunters sometimes put down poisoned food to control natural predators. Don't let your dog far out of your sight or let it roam free, as dogs may be stolen or mistakenly shot by hunters.

Veterinary surgeons are well trained in most countries, where there are also kennels, catteries and animal hospitals and clinics, which may provide a 24-hour emergency service, and even pet ambulances and cemeteries. There are also animal welfare organisations in many countries which operate shelters for stray and abused animals, and inexpensive pet hospitals. Health insurance for pets is available in most countries (vet fees can be astronomical) and it's wise to have third-party insurance in case your pet bites someone or causes an accident.

British Pet Owners

On 28th March 2000, Britain introduced a pilot 'Pet Travel Scheme (PETS)' which replaced quarantine for qualifying cats and dogs. Under the scheme, pets must be microchipped (they have a microchip inserted in their neck), vaccinated against rabies, undergo a blood test and be issued with a special health certificate or 'passport'. Note that it can take up to six months to receive a PETS certificate. Pets must also be checked for ticks and tapeworm 24 to 48 hours before embarkation on a plane or ship.

The scheme is restricted to animals imported from rabies-free countries and countries where rabies is under control – initially 24 European countries (the 15 EU countries plus Andorra, Gibraltar, Iceland, Liechtenstein, Monaco, Norway, San

Marino, Switzerland and the Vatican), but has now been extended to Australia, New Zealand, Cyprus, Malta and a number of other rabies-free islands. It may also be extended to North America, although the current quarantine law will remain in place for pets coming from Eastern Europe, Africa, Asia and South America. The new regulations cost pet owners around £200 ($300) for a microchip, rabies vaccination and blood test, plus £60 ($90) per year for annual booster vaccinations and around £20 ($30) for a border check. Shop around and compare fees from a number of veterinary surgeons. To qualify, pets must travel by sea via Dover or Portsmouth, by train via the Channel Tunnel or via Heathrow airport (only certain carriers are licensed to carry animals and they can usually take only one animal per flight). Additional information is available from the Department of the Environment, Food and Rural Affairs (DEFRA, formerly MAFF, ☎ UK 0845-933 5577, ⊠ pets.help line@defra.gsi.gov.uk).

British owners must complete an Application for a Ministry Export Certificate for dogs, cats and other rabies-susceptible animals (form EXA1), available from the DEFRA, Animal Health (International Trade) Division B, Hook Rise South, Tolworth, Surbiton, Surrey KT6 7NF, UK (☎ 020-8330 4411). A health inspection must be performed by a licensed veterinary officer before you're issued with an export health certificate valid for 30 days.

LEARNING THE LANGUAGE

Learning the local language isn't usually necessary if you spend only a few weeks a year abroad, but may be essential if you spend long periods in a country or live there permanently and wish to fully integrate into the local community and way of life. If you're unable to speak the local language you will be excluded from everyday situations and may feel uncomfortable and isolated. The most common reason for negative experiences among foreigners abroad, both visitors and residents, is because they cannot or won't speak the local language. Unfortunately many residents (particularly British retirees) make little effort to learn foreign languages beyond the few words necessary to buy the weekly groceries and order a cup of coffee or a beer, and they often live as if they were on a brief holiday. If you're a retiree, you ought to make an effort to learn at least the rudiments of the local language so that you can understand your bills, use the phone, deal with servicemen, and communicate with your local town hall (plus performing myriad other 'daily' chores). If you don't learn the language, you will be continually frustrated in your communications and will be constantly calling on friends and acquaintances to assist you, or even paying people to do jobs that you could quite easily do yourself.

You must usually learn the local language if you wish to make friends among the local inhabitants. Learning the language will also help you to appreciate the local way of life and make the most of your time abroad, and will open many doors that remain closed to resident 'tourists'. Note that your business and social enjoyment and success in a foreign country will usually be directly related to the degree to which you master the local language. **The most important purpose of learning the local language, however, is that in an emergency it could save your life or that of a loved one!**

Although it isn't easy, even the most non-linguistic (and oldest) person can usually acquire a working knowledge of most foreign languages. All that's required is a little hard work and some help and perseverance (or a lot of work if you have only English-speaking colleagues, friends and neighbours). You won't just 'pick it up' (apart from a few words), but must make a real effort to learn. Most people can teach themselves a great deal through the use of books, tapes, videos and even CD and computer-based courses. However, even the best students require some help. **For most people, the key to mastering a language is total immersion.**

Language teaching is big business in most countries, with classes offered by language schools, colleges and universities, private and international schools, foreign and international organisations, local associations and clubs, and private teachers. Courses range from language courses for complete beginners, through special business or culture-oriented courses, to university-level courses leading to recognised diplomas. Universities in most countries organise summer language courses and myriad organisations offer holiday courses all year round, particularly for children and young adults. If you have difficulty learning languages in the traditional way, you could try the 'suggestological' method where the structure is assimilated while you're under deep relaxation – apparently it works!

Don't expect to become fluent in a short time unless you have a particular flair for languages or already have a good command of the local language. Unless you desperately need to learn quickly, it's best to arrange your lessons over a long period. However, don't commit yourself to a long course of study, particularly an expensive one, before ensuring that it's the right course for you. Most schools offer free tests to help you find your correct level and a free introductory lesson. If you already speak a language but need conversational practice, you may wish to enrol in an art or craft course at a local institute or club.

You may prefer to have private lessons, which are a quicker, although more expensive way of learning a language. The main advantage of private lessons is that you learn at your own speed and aren't held back by slow learners or left floundering by the class genius. You can advertise for a teacher in your local newspapers, on shopping centre/supermarket bulletin boards, university notice boards, and through your and your spouse's employers. Don't forget to ask your friends, neighbours and colleagues if they can recommend a private teacher, as personal recommendations are invariably the best.

Remember that, however terrible your language ability, your bad grammar, limited vocabulary and foreign accent will be much better appreciated than your fluent English (or other foreign language). Don't, however, be surprised when the locals wince at your torture of their beloved tongue!

TELEVISION & RADIO

Although many people complain about the poor quality of television (TV) programmes in their home countries, many find they cannot live without a TV when they're abroad. Fortunately the growth of satellite TV in the last few decades has enabled people to enjoy TV programmes in English and a variety of other languages almost anywhere in the world. Cable TV is also available in many countries and often includes foreign-language stations. The quality of local radio (including expatriate stations in some countries) is generally excellent, and if you have a high quality receiver (or a satellite TV system) it's possible to receive radio stations from around the globe. Note that a TV licence is required in most countries and a separate radio licence may also be necessary.

Television Standards

The standards for TV reception aren't the same in all countries. For example, TVs and video cassette recorders (VCRs) operating on the PAL system or the North American NTSC system won't function in France and TVs manufactured for a European market won't operate in North America. Most European countries use the PAL B/G standard, except for Britain, which uses a modified PAL-I system that's incompatible with other European countries. France has its own standard called SECAM-L, which is different from the SECAM standard used elsewhere in the world, e.g. SECAM B/G in the Middle East and North African countries, and SECAM D/K in some eastern European and many African countries.

If you want a TV that will operate in France and other European countries, and a VCR that will play back both PAL and SECAM videos, you must buy a multi-standard TV and VCR. These are widely available in some countries and contain automatic circuitry that switches from PAL-I (Britain), to PAL-B/G (rest of Europe) to SECAM-L (France). Some multi-standard TVs also incorporate the North American NTSC standard and have an NTSC-in jack plug connection allowing you to play back American videos. If you have a PAL TV, it's also possible to buy a SECAM to PAL transcoder that converts SECAM signals to PAL. Some people opt for two TVs, one to receive local programmes or satellite TV and another to play back their favourite videos. A British or US video recorder won't work with a French TV unless it's dual-standard (with SECAM), and although you can play back a SECAM video on a PAL VCR, the picture will be in black and white.

Satellite Television

Wherever you live in the world it's likely that you will be able to receive satellite TV, although the signal strength and number of stations that can be received will depend on your equipment and your location. Note, however, than in a few countries the use of satellite receivers is banned (nervous local authorities don't want their citizens to be influenced by subversive foreign TV broadcasts!).

Europe: The continent best served by satellite TV is Europe where a number of geo-stationary satellites, e.g. Astra and Eutelsat, carry over 60 channels (over 200 with digital TV) broadcasting in a variety of languages. Satellite TV has increased in popularity in Europe in recent years, particularly in countries and regions where there's no cable TV. TV addicts (easily recognised by their antennae and square eyes) are offered a huge choice of English and foreign-language stations, which can be received throughout most of Europe (the dish size required varies). An added bonus is the availability of radio stations via satellite, including the major BBC stations (see **Satellite Radio** on page 51).

Among the many English-language stations available on Astra are Sky One, Movimax, Sky Premier, Sky Cinema, Film Four, Sky News, Sky Sports (three channels), UK Gold, Channel 5, Granada Plus, TNT, Eurosport, CNN, CNBC Europe, UK Style, UK Horizons, the Disney Channel and the Discovery Channel. Other stations broadcast in Dutch, German, Japanese, Swedish and various Indian languages. The signal from many stations is scrambled (the decoder is usually built into the receiver) and viewers must pay a monthly subscription fee to receive programmes. You can buy pirate decoders for some channels. The best served by clear (unscrambled) stations are German-speakers (most German stations on Astra are clear).

BSkyB Television: You must buy a receiver with a Videocrypt decoder and pay a monthly subscription to receive BSkyB or Sky stations except Sky News (which isn't scrambled). Various packages are available costing from around £12 ($18) to around £35 ($50) per month for the premium package offering all movie channels plus Sky Sports. To receive scrambled channels such as Movimax and Sky Sports, you need an address in Britain. Subscribers are sent a coded 'smart' card (similar to a credit card), which must be inserted in the decoder to activate it (cards are periodically updated to thwart counterfeiters). Sky won't send smart cards to overseas viewers, as they have the copyright only for a British-based audience (expatriates need to obtain a card through a friend or relative in Britain). Satellite companies (some of which advertise in the expatriate press) in most countries can supply genuine BSkyB cards, although you must pay a premium.

Digital Television: English-language digital satellite TV was launched on 1st October 1998 by BSkyB in Britain. The benefits include a superior picture, better (CD) quality sound, wide-screen cinema format and access to many more stations (including around ten stations that show nothing but movies). To watch digital TV you require a Digibox and a (digital) dish, which can be purchased at a subsidised price by customers in Britain. Customers have to sign up for a 12-month subscription and agree to have the connection via a phone line (to allow for future interactive services). In addition to the usual analogue channels (see above), BSkyB digital provides BBC 1, BBC 2, ITV, Channel 4 and Channel 5, plus many digital channels (a total of 200 with up to 500 possible later). Ondigital launched a rival digital service on 15th November 1998, which although it's cheaper, provides a total of 'only' 30 channels (15 free and 15 subscription), including BBC 1 and 2, ITV3, Channel 4 and Channel 5. (In late-2001, its future was in doubt.) Digital satellite equipment is offered by a number of satellite companies throughout Europe (although getting a Sky Card isn't easy).

Eutelsat: Eutelsat was the first company to introduce satellite TV to Europe (in 1983) and it now runs a fleet of communications satellites carrying TV stations to over 50 million homes. Until 1995, they broadcast primarily advertising-based, clear access cable channels. However, following the launch in March 1995 of their Hot Bird 1 satellite, Eutelsat hoped to become a major competitor to Astra, although its channels are mostly non-English. The English-language stations on Eutelsat include Eurosport, BBC World and CNBC. Other stations broadcast in Arabic, French, German, Hungarian, Italian, Polish, Portuguese, Spanish and Turkish.

BBC World-wide Television: The BBC's commercial subsidiary, BBC Worldwide Television, broadcasts two 24-hour channels: BBC World (24-hour news and information) and BBC Prime (general entertainment), transmitted via the Eutelsat Hotbird 5 satellite (13° east). BBC World is unencrypted (clear) while BBC Prime is encrypted and requires a D2-MAC decoder and a smartcard, available on subscription from BBC Prime, PO Box 5054, London W12 0ZY, UK (☎ 020-8433 2221, ✉ bbcprime@bbc.co.uk). For further information and a programme guide contact

BBC Worldwide Television, Woodlands, 80 Wood Lane, London W12 0TT, UK (☎ 020-8576 2555). A programme guide is also available on the Internet (🖳 www. bbc.co.uk/schedules) and both BBC World and BBC Prime have websites (🖳 www. bbcworld.com and www.bbcprime. com). When accessing them, you need to enter the name of your country of residence so that schedules are displayed in local time.

Equipment: A satellite receiver should have a built-in Videocrypt decoder (and others such as Eurocrypt, Syster or SECAM if required) and be capable of receiving satellite stereo radio. A system with an 85cm (33in) dish (to receive Astra stations) costs from around £200 ($300), plus installation, which may be included in the price. A digital system is more expensive: for example, a BSkyB system costs around £650 ($1,000) in most European countries (excluding Britain and Ireland). Shop around, as prices vary considerably. With a 1.2 or 1.5m (47 or 59in) motorised dish, you can receive hundreds of stations in a multitude of languages from around the world. If you wish to receive satellite TV on two or more TVs, you can buy a satellite system with two or more receivers. To receive stations from two or more satellites simultaneously, you need a motorised dish or a dish with a double feed antenna (dual LNBs). There are satellite sales and installation companies in most countries, some of which advertise in the expatriate press. Shop around and compare prices. Alternatively, you can import your own satellite dish and receiver and install it yourself. **Before buying a system, ensure that it can receive programmes from all existing and planned satellites.**

Location: To receive programmes from any satellite, there must be no obstacles, e.g. trees, buildings or mountains, between the satellite and your dish, so check before renting or buying a home. Before buying or erecting a satellite dish, check whether you need permission from your landlord, development or local municipality. Some towns and buildings (such as apartment blocks) have regulations regarding the positioning of antennae, although in some countries owners may mount a dish almost anywhere. Dishes can usually be mounted in a variety of unobtrusive positions and can also be painted or patterned to blend in with the background. Note, however, that in some countries, private dishes in apartment blocks are prohibited and have been replaced by a single communal antenna with a cable connection to individual apartments.

Programme Guides: Many satellite stations provide teletext information and most broadcast in stereo. Sky satellite programme listings are provided in a number of British publications such as *What Satellite*, *Satellite Times* and *Satellite TV Europe* (the best), which are available on subscription and from local newsagents in some countries. Satellite TV programmes are also listed in expatriate newspapers and magazines in most countries. The annual *World Radio TV Handbook* edited by David G. Bobbett (Watson-Guptill Publications) contains over 600 pages of information and the frequencies of all radio and TV stations world-wide.

Radio

Radio flourishes in most countries, where it's often more popular than TV. Numerous public and private, local, regional, national and foreign radio stations can be received in most countries, with programme standards varying from excellent to amateurish. There's a wealth of excellent FM (VHF stereo) and AM (medium waveband) stations in the major cities and resort areas in most countries, although in remote rural areas (particularly mountainous areas) you may be unable to receive any FM stations clearly. The long wave (LW) band is little used in most countries, although LW stations are common in Britain and Ireland. A short wave (SW) radio is useful for receiving foreign stations.

Expatriate Stations: There are English and foreign-language commercial radio stations aimed at expatriates in the major cities and resort areas in many countries, where the emphasis is usually on music and chat with some news. Some expatriate stations broadcast in a variety of languages at different times of the day, including English, Dutch, German and various Scandinavian languages. Unfortunately (or inevitably) expatriate radio tries to be all things to all men (and women) and usually falls short, particularly with regard to music, where it's impossible to cater for all tastes. However, it generally provides a good service and is particularly popular among retirees. The main drawback of expatriate radio (and most commercial radio) is its amateurish advertisements, which are obtrusive and repetitive, and make listening a chore. Expatriate radio programmes are published in the expatriate press in many countries.

BBC & Other Foreign Stations: The BBC World Service is broadcast on short wave on several frequencies, e.g. 12095, 9760, 9410, 7325, 6195, 5975 and 3955kHz, simultaneously and you can usually receive a good signal on one of them. The signal strength varies according to where you live, the time of day and year, the power and positioning of your receiver, and atmospheric conditions. The BBC World Service plus BBC Radio 1, 2, 3, 4 and 5 are also available via the Astra (Sky) satellite. For a free BBC World Service programme guide and frequency information, write to BBC World Service (BBC Worldwide, PO Box 76, Bush House, Strand, London WC2B 4PH, UK, ☎ 020-8752 5040). The BBC publishes a monthly magazine, *BBC On Air*, containing comprehensive programme listings for BBC World Service radio, BBC Prime TV and BBC World TV. It's available on subscription from the BBC (On Air Magazine, Room 207 NW, Bush House, Strand, London WC2B 4PH, UK, ☎ 020-7240 4899, ✉ on.air.magazine@bbc.co.uk) and from news-stands in some countries.

Many other foreign stations also publish programme guides and frequency charts, including Radio Australia, Radio Canada, Denmark Radio, Radio Nederland, Radio Sweden International and the Voice of America. Some stations also have websites, where you can often download and hear broadcast material as well as view schedules.

Cable & Satellite Radio: If you have cable or satellite TV, you can also receive many radio stations via your cable or satellite link. For example, BBC Radio 1, 2, 3, 4 and 5, BBC World Service, Sky Radio, Virgin 1215 and many foreign-language stations are broadcast via the Astra satellites. Satellite radio stations are listed in British satellite TV magazines such as *Satellite Times*. If you're interested in receiving radio stations from further afield, you should obtain a copy of the *World Radio TV Handbook* edited by David G. Bobbett (Watson-Guptill Publications).

3.

FINANCE

One of the most important aspects of buying a home abroad and living abroad (even for brief periods) is finance, which includes everything from transferring and changing money to mortgages and local taxes. If you're planning to invest in a property or a business abroad financed with funds imported from another country, it's important to consider both the present and possible future exchange rates (don't be too optimistic!). On the other hand, if you live and work abroad and earn your income in the local currency, this may affect your financial commitments abroad (particularly if the local currency is devalued). **Bear in mind that your income can be exposed to risks beyond your control when you live abroad, particularly regarding inflation and exchange rate fluctuations.**

In some countries, e.g. Spain, all residents and non-resident foreigners with financial dealings there must have a fiscal number (called a *número de identificación de entranjero/NIE* in Spain). Your NIE must be used in all dealings with the Spanish tax authorities, when paying property taxes and in various other transactions. Without an NIE in Spain you cannot register the title deed of a property, open a bank account or take out an insurance policy.

If you own a home abroad, you should employ a local professional, e.g. an accountant or tax adviser, as your representative to look after your local financial affairs and declare and pay your taxes. You can also have your representative receive your bank statements, ensure that your bank is paying your standing orders, e.g. for utility bills, and that you have sufficient funds to pay them. In some countries, e.g. Spain, it's mandatory for non-resident property owners to appoint a fiscal representative, who automatically receives all communications from the local tax authorities.

This section includes information on importing and exporting money, banking, using credit, debit and charge cards, mortgages, taxes (property, income, capital gains, inheritance and gifts), and the cost of living.

IMPORTING & EXPORTING MONEY

Exchange controls have been abolished in the last few decades in most countries, particularly EU countries, and countries that allow property sales to foreigners impose few or no restrictions on the import or export of funds. However, many countries require foreigners to declare the import or export of funds above a certain amount, e.g. £5,000/$7,500, and have restrictions on the amount that can be imported or exported in cash, notes and bearer-cheques in any currency, plus gold coins and bars. Where necessary, it's particularly important to declare large sums, e.g. for the purchase of a home abroad, as it may be impossible to (legally) export funds from some countries if they weren't declared when imported. These regulations are usually designed to curb criminal activities, e.g. money laundering, and tax evasion, and may also apply to travellers stopping in a country for less than 24 hours. In some countries foreigners must declare the origin of funds used for property purchase. **Note that if you don't declare the funds, they may be subject to confiscation.**

International Money Transfers: Making international money transfers between different countries can be a nightmare and can take anything from a few minutes to many weeks (or months if the money gets 'lost'), depending on the banks and countries involved. A bank to bank transfer can usually be made by a 'normal' postal transfer or via a wire or electronic transfer (such as SWIFT). A normal transfer within Europe is supposed to take three to seven days, but in reality it often takes much longer, whereas a SWIFT telex transfer *should* be completed in a few hours, with funds being available within 24 hours. The cost of transfers varies considerably, not only the commission and exchange rates, but also transfer charges.

Most international transfers are slow and costly, even between banks and countries with sophisticated, state-of-the-art banking systems. The average time taken for international transfers within Europe is around five days and some transfers take many weeks or even get lost completely. Banks in some countries are notoriously slow and have been accused of deliberately delaying transfers in order to gain interest on money 'in the pipeline'. The cost of transfers also varies considerably. An EU directive which came into force in 1998 limits banks in EU countries to passing on to customers the costs incurred by sender banks, and money must be deposited in customers' accounts within five working days.

Shop around banks and financial institutions for the best deal and don't be afraid to change your bank if the service provided doesn't meet your requirements. Many banks subscribe to an international electronic network to (hopefully) facilitate fast and inexpensive transfers between members. Of these, one of the best is the Interbank On-Line System (IBOS) network (established 1994), whose 15 members include the Royal Bank of Scotland (UK), Bank of Ireland, Banco Santander Central Hispano (Spain), Banco Santander Portugal, Crédit Commercial de France (France), Kredietbank (Belgium), Nordea Group (Scandinavia), ING Bank (Netherlands), San Paolo-IMI (Italy), Bank One and First Union National Bank (USA), Scotiabank (Canada), Scotiabank Inverlat (Mexico) and ABSA Bank (South Africa). The IBOS network (🖳 www.ibosassociation.com) guarantees transfers within 24 hours. Other networks include Taps (around 20 European countries), the Tipa-Net of Co-Operative banks, and the Eufiserv network of EU savings banks.

You can also make transfers in Europe by euro-giro from post offices, which takes three days and is available between most EU countries plus Switzerland. Telegraphic transfers can be made via specialist companies such as Western Union, both within Europe and to North America, which is the quickest and safest method, but also one of the most expensive. American Express (AE) card holders can send money via the AE Moneygram service between AE offices in Europe and North America, and between European countries in as little as 15 minutes. Western Union operates a similar service between Western Union offices, although both are expensive, e.g. fees amounting to 5 to 10 per cent of the amount transferred.

Yet another way to transfer money is via a bank draft, which should be sent by registered mail. Note, however, that in the unlikely event that it's lost or stolen, it's impossible to stop payment and you must wait six months before a new draft can be issued. In some countries, bank drafts aren't treated as cash and must be cleared like personal cheques. It's also possible to send a cheque drawn on a personal account, although both of these take a long time to clear (usually a matter of weeks) and fees can be high. When transferring small amounts it's better to use a cheque or money order. **If you intend to send a large amount of money abroad for a business transaction such as buying a property, you should ensure you receive the commercial rate of exchange rather than the tourist rate.**

Personal Cheques: It's often possible to pay a cheque drawn on your home bank into a bank account abroad, e.g. in Europe, although they can take a long time to clear. A personal cheque drawn on a European or American bank can take three or four weeks to clear, as it must be cleared with the paying bank. However, some banks allow customers to draw on cheques issued on foreign banks from the day they're paid into a client's account. Many foreigners living abroad keep the bulk of their money in a foreign account (perhaps in an off-shore bank) and draw on it using a cash or credit card when abroad. This is a convenient solution for holiday home owners (although you still need a local bank account to pay your local bills).

Postcheques: Giro postcheques issued by European post offices can be cashed (with a guarantee card) for £125 (or the foreign currency equivalent) at post offices in most European countries.

Footnote: In many countries, there isn't a lot of difference in the cost between buying foreign currency using cash, buying travellers' cheques or using a credit card to obtain cash. However, many people simply take cash when travelling abroad, which is asking for trouble, particularly if you have no way of obtaining more cash, e.g. with a credit card. **One thing to bear in mind when travelling anywhere is not to rely on only one source of funds!**

BANKING

Although it's possible to own and use a home abroad without having a local bank account, making use of credit cards and traveller's cheques, this isn't wise and is an expensive option. In any case, home owners usually need a local bank account to pay their utility and tax bills, which are best paid by direct debit. If you have a holiday home abroad, you can usually have all documentation, e.g. cheque books and statements, sent to your permanent home address. Many foreign banks have branches abroad, although only a few British banks, e.g. Barclays, have extensive networks, notably in France and Spain. Note, however, that foreign banks abroad operate in the same way as local banks, so you shouldn't expect, for example, a branch of Barclays or Deutsche Bank in Spain to behave like a branch in Britain or Germany.

Non-residents can open a bank account in most countries by correspondence, although it's best done in person in the country concerned. Ask your friends, neighbours or colleagues for their recommendations and just visit the bank of your choice and introduce yourself. You must provide proof of identity, e.g. a passport or identity card, your address abroad and in some countries, e.g. Spain, a fiscal number. If you open an account while in your home country, you must obtain an application form from an overseas branch of your chosen bank or from a bank abroad. If you open an account by correspondence, you will also need to provide a reference from your current bank (which may be necessary in any case).

Note that banks in most countries make few or no concessions to foreign customers, e.g. the provision of general information and documentation such as statements in foreign languages and staff who speak foreign languages. However, some banks offer a multilingual service and go out of their way to attract foreign customers. In some countries there are restrictions regarding the type of accounts a non-resident foreigner may open.

Note that overdrawing a bank account in many countries is a criminal offence and offenders can be barred from maintaining a bank account; it will also severely damage your credit rating.

Offshore Banking

If you have a sum of money to invest or wish to protect your inheritance from the tax man, it may be worthwhile looking into the accounts and services (such as pensions and trusts) provided by offshore banking centres in tax havens such as the Channel Islands (Guernsey and Jersey), Gibraltar and the Isle of Man (around 50 locations world-wide are officially classified as tax havens). The big attraction of offshore banking is that money can be deposited in a wide range of currencies, customers are usually guaranteed complete anonymity, there are no double-taxation agreements, no withholding tax is payable, and interest is paid tax-free. Many offshore banks also offer telephone banking (usually seven days a week) and some provide Internet banking.

A large number of American, British and other European banks and financial institutions provide offshore banking facilities in one or more locations. Most institutions offer high-interest deposit accounts for long-term savings and investment portfolios, in which funds can be deposited in any major currency. Many people living abroad keep a local account for everyday business and maintain an offshore account for international transactions and investment purposes. **However, most financial experts advise investors never to rush into the expatriate life and invest their life savings in an offshore tax haven until they know what their long-term plans are.**

Accounts have minimum deposits levels which usually range from £500 to £10,000 ($750 to $15,000), with some as high as £100,000 ($150,000). In addition to large minimum balances, accounts may also have stringent terms and conditions, such as restrictions on withdrawals or high early withdrawal penalties. You can deposit funds on call (instant access) or for a fixed period, e.g. from 90 days to one year (usually for larger sums). Interest is usually paid monthly or annually. Monthly interest payments are slightly lower than annual payments, although they have the advantage of providing a regular income. There are usually no charges provided a specified minimum balance is maintained. Many accounts offer a debit card, e.g. Mastercard or Visa, which can be used to obtain cash via ATMs throughout the world.

When selecting a financial institution and offshore banking centre, your first priority should be for the safety of your money. In some offshore banking centres all bank deposits are guaranteed up to a maximum amount under a deposit protection scheme, whereby a maximum sum is guaranteed should a financial institution go to the wall (the Isle of Man, Guernsey and Jersey all have such schemes). Unless you're planning to bank with a major international bank (which is only likely to fold the day after the end of the world!), you should always check the credit rating of a financial institution before depositing any money, particularly if it doesn't provide deposit insurance. All banks have a credit rating (the highest is 'AAA') and a bank with a high rating will be happy to tell you (but get it in writing). You can also check the rating of an international bank or financial organisation with Moody's Investor Service. You should be wary of institutions offering higher than average interest rates, as if it looks too good to be true it probably will be – like the Bank of International Commerce and Credit (BICC) which went bust in 1992.

CREDIT, DEBIT & CHARGE CARDS

'Plastic money' in the form of debit, credit and charge cards is widely used in most countries, where banks are fast creating a cashless society. Debit cards are issued by most banks and most can be used abroad via the Visa and Mastercard networks. Most foreign banks also issue debit cards. With a debit card cash withdrawals and purchases are automatically debited from a cheque or savings account. All withdrawals or purchases are shown on your monthly statement and you cannot usually run up an overdraft or obtain credit.

Cards allow holders to withdraw cash, e.g. £100 to £500 ($150 to $750), or the foreign currency equivalent per day from automated teller machines (ATMs) and obtain account balances and mini-statements. Cash can also be obtained from the ATMs of other networks (other than the one your card belongs to), although there's usually a fee. Most ATMs accept a bewildering number of cards, which may be illustrated on machines, including credit (Eurocard, Mastercard, Visa) and charge cards (Amex, Diners Club). Note that although foreign debit cards such as those belonging to the Visa network can be used to obtain cash abroad, they may be treated as credit cards and a charge levied.

Credit and charge cards are usually referred to collectively as credit cards, although not all cards are real credit cards, where the balance can be repaid over a period. Visa and Mastercard are the most widely acceptable credit cards in most countries and are issued by most banks. Charge cards such as American Express and Diners Club aren't widely accepted in some countries, particularly by small businesses (who wisely prefer cash, which cannot be traced by the tax authorities!).

Note that when using a credit card in some countries, e.g. France, you usually need to enter a PIN number into a machine, without which you're unable to use your credit card. You also need a PIN number to withdraw cash abroad from an ATM with a credit card (there's a limit to the amount that can be withdrawn). Note that using a foreign credit card to obtain cash abroad is usually expensive as there's a standard charge, e.g. 1.5 per cent, plus a high interest rate which is usually charged from the day of the withdrawal. Never assume that a particular business (such as a restaurant) accepts a particular credit or charge card or you may discover to your embarrassment that: 'that *won't* do nicely sir'! Note that small businesses in many countries don't accept credit cards.

Even if you shun credit cards in your home country they can be particularly useful when abroad, for example for paying for travel tickets, car rentals and hotel bills. They also offer safety, security and convenience, although you should be wary of bogus charges and carefully scrutinise your statements. **You shouldn't, however, rely solely on credit cards for obtaining cash or paying bills when travelling abroad.**

MORTGAGES

Mortgages or home loans for those buying a home abroad may be available in your home country, the country where the property is situated, and possibly also from financial institutions in offshore banking centres. The amount that can be borrowed varies according to the country where the property is situated, the country where the loan is to be raised, the lender, and, not least, the financial standing of the borrower.

In recent years, lenders have tightened their lending criteria because of the repayment problems experienced by many recession-hit borrowers in the '90s, and some lenders apply strict rules regarding income, employment and the type of property on which they will lend. Foreign lenders such as banks in offshore financial centres also have strict rules regarding the nationality and domicile of borrowers, and the percentage they will lend. In theory lenders based in European Union (EU) countries are allowed to make loans anywhere within the EU, but in practice a single market doesn't exist.

In some countries, e.g. France, the law doesn't permit banks to offer mortgages or other loans where repayments are more than one third of net income (which includes existing mortgage or rental payments). Joint incomes and liabilities are included when assessing a couple's borrowing limit (usually a bank will lend to up to three joint borrowers). Most banks require proof of your monthly income and all outgoings such as mortgage payments, rent and other loans and commitments. Proof of income includes three month's pay slips for employees, confirmation of income from your employer and tax returns. If you're self-employed, you usually require an audited copy of your balance sheets and trading accounts for the past three years, plus your last tax return. Foreign banks aren't particularly impressed with accountants' letters. If you want a mortgage to buy a property for commercial purposes, you must usually provide a detailed business plan. In most countries it's customary for a property to be held as security for a loan, i.e. the lender takes a first charge on the property which is recorded at the property registry.

Mortgages are granted on a percentage of a property's valuation, which itself may be below the actual market value. The maximum mortgage granted in most countries is 70 to 80 per cent of the purchase price, although it can be as low as 50 to 60 per cent for non-residents and buyers of second homes. Banks may also offer non-status loans of around 50 per cent, where no proof of income is required. Loans may be repaid over five to 30 years, depending on the lender and country, although the usual term in most countries is 10 to 20 years for residents and possibly less for non-residents. Repayment mortgages are the most common type in most countries, although endowment and pension-linked mortgages are also available in some countries. Repayments are usually made monthly or quarterly, although bi-weekly payments (which reduce the overall cost considerably) are also possible in some countries.

Note that you must add expenses and fees (see **The Fees** on page 89), totalling from 5 to 20 per cent of the purchase price (depending on the country) to the cost of a property. There are various fees associated with mortgages, e.g. all lenders charge an 'arrangement' fee and although it's unusual to have a survey in most countries, lenders usually insist on a 'valuation survey' before they grant a loan. **Always shop around for the best interest rate *and* ask the effective rate including *all* commissions and fees.**

Buying Through an Offshore Company: This is (not surprisingly) popular among non-resident property buyers in many countries, as they can legally avoid paying wealth tax, inheritance tax and capital gains tax. Buyers can also avoid transfer tax or stamp duty when buying a property owned by an offshore company, which can be a good selling point. However, it isn't possible in many countries and the owners of properties purchased through offshore companies in some countries, e.g. Spain, have been required to register their ownership with the authorities in recent years or face punitive taxes. However, there are still legitimate advantages for buying through an offshore company in some countries, although you should obtain expert advice from an experienced lawyer before doing so.

Mortgages for Second Homes: If you have equity in an existing home it may be more cost effective to remortgage (or take out a second mortgage) on that property, rather than take out a new mortgage for a home abroad. It entails less paperwork and therefore lower legal fees and a plan can be tailored to meet your individual requirements. Depending on your equity in your existing property and the cost of a home abroad, this may also enable you to pay cash for a second home. The disadvantage of remortgaging or taking out a second mortgage is that you reduce the amount of equity available in a property, which may be useful if you need to raise cash in an emergency. Note that when a mortgage is taken out on a home abroad, it's usually charged against the property and not the individual borrower, which may be important if you get into repayment difficulties.

Foreign Currency Loans: It's generally recognised that you should take out a mortgage in the currency in which your income is paid or in the currency of the country where a property is situated. However, it's also possible to obtain a foreign currency mortgage in major currencies such as £sterling, $US, Swiss francs or euros. In previous years, high interest rates in many countries meant that a foreign currency mortgage was a good deal. **However, you should be extremely wary of taking out a foreign currency mortgage, as interest rate gains can be wiped out overnight by currency swings and devaluations.**

The advantage of having a mortgage in the currency in which your income is paid is that if the currency is devalued against the currency of the country where you own a property, you will have the consolation that the value of your home abroad will (theoretically) have increased by the same percentage when converted back into your 'income' currency. When choosing between various currencies, you should take into account the costs, fees, interest rates and possible currency fluctuations. Regardless of how you finance the purchase of a home abroad, you should always obtain professional advice. Note that if you have a foreign currency mortgage, you must usually pay commission charges each time you transfer currency to pay your mortgage or remit money abroad. If you let a home abroad, you may be able to offset the interest on your mortgage against rental income, but only pro rata. If you raise a mortgage outside your home country or in a foreign currency, you should be aware of any impact this may have on your tax allowances or liabilities.

Payment Problems: If you're unable to meet your mortgage payments, some lenders will renegotiate mortgages so that payments are made over a longer period, thus allowing you to reduce your payments. Although interest rates have fallen dramatically in recent years, many lenders are slow to reduce their interest rates for existing borrowers and some try to prevent existing mortgage holders transferring to another lender offering a lower rate by imposing prohibitive fees. However, some countries have introduced legislation to enable borrowers with fixed rate mortgages to change their mortgage lender or re-negotiate a mortgage with their existing lender at a greatly reduced cost. In some countries a mortgage can be taken over (assumed) by the new owner when a property is sold, which can be advantageous for a buyer. If you stop paying your mortgage, your lender can embargo your property and could eventually forcibly sell it at auction.

Tax relief: Note that residents in many countries receive tax relief on mortgages, which may include both capital and interest repayments, therefore it may pay you to have a mortgage when living abroad, even when you can afford to pay cash. Some countries, e.g. Britain, allow taxpayers to deduct the interest on a mortgage taken out on an overseas home.

TAXES

Before buying a home abroad, you should investigate the taxes levied on non-resident property owners such as property taxes (rates), residential tax, capital gains tax, wealth tax and inheritance tax. If you plan to live abroad permanently, you will also need to compare income tax rates, social security and other taxes incurred by residents. For many people, moving abroad is an opportunity to reduce their overall taxes, particularly when moving from a high to a low-tax country, when the timing of a move can be decisive. Some countries encourage foreigners, e.g. retirees, to take up residence by offering tax incentives. Note that in most countries, taxes are payable on property transactions, which can increase the cost of buying a property considerably (see **The Fees** on page 89).

Property Taxes

Property taxes (also called real estate taxes or rates) are levied by local authorities in most countries and are payable by all property owners, irrespective of whether they're residents or non-residents. In some countries an additional 'residential' or local income tax is also paid by residents. Property taxes pay for local services which may include garbage collection, street lighting, sanitary services, e.g. street and beach cleaning, local schools and other community services, local council administration, social assistance, community substructure, cultural and sports amenities, and possibly water rates. Before buying a property, check the tax rate with the local town hall, as rates usually vary from community to community.

Property tax is usually payable irrespective of whether a property is inhabited, provided it's furnished and habitable. It may be split into two separate amounts, one for the building and another for the land, with tax on the land payable irrespective of whether it's built on or not. Before buying a property you should check that there are no outstanding property taxes for the current or previous years, as in many countries the new owner assumes all unpaid property related taxes and debts (you can, however, reclaim the tax from the previous owner - if you can find him!). When you buy a property in any country, your ownership must be registered at the local land registry, which is usually done by the public notary officiating at the completion of the sale.

Property taxes are normally based on the fiscal or notional letting value of a property, which is usually lower than the actual purchase price or a property's market value. If the fiscal value of your property increases greatly, check that it has been correctly calculated. You can appeal against the valuation of your property if you believe it's too high, particularly if it's higher than that of similar properties in the same area. Note, however, that an appeal must be lodged within a limited period (check with the local town hall). **It's important that the fiscal value of your property is correct, as in some countries, e.g. Spain, a number of taxes are linked**

to this value such as property letting tax, wealth tax, transfer tax on property sales and inheritance tax.

Valuation: Property values are calculated according to a variety of measurements and evaluations which usually include the area of the property (i.e. the built or living area, terraces, outbuildings, garage and land areas), building and zoning restrictions in the area, the quality and date of construction, the proximity to services, e.g. mains water, electricity and gas, and roads, and the location. You can check that your property is correctly specified at the local town hall or land registration office, where a dossier is maintained for all properties. This usually contains official papers, plans, and photographs relating to a property. Carefully check that all the information recorded is correct, as errors are fairly common in some countries. Note that property valuations may be adjusted periodically to account for inflation.

Tax Rates: Tax rates are usually expressed in a variety of ways, e.g. as a percentage such as 0.5 to 1.5 per cent, by which the fiscal value is simply multiplied to obtain the annual tax due. The rate may depend on both the population of the municipality and the level of public services provided, and can vary considerably for similar properties located in different areas. If a municipality has invested heavily in civic amenities, e.g. indoor sports complexes (with swimming pools, gymnasiums, etc.) and cultural centres, then property taxes may be increased dramatically to pay for them. Therefore a high property tax may be a good rather than a bad sign, although it may also indicate that the local council is dishonest or profligate.

Payment: Note that town halls in some countries don't send out bills and it's the property owner's responsibility to discover the amount due and when it's payable. If you're a non-resident, you should pay your property tax (and other local taxes and utility bills) by direct debit from a local bank account. You can also employ a local property management company or representative to pay your property tax and other bills relating to your property. If property tax isn't paid on time, a surcharge may be levied in addition to interest, plus possible collection costs. If you get into debt and are unable to pay your property tax, you should talk to your local tax office. They will be pleased to know that you haven't absconded and will usually be willing to agree a payment schedule.

Non-payment: If you 'forget' to pay your property taxes or refuse to pay them, your property can (after a certain period) be seized and sold at auction, often for a fraction of its market value. In some countries there have been cases of foreigners returning after a long absence to find that their property has been sold to pay unpaid taxes. Local authorities may also have the power to seize vehicles and place garnishment orders on bank accounts. **There's little sympathy among local residents with those who blatantly avoid paying property taxes, as other owners must bear the burden (through increased taxes) or municipalities are forced to cut services.**

Other Local Taxes: Note that the local authorities in some countries may also levy special fees for services such as beach cleaning or sewerage. Other taxes may include a regional or sundry tax, which may be levied on properties located in popular tourist areas where local authorities fund special amenities and pay for the upkeep of showpiece gardens, parks and other 'attractions'. In France (and some other countries) there's an additional property based 'residential' tax (*taxe d'habitation*), which is payable by anyone who lives in a property, whether as an owner, tenant or rent free.

Wealth Tax

Some countries levy a wealth tax, although this is usually applicable only to residents. Spain is a notable exception, where wealth tax also applies to non-resident property owners. Your wealth is generally calculated by totalling your assets and deducting your liabilities. When calculating your wealth tax, you must include the value of all assets including property (real estate), vehicles, boats, aircraft, business ownership, cash (e.g. in bank accounts), life insurance, gold bars, jewellery, stocks, shares and bonds. If you fail to declare your total assets you can be fined. Assets that are exempt from wealth tax usually include *objets d'art* and antiques (provided their value doesn't exceed certain limits), the vested rights of participants in pension plans and funds, copyrights (so long as they remain part of your net worth), assets forming part of a country's historical heritage, and 'professional assets' in a business. Deductions are usually made for mortgages, business and other debts, and wealth tax paid in another country.

The level at which wealth tax is applicable varies greatly according to the country and whether you're a resident or non-resident. For residents in Spain it's payable on assets above €108,182 (although a couple are each entitled to the exemption, making a combined exemption of €216,364) while in France no tax is payable on assets below €700,000. Wealth tax may depend on your domicile, e.g. if you're domiciled in France, the value of your estate is based on your world-wide assets. If you're resident in France but not domiciled there, the value of your estate is based only on your assets in France.

Capital Gains Tax (CGT)

Capital gains tax is payable on the profit from sales of certain assets in most countries, which usually includes property (real estate) and may also include antiques, art and jewellery, stocks, bonds and shares, household furnishings, vehicles, coin and stamp collections and other 'collectibles', gold, silver and gems, and the sale of a business. International tax treaties usually decree that capital gains on property is taxable in the country where it's located.

Note that if you move abroad permanently and retain a property in your home country, this may affect your position regarding capital gains there. Had you sold your foreign home before moving abroad, you would have been exempt from CGT as it would have been your principal residence. However, if you establish your principal residence abroad, your property in your home country becomes a second home and thus liable to CGT when it's sold. Capital gains tax can be a complicated subject and you should always obtain legal advice before buying a property abroad. **Note that the tax authorities in many countries co-operate to track down those attempting to avoid capital gains tax.**

Most countries have an exemption if gains don't exceed a certain figure, e.g. €900 in France and €1,200 in Spain, in a calendar year. Certain gains are exempt and these may include gains as a result of the death of a taxpayer, gifts to government entities, donations of certain assets in lieu of tax payments, and the contribution of assets in exchange for a life annuity for those aged over 65. Capital losses can usually be offset against capital gains, but not against ordinary income, and it's usually possible to carry forward capital losses (or a percentage) in excess of gains and offset them against future gains for a limited period. In most countries capital gains are treated as ordinary income for residents.

A property capital gain is based on the difference between the purchase price and the sale price. However, in most countries there are exemptions, which usually depend on the number of years a property has been owned. If an asset has been owned for less than a certain period, e.g. two years in France and Spain, capital gains are taxed in full. Most countries allow a tax exemption (called indexation relief) on the sale of your principal residence (e.g. Britain and France), although some (such as Spain and the USA) allow an exemption only if you buy another home within two years, and levy tax on any profits that aren't re-invested. In the USA, if you're over 55 you can make a one-time, tax-free profit of $125,000 on the sale of your principal residence before becoming liable for CGT. Note that in some countries you're exempt from CGT on a second home if you don't own your main residence, i.e. if you're a tenant or leaseholder, although this may apply only to the first sale of a second home.

In some countries, capital gains made by non-residents are taxed at a flat rate, e.g. 35 per cent in Spain, and there may be no reduction for the length of time you've owned a property. However, in most countries the amount of CGT payable is reduced the longer you've owned a property until it's no longer applicable, e.g. after 32 years in France and ten years in Spain. Where applicable, a sum may be withheld by the official handling the sale in lieu of capital gains tax or the buyer must retain a percentage when the seller is a non-resident, e.g. 5 per cent in Spain.

You should keep all bills for the fees associated with buying a property, e.g. lawyer, estate agent and surveyor, plus any bills for renovation, restoration, modernisation and improvements of a second home, as these can usually be offset against CGT and may be index-linked. If you work on a house yourself, you should keep a copy of all bills for materials and tools, as these may also be offset against CGT. Losses on rentals may also be able to be carried forward and offset against a capital gain when a property is sold. Costs relating to a sale can also usually be offset against any gain, as can interest paid on a loan taken out to purchase or restore a property. In some countries you can protect yourself and your survivors from capital gains tax by bequeathing appreciated property, rather than giving it away while you're alive.

Inheritance & Gift Tax

Dying doesn't free you entirely from the clutches of the tax man and most countries impose an inheritance (also called estate tax or death duty) and gift tax on the estate of a deceased person. Usually both residents and non-residents are subject to inheritance tax if they own property abroad. The country where you pay inheritance and gift tax is usually decided by your domicile. If you're living permanently abroad at the time of your death, you will be deemed to be domiciled there by the local tax authorities. If you're domiciled abroad, then inheritance and gift tax payable there will apply to your world-wide estate (excluding property), otherwise it applies only to assets held abroad, such as a holiday home. It's important to make your domicile clear so that there's no misunderstanding on your death.

Inheritance Tax: In many countries, e.g. France and Spain, inheritance tax is paid by the beneficiaries and not by the deceased's estate. This may mean that if you inherit a home abroad, you will need to sell it to pay tax. The rate of inheritance tax payable usually depends upon the relationship between the donor and the recipient, the amount inherited, and (in some countries) the current wealth of the recipient. Direct descendants and close relatives of the deceased usually receive an allowance before they become liable for inheritance tax. Some countries have strict succession laws (although they aren't always applied to foreigners) regarding to whom you can leave your assets. To take advantage of lower tax rates, you should leave property to your spouse, children or parents, rather than someone who's unrelated.

In many countries there are a number of ways to avoid or reduce inheritance tax, including buying property through an offshore company or trust. Note that most countries don't recognise the rights to inheritance of a non-married partner, although there are a number of solutions to this problem, e.g. a life insurance policy. Some bequests are exempt from inheritance tax, including certain types of properties and legacies to charities and government bodies.

Gift Tax: Gift tax is calculated in the same way as inheritance tax, according to the relationship between the donor and the recipient and the size of the gift. A reduction is usually granted according to the age of the donor (generally the younger the donor the larger the reduction).

It's important for both residents and non-residents owning a home abroad to decide in advance how they wish to dispose of it. If possible, this should be decided *before* buying a home or other property abroad, as it can be complicated and expensive to change later. There are many ways to limit or delay the impact of inheritance laws, including inserting a clause in a property purchase contract allowing a property to be left in its entirety to a surviving spouse without being shared among the children. A surviving spouse can also be given a life interest in an estate in preference to children or parents, through a 'gift between spouses'.

Inheritance law is a complicated subject and professional advice should be sought from an experienced lawyer who's familiar with the inheritance laws of the country where you plan to buy (or own) a home and any other countries involved. Your will is a vital component in ensuring that inheritance and gift tax is kept to a minimum or delaying its payment.

Income Tax

Income tax is mainly of interest (or concern!) to those planning to live or work abroad permanently, as non-residents are usually only liable to pay income tax in a country when they receive income from a local source. Most countries levy income tax on income earned by non-residents such as the income from letting a home. If you're planning to live or work abroad permanently you should also take into account social security contributions, which are very high in some countries, particularly for the self-employed. If you're planning to work or start a business abroad, you should seek expert tax advice, both in your present country of residence regarding your tax liability there and the country where you plan to work. Note that the combined burden of income tax, social security and other taxes can make a considerable hole in your income in some countries.

Liability: Your liability to pay income tax in a country where you own property depends on whether you earn any income from your property or have income arising in that country and how long you're resident there each year. In some countries, e.g. Spain, all home owners must pay an imputed 'letting' tax based on the value of their property, irrespective of whether they receive any income from it. Under the law of most countries you become a fiscal resident (liable to income tax) if you spend 183 days there during a calendar year *or* your main centre of economic interest, e.g. investments or business, is there. Temporary absences are usually included in the calculation of the period spent abroad, unless residence is shown to have been in another country for 183 days in a calendar year. If your spouse (and dependent minor children) normally resides in a country where you have a home, has a residence permit and isn't legally separated from you, you may also be considered to be a tax resident in that country (unless you can prove otherwise). Some countries restrict the visits of non-residents over a certain period, e.g. Britain limits visits by non-residents to 182 days in any tax year *or* an average of 91 days per tax year over four consecutive tax years.

Dual Residence: It's possible for some people to have 'dual residence' and be tax resident in two countries simultaneously, in which case your 'tax home' may be resolved under the rules of international treaties. Under such treaties you're considered to be resident in the country where you have a permanent home. If you have a permanent home in both countries, you're deemed to be resident in the country where you have the closest personal and economic ties. If your residence cannot be determined under the above rules, you're deemed to be resident in the country where you have your habitual abode. If you have your habitual abode in both or in neither country, you're deemed to be resident in the country of which you're a citizen. Finally, if you're a citizen of both or neither country, the authorities of the countries concerned will decide your tax residence between them by mutual agreement.

Double Taxation: Residents in most countries are taxed on their world-wide income, subject to certain treaty exceptions. Non-residents are usually taxed only on income arising in a particular country, e.g. non-residents of France only pay tax on income arising in France. Citizens of most countries are exempt from paying taxes in their home country when they spend a minimum period abroad, e.g. one year. Many countries have double taxation treaties with other countries that are designed to ensure that income that has been taxed in one treaty country isn't taxed again in another. The treaty establishes a tax credit or exemption on certain kinds of income, either in the country of residence or the country where the income is earned.

Double taxation treaties vary with the country, for example the UK has treaties with most of the countries featured in this book (see **Chapter 6**). Where applicable, a double-taxation treaty prevails over domestic law. However, even when there's no double taxation agreement between two countries, you can still obtain relief from double taxation. When there's no double taxation agreement, tax relief is provided through direct deduction of any foreign tax paid or through a 'foreign compensation' formula. Note that if your tax liability in one country is less than in another, you may be required to pay the tax authorities the difference in the country where you're resident. If you're in doubt about your tax liability in your home country or a country where you own property, contact your nearest embassy or consulate for information. The USA is the only country that taxes its non-resident citizens on income earned abroad (US citizens can obtain a copy of a brochure, *Tax Guide for Americans Abroad*, from American consulates).

Moving Abroad: Before leaving a country for good, you must usually pay any tax due for the previous year and the year of departure, and you may also need to apply for a tax clearance. A tax return must usually be filed prior to departure and must include your income and deductions for the current tax year up to the date of departure. The local tax office will calculate the taxes due and provide a written statement. In some countries a tax clearance certificate is necessary to obtain a 'sailing or departure permit' or an exit visa. A shipping or removal company may also need official authorisation from the tax authorities before they can ship your effects abroad.

Tax Havens: If you're looking for a tax haven or a low tax country you should investigate buying a home in Andorra, the Caribbean islands (e.g. Bahamas, Bermuda or the Cayman Islands), the Channel Islands, Cyprus, the Isle of Man, Gibraltar, Liechtenstein, Malta, Monaco or Switzerland. Note that you need a *very* large bank balance to purchase a property and become a resident in some low-tax countries, e.g. the Caribbean, the Channel Islands, Monaco and Switzerland. You should also be aware that owning a home in a particular country won't necessarily qualify you for a residence permit and that to qualify as a resident you must usually spend at least 183 days a year in a country.

Planning: If you're planning to move abroad permanently, you should plan well in advance, as the timing of a move can make a big difference to your tax liabilities, both in your present and your new country of residence. Investigate beforehand what you need to do to become a non-resident in your current country of residence and how long you will need to be resident in your new home to qualify as a resident for tax purposes. In most countries you automatically become liable for income tax if you spend longer than six months (183 days) there during a calendar year.

If you intend to live abroad permanently, you should notify the tax authorities in your previous country of residence well in advance. You may be entitled to a tax refund if you leave during the tax year, which usually requires the completion of a tax return. The authorities may require evidence that you're leaving the country, e.g. evidence of a job abroad or of having purchased or rented a property abroad. If you move abroad to take up a job or start a business, you must register with the local tax authorities soon after your arrival.

COST OF LIVING

No doubt you would like to estimate how far your money will stretch abroad and how much you will have left after paying your bills. The cost of living has risen considerably in most countries in the last decade or so, and some Mediterranean countries that previously enjoyed a relatively low cost of living are no longer quite so attractive, particularly for retirees. On the other hand, foreigners whose income is paid in 'hard' currencies, such as those of most northern European countries and North America, have seen their incomes (when converted to local currencies) in many countries rise sharply in recent years. If anything, the difference in the cost of living between 'rich' North American and northern European countries (where most holiday home buyers and retirees come from) has remained the same or has widened in favour of the richer countries.

If you spend only a few weeks abroad each year, you won't be too concerned about the local cost of living. However, if you plan to live abroad permanently you should ensure that your income is, and will remain, sufficient to live on bearing in mind devaluations (if your income isn't paid in local currency), inflation, and extraordinary expenses such as medical bills or anything else that may drastically reduce your income (such as stock market crashes and recessions). Note that if your pension is paid in a currency that's devalued, this could have a catastrophic affect on your standard of living (as it did on British residents abroad when sterling was effectively devalued by some 20 per cent in 1992 after Britain withdrew from the European Monetary System). Note also that some countries, e.g. Britain, freeze the pensions of state pensioners living in certain countries.

It's difficult to calculate an average cost of living for any country as it depends on each individual's particular circumstances and life-style and where you live. It's generally cheaper to live in a rural area than in a large city or a popular resort area (and homes are also much cheaper). The actual difference in your food bill will depend on what you eat and where you lived before moving abroad. Food in most southern European and Mediterranean countries is cheaper than in most northern European countries, although North Americans will find it costs around the same or more. The equivalent of around £150 ($225) should feed two adults for a month, including inexpensive local wine, but excluding fillet steak, caviar and expensive imported foods.

A couple owning their home (with no mortgage) in many popular 'retirement' countries can 'survive' on a net income of as little as £300 ($500) a month (some pensioners live on less) and most people can live quite comfortably on an income of £500 ($750) a month. In fact many northern Europeans (particularly Scandinavians) and North Americans find that if they live modestly without overdoing the luxuries, their cost of living is around half that in their home country.

Comparing prices and where feasible shopping abroad (possibly by mail) for expensive items can yield huge savings. It may also be possible to make savings by buying clothes, general household items, furniture and furnishings, and even your car abroad. Where possible, foreign newspapers and magazines should be purchased on subscription. If you have a tight budget, you should avoid shopping in fashionable towns or shopping centres and 'tourist-oriented' shops (which abound in some countries and may include supermarkets in areas inhabited mainly by foreigners). Ask the locals where to shop for the lowest prices.

4.

FINDING YOUR DREAM HOME

Having decided the country where you plan to buy a home, your next decision is to choose the area and the type of home to buy. If you're unsure where and what to buy, the best decision is usually to rent a property for a period, e.g. six months or a year (see page 74). The secret of successfully buying a home abroad is research, research and more research. You may be fortunate and buy the first property you see without doing any homework and live happily ever after. However, a successful purchase is much more likely if you thoroughly investigate a country, its regions, the range of property available, prices and relative values, and the procedure for buying property. It's a wise or lucky person who gets his choice absolutely right first time, but you will have a much better chance if you do your homework thoroughly.

This chapter is designed to help you decide what sort of home to buy and, most importantly, its location. It will help you avoid problems and contains information about the cost, contracts, conveyancing, deposits, fees, legal advice, choosing the location, community properties, renovation and restoration, guarantees, utilities, planning permission, heating and air-conditioning, security, renting, garages, surveys, estate agents, building your own home, timesharing (and other part ownership schemes), moving house, property income, and, last but not least, selling a home.

AVOIDING PROBLEMS

The problems associated with buying property abroad have been highlighted in the last few decades, during which the property market in many countries has gone from boom to bust and back again. The laws regarding the purchase and sale of property in some countries are full of holes and an open invitation for dishonest sellers to exploit a foreign buyer's ignorance. On occasion some observers have even gone as far as to advise people *not* to buy in certain countries. However, although the pitfalls must never be ignored, buying property in most countries needn't be a gamble. There are millions of foreign property owners owning property in a large number of countries, the vast majority of whom are happy with their purchases and encountered few or no problems when buying their homes. This should be borne in mind when you hear or read horror stories concerning foreign property buyers abroad.

However, it cannot be emphasised too strongly that anyone planning to buy (or sell) property abroad *must* take expert, independent legal advice. *Never* sign anything or pay any money until you've sought legal advice in a language in which you're fluent from an experienced lawyer (preferably someone who has been highly recommended). If you aren't prepared to do this, you shouldn't even think about buying a home abroad!

The majority of people buying a home abroad don't obtain independent legal advice and most people who experience problems take no precautions whatsoever when purchasing property. Of those that do take legal advice, many do so only after having already paid a deposit and signed a contract or, more commonly, after they've run into problems. You will find the relatively small cost (in comparison to the cost of a property) of obtaining legal advice to be excellent value for money, if only for the peace of mind it affords. Trying to cut corners to save 'a few pence' on legal costs is foolhardy in the extreme when a large sum of money is at stake. **However, be careful who you employ, as in some countries lawyers are part of the problem rather than the solution!**

It definitely *isn't* wise to rely solely on advice given by those with a financial interest in selling you a property, such as a developer or agent, although their advice may be excellent and totally unbiased. You can find professionals who speak English and other foreign languages in all countries, and many expatriate professionals also practise abroad. However, when dealing with a fellow countryman you should never assume that he'll offer you a better deal or do a better job than a local national. **In fact most frauds are perpetrated by foreigners on their fellow countrymen.** Deal only with reputable and registered estate agents, as it isn't unknown for bogus agents or owners to sell the same house to a number of people and disappear with the money!

There are a number of flaws in the legal procedures for buying property in some countries, some of which are unique to that particular country. Professionals operating in many countries aren't required to have liability insurance, developers are sometimes grossly under-funded (hence the large number of bankruptcies during the recession in the '90s), and some countries attract more than their fair share of crooks and fraudsters. On the other hand, buyers must also accept their share of blame. Some do incredibly irresponsible things, such as literally handing over 'bags of cash' to agents and owners without any security. **It's hardly surprising that people are defrauded!**

Among the many problems experienced by buyers are properties purchased without a legal title, properties built (or extended) illegally without planning permission, properties sold that are subject to mortgages or embargoes, properties with missing infrastructure, properties sold to more than one buyer, and even properties sold that don't exist! Checks must be made both before signing a contract *and* before signing the deed of sale. Note that if you get into a dispute over a property deal it can take many years to have it resolved via the courts, and even then there's no guarantee that you will ever receive satisfaction.

In many countries, e.g. Spain, there's a law of subrogation, whereby property debts, including mortgages, local taxes and community charges, remain with a property and are inherited by a buyer. This is an open invitation to dishonest sellers to 'cut and run'. It's possible, of course, to check whether there are any outstanding debts on a property and this should be done by your legal advisor. However, it may be impossible to prevent a seller fraudulently taking out a loan on a property after you've made a check. In some countries, problems arise when people buy unfinished properties (i.e. buying off plan) or properties on unfinished developments. A 'finished' property is a property where the building is complete in every detail (as confirmed by your own architect or legal advisor), all communal services have been completed, and *all* infrastructure is in place such as roads, parking areas, lighting, landscaping, water, sewerage, swimming pools, tennis courts, electricity (individual meters) and telephone lines.

In view of the problems associated with buying off plan in some countries, such as the difficulty in ensuring that you actually receive what's stated in the contract and that the developer doesn't go broke, some experts advise buyers against buying an unfinished property. On the other hand, in most countries there are excellent legal safeguards for buyers buying off plan and it's a common practice - in fact it's often the only way to buy in a popular development. **However, you should *always* ensure that payments are secured by a cast-iron guarantee!**

RENTING

If you're uncertain about exactly what you want, how much you wish to pay and where you want to live, it's wise to rent a furnished property for six months or a year in order to reduce the chances of making a costly error when buying in an unfamiliar country or region. If possible, you should rent a similar property to that which you're planning to buy, during the time of year when you plan to occupy it. If you're looking for a permanent home, it's wise to rent during the worst part of the year (weather-wise) and either outside the main tourist season (in 'remote' parts) or at the height of the season (in a popular resort). If you're planning to buy a property in a resort area, long-term rentals are usually good value, particularly during the winter months. If you're looking for a rental property for a long let, e.g. six months, it's wise not to rent unseen, but to rent a holiday apartment for a few weeks to allow you time to look around for a long-term rental.

Renting allows you to become familiar with the weather, the amenities and the local people, to meet other expatriates who have made their home there and ask them about their experiences, and not least, to discover the real cost of living for yourself. Provided you still find the area alluring, this will also allow you plenty of time to look around for a permanent home at your leisure. **The wrong decision regarding location is one of the main causes of disenchantment among foreigners who have purchased property abroad.** Renting 'buys' you time to find your dream home at your leisure.

In most countries there's a huge range of properties for rent at all prices including cottages, apartments, villas, bungalows, mobile homes, chalets, and even castles and manor houses. The most elaborate dwellings have private swimming pools, tennis courts and acres of private parkland, although you may need to rob a bank to pay the rent! Standards vary considerably, from dilapidated ill-equipped cottages in rural areas to beach-side, luxury villas with every modern convenience. However, most properties are well-equipped with everything required, although you should check whether bed linen and towels are provided, and whether there's a washing machine, television or anything else you consider essential.

There's usually a wide selection of properties for rent in most countries, particularly during winter, when rates are usually relatively low for long lets. Properties are advertised in local newspapers and magazines, particularly expatriate publications, and can also be found through property publications in individual countries such as France, Spain and the USA. You can place a 'wanted' advertisement in a local newspaper or magazine, although you shouldn't rely on finding a rental this way. One of the best places to start looking for a rental home is in the wealth of catalogues available at travel agents and in lists provided by national tourist offices. Many estate agents also offer rentals, and developers in many countries rent properties to potential buyers.

Home Exchange: An alternative to renting is to exchange your home with one abroad for a period. This way you can experience home living abroad for a relatively small cost and may save yourself the expense of a long-term rental. Although there's an element of risk involved in exchanging your home with another family (depending on whether your swap is made in heaven or hell!), most agencies thoroughly vet clients and have a track record of successful swaps. There are home exchange agencies in most countries, many of which are members of the International Home Exchange Association (IHEA). There are many home exchange companies in the USA, including HomeLink International (over 20,000 members in some 50 countries), Box 47747, Tampa, FL 33647, USA (☎ 0800-6383841 or 0813-975 9825, 🖥 www.homelink.org with links to 18 national websites). Home exchange companies in Britain include HomeLink International (part of the Homelink International organisation), Linfield House, Gorse Hill Road, Virginia Water, Surrey GU25 4AS, UK (☎ 01344-842642, 🖥 www.homelink.org.uk), which publishes a directory of homes and holiday homes for exchange, Home Base Holidays, 7 Park Avenue, London N13 5PG, UK (☎ 020-8886 8752, 🖥 www.homebase-hols.com) and Intervac International, c/o Rhona Nayar, Coxes Hill Barn, North Wraxall, Chippingham, Wilts. SN14 7AD, UK (☎ 01225-892011, 🖥 www.intervac.co.uk).

WHAT SORT OF PROPERTY?

Many foreigners buying property abroad are seeking a second home for family holidays or as a weekend retreat, perhaps with a view to retiring or living there permanently in the future. However, an increasing number of people buy a home abroad to retire, work or start a business, or even to commute to a job in a neighbouring country. If you're buying a holiday home that will be occupied for only a few weeks a year, you may be satisfied with a studio or a one-bedroom apartment. On the other hand, if you're looking for a permanent family home you may decide that nothing less than a four-bedroom villa with a swimming pool will suffice. Before buying a home abroad, you should have a clear idea of your long-term plans and goals (see **Choosing the Location** on page 90).

For many foreign buyers, buying a home abroad provides the opportunity to buy a home of a size or style they couldn't afford in their home country. However, a common mistake when buying a rural property in some countries, e.g. France, is to buy a house that's much larger than you need with acres of land, simply because it appears to offer good value. Bear in mind that a large property, particularly an older property, requires a lot of work to maintain it and keep it clean, particularly when it has a large garden and a swimming pool. Can you do it on your own or afford to employ someone to do it for you? Don't on the other hand, buy a property that's too small, as extra space can easily be swallowed up. Bear in mind that when you have a home abroad, you will inevitably discover that you have many more relations and friends than you ever thought possible!

Buying a huge house with a few acres of land may seem like a good investment, but should you wish to sell, buyers may be thin on the ground, particularly if the price has doubled or trebled after the cost of renovation. In most areas there's only a limited market for renovated rural property. Although there are usually plenty of buyers in the lower £50,000 ($75,000) price range, they become much scarcer over £100,000 ($150,000) or more unless a property is exceptional, i.e. outstandingly attractive in a popular area and with a superb location. In some areas even the most desirable properties remain on the market for a number of years.

What sort of home are you looking for? An apartment or a detached house? Old or new, or perhaps something in need of renovation? Country or town, coast or inland? Do you want a mature garden, a pool or a large plot of land? As when buying property anywhere, it's never wise to be in too much of a hurry. Have a good look around in the area you've chosen and get a clear picture of the relative prices and the types of properties available. There's a huge range of properties available, ranging from derelict farmhouses to modern townhouses and apartments with all modern conveniences, from crumbling castles requiring complete restoration to new luxury villas. You can also buy a plot of land and have an individual, architect-designed house built to your own specifications.

There's no shortage of properties for sale in most countries (indeed, in many areas there's a glut) and whatever kind of property you're looking for, you'll have an abundance to choose from. Wait until you find something you fall head over heels in love with and then think about it for a while before rushing headlong to the altar! One of the best things about buying property in most countries is that there's always another 'dream' home around the next corner - and the second or third dream home is often even better than the first. Better to miss the 'opportunity of a lifetime' than end up with an expensive pile of stones around your neck. See also **Choosing the Location** on page 90.

Old Properties

If you want a property with abundant charm and character, a building for renovation or conversion, outbuildings, or a large plot of land, then you must usually buy an 'old' property. In many countries (particularly France and Italy) it's still possible to buy an old 'derelict' property for as little as £20,000 ($30,000), although you will need to carry out major renovations and restoration, which will usually double or treble the price. Because the purchase price of unrestored buildings is usually low, many foreign buyers are lulled into a false sense of security and believe they're getting a bargain, without investigating the renovation costs. **Bear in mind that renovation or conversion costs are invariably more than you imagined or planned!**

As with most things in life, you generally get what you pay for, so don't expect a modern or restored country property for £20,000 ($30,000). At the other end of the scale, for those who can afford them there's a wealth of beautiful mini castles, spacious manor houses and luxurious country houses, many costing no more than an average three or four-bedroom townhouse in some countries. However, if you aspire to live the life of the landed gentry in your own castle, bear in mind that the reason many are on the market and appear to be so reasonably priced, is that the cost of restoration and upkeep is *astronomical!*

Although property is generally less expensive in southern European and Mediterranean countries than in northern Europe and North America, most old country houses require complete renovation and modernisation. Some are even lacking in basic services such as electricity, gas, a reliable water supply and sanitation. If you're planning to buy a property that needs restoration or renovation, always obtain an *accurate* estimate of the cost *before* signing the contract. As a rough guide, a property in need of total restoration is likely to cost *at least* as much to restore as it does to buy, and it isn't unusual for restoration costs to be as much as two or three times the purchase price. If you aren't into do-it-yourself in a big way, you may be far better off buying a new or recently built property or one that has already been partly or wholly restored. If you need to pay for total restoration, the cost may be prohibitive and is rarely recovered when you sell (see **Renovation & Restoration** on page 102).

Don't buy a derelict property unless you have the courage, determination and money to overcome the many problems you will certainly face (it isn't for the faint-hearted!). In some countries you will also need to do battle with obstructive local bureaucrats and negotiate arcane planning laws of Byzantine complexity. **Taking on too large a task in terms of restoration is a common mistake made by foreign buyers in some countries, e.g. France and Italy.** Unless you're prepared to wait or live in a caravan for a long time, it's better to spend a bit more and buy something habitable but untidy, rather than a property that needs completely gutting before it can be lived in.

Bear in mind that if you buy and restore a property with the intention of selling it for a profit, you must take into account not only the initial price and restoration costs, but also the fees and taxes included in the purchase cost, plus capital gains if it's a second home. It's often more difficult to sell a renovated property at an above average market price (irrespective of its added value) than it is a modern property. The local inhabitants in many countries have little interest in old restored properties, which may be an important point if you need to sell in a hurry. If you want to make a profit, you're often better off buying or building a new house.

Resale Properties

Resale or second-hand properties are often good value abroad, particularly in resort areas, where many apartments and townhouses are sold fully furnished, although the quality of furnishings varies considerably (from beautiful to junk) and may not be to your taste. Note, however, that 'luxury' apartments and villas, e.g. costing upwards of £150,000 ($200,000), are rarely sold furnished. With a resale property you can see exactly what you will get for your money (unlike when buying off plan), most problems will have been resolved, and previous owners may have made improvements or added a swimming pool, which may not be fully reflected in the asking price.

You will also save on the cost of installing water and electricity meters and telephone lines, or the cost of extending these services to a property. Note that if you need a telephone, either for business or personal reasons, you may need to buy a resale property with a telephone line, as it can take months to have a line installed in some countries. When buying a resale property in a development (see **Community Properties** on page 84), you should ask the neighbours about any problems, community fees, planned developments and anything else that may affect your enjoyment of the property. Most residents are usually happy to tell you, unless of course they're trying to sell you their own home!

You should consider having a survey (see page 86) done on a resale property, particularly an old house, which may have been built with inferior materials. Common problems include rusting water pipes, poor wiring, humidity and rising damp, uneven flooring, collapsing façades, subsidence, and cracked internal and external walls. Some of these problems are even evident in developments less than five years old! The cost of a survey is a small price to pay for the peace of mind it provides.

Owners often advertise their property directly in the local expatriate press or simply by putting a for sale sign in the window. Note that although it may be cheaper buying directly from an owner, particularly when he's forced to sell, you should employ a lawyer to carry out the necessary checks (see page 95). If you're unsure of the value of a property, you should obtain an independent valuation from an experienced local valuer.

New Properties

New properties are widely available in most countries and include coastal and city apartment and townhouse complexes, golf, marina and winter sports developments, and a wide range of individually-designed, detached and semi-detached houses, chalets and villas. Many new properties are part of purpose-built, leisure developments, particularly in southern Europe and Mediterranean islands. These are often located on the coast and encompass a golf course, swimming pool, tennis courts, a gym or fitness club and a restaurant. If you're looking for a home providing sports and other facilities, such as a golf course or a marina, check the lifetime or annual fees (which may be included in the cost of a property), as they can be very high.

Note that many new developments are planned as holiday homes and may not be attractive as permanent homes. If you're buying an apartment or house that's part of a development or complex, check whether your neighbours will be mainly local nationals or foreigners. Some foreigners don't wish to live in a community consisting mainly of their fellow countrymen (or other foreigners) and this may also deter buyers when you wish to sell. On the other hand, many foreigners don't want to live in a local community, particularly if they don't speak the local language.

The quality of new homes in many countries is extremely variable and it's often poorer in southern European and Mediterranean countries than in northern Europe and North America. The best (and most expensive) properties in some countries are often built by foreign builders, many of whom use high quality imported materials and fittings, e.g. doors, windows and bathroom and kitchen suites, to ensure a high standard. The quality of a building and the materials used is usually reflected in the price, so when comparing prices make sure that you're comparing similar quality. Less expensive properties aren't usually the best built, although there are exceptions. If you want a permanent rather than a holiday home, you're better off opting for quality rather than quantity.

In many countries the word 'luxury' is used very loosely and should be taken with a pinch of salt. A true luxury property will include features such as a full-size, fully fitted kitchen (possibly with microwave, hob/oven with extractor hood, dishwasher, fridge/freezer and washing machine), utility room, large bathrooms, usually en suite to all bedrooms, bedroom dressing areas, separate shower room(s), air-conditioning and central heating (possibly under-floor) in the lounge and bedrooms, double glazing and shutters (possibly electric) on all windows, cavity walls (for sound deadening and cooling), fireplaces, wall safes, ceramic tiled floors in bathrooms and kitchens, and marble-tiled floors in other rooms, fitted carpets in all bedrooms and dressing rooms, built-in mirror-fronted wardrobes, satellite TV, telephone outlets, 24-hour security and resident concierge, panic call buttons and intercom to concierge, automatic lifts, basement car parking, and a lockable basement storage room.

Luxury properties that are part of a community development (see page 84) also usually have a wide range of quality community facilities such as indoor (heated) and outdoor swimming pools, tennis courts and beautiful landscaped gardens. Some properties have an associated golf or country club offering a wide range of facilities which may include golf, tennis and squash courts, health spa, gymnasium, sauna, jacuzzi, snooker, indoor bowling and swimming pools, plus a restaurant and bar. Most community developments have their own sales' offices, which usually offer a full management and rental service to non-resident owners. If you wish to furnish a property solely for letting, furniture packages are available and are usually good value for money (some estate agents will also furnish properties for their clients).

Although new properties may lack the charm and character of older buildings, they often offer attractive financial and other advantages. These may include a smaller deposit, lower conveyancing fees, lower property taxes, a builder's guarantee, no costs or problems associated with renovation or modernisation, and a wide range of fixtures and fittings. If required, a new property can usually be let immediately. It's also often cheaper to build new rather than restore a derelict property, as the price is fixed, unlike the cost of renovation which can soar way beyond original estimates (as many buyers discover to their cost). On the other hand, new homes are often smaller than old properties and are generally built on smaller plots of land.

If you're buying a new apartment or house off plan, you may be able to choose your bathroom suite, kitchen, fireplace, wall and floor tiles, and carpet in bedrooms, which may be included in the price. You can also choose the decoration and may even be able to alter the interior room layout of the property, although this will increase the price. New homes also usually contain a high level of 'luxury' features such as tiled kitchens, deluxe bathroom suites, fitted cupboards, fitted kitchens (with dishwashers, cookers and refrigerators), smoke and security alarms, and optional co-ordinated interior colour schemes. If you're buying a swimming pool with your home, you should check that it isn't overpriced. Note, however, that many builders won't allow buyers to install a pool simultaneously with a home unless it's purchased through them.

In most countries new properties are covered by a builder's warranty, e.g. for 10 or 15 years, against structural defects and it's usually against the law to sell a new house without a guarantee. Other systems and equipment, e.g. the electrical, plumbing, and ventilation systems, are usually covered by a minimum two-year guarantee. In some countries an architect is also responsible for ten years for defects due to instructions given to the builder or problems relating to a plot of land, e.g. subsidence. In most countries a developer, builder and architect must have financial bank guarantees, and stage payments and completion times are strictly monitored.

When you have a limited warranty, such as the first two years of a builder's warranty, you should ensure that any claims for defects are made during the relevant period, e.g. a claim for poor workmanship may need to be made in the first year. If necessary (and to support a claim), have a professional inspection carried out before the warranty expires. **Whether you have a warranty or not, the most important consideration when buying a new home is the reputation and integrity of the builder or developer.** Ask the builder or developer what other homes and developments he has built and ask owners about any problems they've had and whether they're satisfied.

Note, however, that in some countries there are no guarantees for buyers against faults in workmanship or materials, such as exist in northern Europe and North America. A small minority of builders and developers in some countries deliberately cut corners, and use inferior or illegal building materials and methods to save time and money. Problems may not come to light for many years, if at all, and when they do the perpetrators know that they can usually avoid responsibility (unless a building collapses completely). If you do have problems you must usually be extremely patient and persistent to obtain satisfaction.

Note that because of the problems associated with buying off plan or buying unfinished properties in some countries, some experts advise people not to buy a property that isn't totally complete with all the infrastructure in place (see **Avoiding Problems** on page 72). In some countries, investigations have shown that almost half of all new properties have construction defects or deficiencies and in one third of cases the contract conditions aren't met, particularly regarding the completion date and the quality of materials used.

Building a House

If you want to be far from the madding crowd, you can buy a plot of land and have an individual architect-designed house built to your own design and specifications or to a standard design provided by a builder. However, having a home built in some countries isn't recommended for the timid. Red tape and the eccentric ways of doing business can make building your own home a nightmare and it's fraught with problems in some countries.

The cost of land varies considerably with the country and region. In rural areas land usually costs from £50 to £100 ($75 to $150) per m² and building costs in most countries range from around £250 to £500 ($400 to $750) per m², according to the quality and location. This means that a plot of 500m² (the smallest plot size in most countries) costs between £25,000 and £50,000 ($40,000 to $75,000) and to build a 100m² home costs a further £25,000 to £50,000. In many countries it's possible to buy a plot of land and build a bigger and better villa for less than the cost of a resale property. You can not only design your own home, but can ensure that the quality of materials and workmanship are first class.

When planning to build your own home, take into account all associated costs including the cost of providing services such as water, electricity and telephone to a property. Note that most quotes are estimates only and that the cost can escalate wildly as a result of contract clauses and changes made during building work. If you want a house built abroad exactly to your specifications, you will usually need to personally supervise it every step of the way or employ a local agent, architect or engineer to do it for you. Note that without close supervision it's highly unlikely that your instructions will be followed in some countries.

You must take the same care when buying building land as you would when buying a property. The most important point when buying land is to ensure that it has been approved for building and that the plot is large enough for the house you plan to build. Check also that it's suitable for building as it may be too steep or require prohibitively expensive foundations (particularly in areas affected by earthquakes or subsidence). You should also check that services such as water, gas (if applicable), electricity and telephone are nearby. Always get confirmation in writing from the local town hall that land can be built on and has approval for road access. Check whether there are any conditions or restrictions regarding building permission, e.g. time limits, and height and size limitations, or regulations regarding the employment of a local architect or builder. Before buying land for building or a property that you wish to modernise or extend, ensure that the purchase contract is contingent on obtaining a building licence or planning permission from the local authorities. **You *must* obtain the title deed for the land before signing a building contract.**

Discuss your requirements with a surveyor or architect and your legal advisor *before* signing a contract or paying any money. Some companies provide a surveying service for around 10 per cent of the building contract price. Architects from European Union (EU) countries can work in other EU countries and there are a number of British and other foreign architects operating in countries that are popular with foreign buyers. Note that if planning permission is flawed, you may find that you're responsible for improving roads, adding pavements, street lighting, electricity installations and sewage disposal (among other things).

In many countries it's common to choose an inclusive land and house deal offered by a developer, rather than buying the land and employing an architect and builder to design and build your home. Many developers have a number of developments that are divided into plots and offer what is often termed 'custom building'. This means that you choose the site and size of your plot, e.g. 1,000m² or half an acre, and select a house design from a range of standard designs. You can usually choose or modify the location of bathrooms, bedrooms and kitchens and even adapt the exterior to your taste. You can also choose the colour of the carpets (which may be included in the price), roof tiles, exterior and interior paint, interior tiles and plumbing fixtures. Optional custom services may include installing a swimming pool or tennis court and landscaping.

Retirement Homes & Sheltered Housing

Sheltered housing (purpose-built retirement developments) and retirement communities are well established in the USA and are becoming increasingly common in Europe, particularly in Britain, France and Spain. In southern European countries, most developments are built and managed by foreign companies for foreigners, as the local inhabitants prefer to live among their family and friends in their 'twilight' years. Some sheltered housing developments are designed for elderly people, e.g. aged 75 plus, often with limited mobility.

Developments usually consist of one and two-bedroom apartments or a combination of apartments, townhouses and villas, which can be purchased freehold or leasehold, i.e. a lifetime occupancy. Properties usually have central heating, air-conditioning, fully-fitted kitchens and satellite television. A wide range of communal facilities and services are usually provided and may include medical and dental clinics (possibly with a resident doctor and dentist), nursing facilities, lounges, laundry, housekeeping, sauna, jacuzzi, restaurant, bar, meal delivery, handyman, mini-supermarket, post and banking, guest apartments, free local transport, 24-hour security with closed-circuit television, intercom service, personal emergency alarm system and a 24-hour multi-lingual reception. Sports and leisure facilities may include swimming pools, tennis courts, lawn bowling, gymnasium, video room, library and a social club.

All sheltered housing developments levy monthly service charges, which can run into hundreds or even thousands of pounds a month. It's important to ensure that you can afford (and will continue to be able to afford) the fees, which may increase annually. The fees may include a number of weeks' (e.g. six) nursing care a year (usually per illness) in a residents' nursing home or even unlimited nursing care in some communities. Note, however, that sheltered housing and retirement communities aren't nursing homes, which are prohibitively expensive in most countries.

Timeshare & Other Part-Ownership Schemes

If you're looking for a holiday home abroad, you may wish to investigate a scheme that provides sole occupancy of a property for a number of weeks each year. These include co-ownership, leaseback, timesharing and a holiday property bond. Don't rush into any of these schemes without fully researching the market and before you're absolutely clear what you want and what you can realistically expect to get for your money.

Co-ownership: Co-ownership includes schemes such as a group of people buying shares in a property-owning company and co-ownership between family, friends or even strangers. Co-ownership allows you to recoup your investment in savings on holiday costs while retaining equity in a property. A common deal is a four-owner scheme (which many consider to be the optimum number of co-owners), where you buy a quarter of a property and can occupy it for up to three months a year. However, there's no reason why there cannot be as many as 12 co-owners, with a month's occupancy each per year (usually divided between high, medium and low seasons).

Co-ownership offers access to a size and quality of property that would otherwise be unimaginable, and it's even possible to have a share in a substantial mansion, where a number of families could live together simultaneously and hardly ever see each other if they didn't want to. Co-ownership can be a good choice for a family seeking a holiday home for a few weeks or months a year and has the added advantage that (because of the lower cost) a mortgage may be unnecessary. Note that it's cheaper to buy a property privately with friends than to buy from an agent or developer who offers this sort of scheme, in which case you may pay well above the market value for a share of a property (check the market value of a property to establish whether it's good value). Co-ownership is much better value than a timeshare and needn't cost much more. Note, however, that a water-tight contract must be drawn up by an experienced lawyer to protect the co-owners' interests.

One of the best ways to get into co-ownership, if you can afford it, is to buy a property yourself and offer shares to others. This overcomes the problem of getting together a consortium of would-be owners and trying to agree on a purchase in advance, which is difficult unless it's just a few friends or family members. Many people form a local company to buy and manage a property, which can in turn be owned by a company in the co-owners' home country, thus allowing any disputes to be dealt with under local law. Each co-owner receives a number of shares according to how much he has paid, entitling him to so many weeks' occupancy a year. Owners don't need to have equal shares and can all be made direct title holders. If a co-owner wishes to sell his shares, he must usually give first refusal to the other co-owners, although if they don't wish to buy them and a new co-owner cannot be found, the property will need to be sold.

Sale & Leaseback: Leaseback or sale and leaseback schemes are designed for those seeking a holiday home for a limited number of weeks each year. Properties sold under a leaseback scheme are located in popular resort areas, e.g. golf, ski or coastal resorts, where self-catering accommodation is in high demand. Buying a property through a leaseback scheme allows a purchaser to buy a new property at less than its true cost, e.g. 30 per cent less than the list price. In return for the discount the property must be leased back to the developer, usually for around ten years, so that he can let it as self-catering holiday accommodation. The buyer owns the freehold of the property and the full price is shown in the title deed.

The purchaser is also given the right to occupy the property for a period each year, usually six or eight weeks, spread over high, medium and low seasons. These weeks can usually be let to provide income or possibly be exchanged with accommodation in another resort (as with a timeshare scheme). The developer furnishes and manages the property, and pays for maintenance and utilities, etc. during the term of the lease, even when the owner occupies the property. Note that it's important to have a contract checked by a legal expert to ensure that you receive vacant possession at the end of the leaseback period, without having to pay an indemnity charge, otherwise you could end up paying more than a property is worth. In some cases you can buy out of a sale and leaseback scheme after a period, e.g. two years.

Timesharing: Also known as holiday ownership, vacation ownership, co-ownership or holidays for life, timesharing is a popular form of part-ownership, although there are few timeshare resorts in Greece and Cyprus compared with, for example, Spain. The best timeshare developments are on a par with luxury hotels and offer a wide range of facilities, including bars, restaurants, entertainment, shops, swimming pools, tennis courts, health clubs, and other leisure and sports facilities. If you don't wish to holiday in the same place each year, you should choose a timeshare development that's a member of an international organisation such as Resort Condominium International (RCI) or Interval International (II), which allow you (usually for an additional fee) to exchange your timeshare with one in another area or country.

Timesharing has earned a poor reputation in some countries, although things have improved in recent years since the introduction of new EU regulations to protect buyers, including a requirement that buyers have secure occupancy rights and that their money is properly protected prior to the completion of a new property. Timeshare companies are required to disclose information about the vendor and the property and to allow prospective buyers a ten-day 'cooling off period', during which they may cancel a sales agreement they've signed without penalty. Timeshare purchases can now be registered with a notary and inscribed in the registry at the buyer's request (it isn't mandatory). A guarantee must be provided by the timeshare company that a property is as advertised and, where applicable, the contract must be in the language of the EU country where the buyer is resident or the language of the buyer's choice (you cannot sign away any of your rights irrespective of what's written in the contract). If a new contract isn't in accordance with the new law, it's null and void.

The best timeshares cost around €12,000/CY£8,000 or more for one week in a one or two-bedroom apartment in a top-rated resort, to which must be added annual management fees of €225 to 300/CY£150 to 200 or more for each week and other miscellaneous fees. Most experts believe that there's little or no advantage in a timeshare over a normal holiday rental and that it's simply an expensive way to pay for your holidays in advance. It doesn't make sense to tie up your money for what amounts to a long-term reservation on an annual holiday (usually you don't actually 'own' anything). Most financial advisers believe that you're better off putting your money into a long-term investment, where you keep your capital and may even earn sufficient interest to pay for a few weeks' holiday each year. For example, €12,000/CY£8,000 invested at just 5 per cent yields €600/CY£400 a year, which when added to the saving on management fees makes a total of around €900 or CY£600 – sufficient to pay for a week's holiday in a self-catering apartment outside the 'high season' almost anywhere.

Often timeshares are difficult or impossible to sell at any price. Note that there's no real resale market for timeshares, and if you need to sell you're highly unlikely to get your money back. If you want to buy a timeshare, it's best to buy a resale privately from an existing owner or a timeshare resale broker, when they sell for a fraction of their original cost. When buying privately, you can usually drive a hard bargain and may even get a timeshare 'free' simply by assuming the current owner's maintenance contract. Further information about timesharing can be obtained from the Timeshare Council (☎ UK 020-7821 8845) and the Timeshare Helpline (☎ UK 020-8296 0900) in Britain. The Timeshare Consumers Association (Hodsock, Worksop, Notts, S81 0TF, UK, ☎ 01909-591100, ✉ tca@netcomuk.co.uk) publishes a useful booklet entitled Timeshare: Guide to Buying, Owning and Selling.

Holiday Property Bond: A holiday property bond is a good alternative to timesharing for those with a minimum of around GB£2,000 to invest. Holiday Property Bond (operated by the Villa Owners Club, HPB House, Newmarket, Suffolk CB8 8EH, UK, ☎ 01638-660066) owns over 600 properties in many countries, including Greece and Cyprus. Each GB£1 invested is equal to one point and each week's stay in a property is assigned a points rating depending on its size, location and the time of year. There are no extra fees apart from a small 'user' charge when occupying a property to cover cleaning and utility costs. Furthermore, there's a buy-back guarantee after two years, when an investment can be sold at its current market value.

Community Properties

In most countries, properties with common elements shared with other properties, whether a building, amenities or land, are owned through a system of co-ownership or community ownership. This includes apartments, townhouses and detached homes on a private estate with communal areas and facilities such as swimming pools, tennis courts and gardens. In the USA, condominiums are community properties in this sense, but co-operative apartments aren't, as apartment owners own a number of 'shares' (depending on the size of their apartments) in the corporation that owns the building. In general, the only properties that don't belong to a community are detached houses on an individual plot in a street or a house on a plot of rural land. In some countries, e.g. Britain, there's a system of leasehold, where the owner of the freehold of an apartment block sells leases for a number of years, e.g. 99 to 999. Leasehold properties are often community properties.

Owners of community properties own not only their homes, e.g. an apartment or townhouse, but also a share of the whole complex including the communal parts of a building (e.g. lifts, hallways and passages), gardens, roads, swimming pools, tennis courts and other sports facilities. Some communal areas (such as roads) may be cared for by the local municipality, provided it has given planning permission and included the development in its general plan for the municipality. Owners of community properties must pay service charges or community fees for the upkeep of communal areas and for communal services. Fees are calculated according to each owner's 'share' of a development or apartment building, usually based on the size of properties, e.g. in m^2. For example, ten properties of equal size in an apartment block would each pay 10 per cent of community fees. The percentage to be paid is detailed in the property deed. Shares not only determine the proportion of fees to be paid, but also voting rights at general meetings.

Community fees usually go towards road cleaning, green zone maintenance (including communal and sometimes private gardens), cleaning, decoration and maintenance of buildings and lifts, caretaking (e.g. porter or concierge), communal lighting in buildings and grounds, water supply (e.g. swimming pools, gardens), swimming pool maintenance, insurance, administration fees, urbanisation rates, maintenance of radio and television aerials, satellite TV charges, and refuse collection. If central heating and hot water are provided communally, the cost is divided according to the share of the utility allocated to each property. **Always check the level of general and special charges before buying a community property.** Fees are usually billed two or three times a year and adjusted at the end of the year when actual expenditure is known and annual accounts have been approved by the owners' committee. If you're buying an apartment from a previous owner, always ask to see a copy of the receipts for fees paid in previous years, as owners may be 'economical with the truth' when stating the fees.

The management and co-ownership of a community development is usually regulated by law and the rules are contained in a 'rules of co-ownership' document. Before buying a community property you should obtain a copy of both the rules governing the division of property and the community rules, and if you don't understand them have them explained. In some countries owners must form a 'community of owners' and it isn't wise to buy a property in a development where there isn't one. The rules allow owners to run their community in accordance with the wishes of the majority, while at the same time protecting the rights of the minority. They usually include such things as noise levels, the keeping of dogs (often prohibited), refuse disposal, use of swimming pools, car parking, children's games and the hanging of laundry.

Community fees vary considerably according to the communal facilities provided. For example, fees for a large luxury penthouse in a prestige development may be well over £2,000 ($3,000) a year, whereas for a small studio apartment in a small block they may be as little as £100 ($150) a year. Some luxury developments (with extensive sports and social facilities) have *very* high annual maintenance fees, e.g. £1,000 ($1,500) for a studio apartment and over £3,000 ($4,500) for a three-bedroom villa! There often appears to be no logical reason for the fees charged in some countries, with fees for similar properties in similar communities differing by as much as 300 per cent. Note, however, that high fees aren't necessarily a negative point (assuming you can afford them), provided you receive value for your money and the community is well managed and maintained. **Note that the value of a community property depends to a large extent on how well the development is maintained and managed.**

If you're buying a holiday apartment that will be vacant for long periods (particularly in winter), don't buy in a block where heating and/or hot water charges are shared, although this isn't standard practice in most countries. You should also ask whether there are any rules regarding letting or leaving a property unoccupied for any length of time. You may also wish to check how many properties share the communal facilities, e.g. a large swimming pool won't look so inviting when 100 people are using it, and getting a game of tennis may be difficult during peak periods.

Note that in some countries, old run-down apartment blocks can have their community fees increased substantially to pay for new installations and repairs (such as a mains water supply, sewage connection or structural repairs). Always enquire about any planned work and obtain a copy of the minutes of the last annual meeting where important matters are bound to have been raised. Some communities have severe debt problems because of non-payment of fees or problems relating to the provision of services and many have infrastructure problems. If an owner doesn't pay his community fees, his property can be embargoed by the community of owners and if he continues to refuse to pay it can eventually be forcibly sold at auction.

In many 'unfinished' community developments, owners have been required to pay for the absent or inadequate infrastructure (which they've already paid for in the purchase price), with costs often running into many thousands of pounds or dollars per owner. In some communities, owners have been fighting (unsuccessfully in most cases) for years to get their infrastructure completed. **In view of the problems encountered by buyers in some countries, some experts advise people not to buy a property in an unfinished community, where the infrastructure isn't completed.** Beware also of purchase contracts containing an 'open-ended cheque' to the developers for costs associated with the repair and upkeep of a development.

SURVEY

When you've found a property that you like, you should make a close inspection of its condition. Obviously this will depend on whether it's a shell in need of complete restoration, has been partly or totally modernised or restored, or is a new building. A common problem with restored properties is that you don't usually know how well the work has been done, particularly if the previous owner did it himself. If work has been carried out by professional builders, you should ask to see the bills, as building work in many countries is guaranteed, e.g. for ten years.

Some simple checks you can do yourself include testing the electrical system, plumbing (plus the septic tank, if applicable), mains water, hot water boiler, central heating and air-conditioning. Don't assume that these are functional, but check them yourself. If a property doesn't have electricity, mains gas, mains water or a telephone link, check the nearest connection point and the cost of extending the service to the property. An older building may show signs of damage and decay, such as bulging or cracked walls, damp, missing roof slates and rotten woodwork. In some countries, certain areas are liable to subsidence, radiation (which can cause cancer) and wood-boring insects such as termites. In hot climates, infestations of cockroaches, ants, termites and other insects are common in many areas, even in fairly new buildings. If you find or suspect problems, you should have the property checked by a builder or have a full structural survey carried out by a technical architect, engineer or surveyor.

Surveys aren't usually performed prior to purchase in most countries, particularly on a property built in the last 10 or 20 years, often because the vendor must usually certify that a property is free from 'hidden defects'. However, if a vendor can show that he was ignorant of any defects, he may not be held responsible. If you're buying a detached villa, farmhouse or village house, especially one built on the side of a mountain, it's always wise to have a survey carried out. Many older properties were built with inferior materials, and common problems include rusting water pipes, poor wiring, defective plumbing and drains, rising damp, dry and wet rot, uneven flooring, collapsing façades, subsidence, woodworm and termites, bulging walls, and cracked internal and external walls. In fact, in some countries serious problems can often be found in properties built in the boom years of the '70s and '80s and even in properties less than five years old. Generally if you would have a survey carried out if you were buying the same property in your home country, you should have one done abroad.

You can make a 'satisfactory' survey a condition of the preliminary contract, although this isn't common practice in most countries and the vendor may refuse or insist that you carry out a survey *before* signing the contract. Some lenders insist on a 'survey' before approving a loan, although this usually consists of a perfunctory valuation to ensure that a property is worth the agreed price. Always discuss with a surveyor exactly what will be included in the survey, and most importantly, what will be excluded (you may need to pay extra to include certain checks and tests).

You may prefer to employ a foreign surveyor practising in the country where the property is located (who will write a report in English), rather than a local surveyor. On the other hand, a local surveyor may have a more intimate knowledge of local properties and building methods. Whoever you employ, you should ensure that he's experienced in the idiosyncrasies of local properties and has professional indemnity insurance (which means you can confidently sue him if he does a bad job!).

THE COST OF PROPERTY

One of the things which attracts many property buyers to foreign countries is the relatively low cost of homes compared with their home countries. However, you should bear in mind that there are high fees (see page 89) associated with property purchase in some countries, which can add as much as 20 per cent to the purchase price. When buying a home abroad you should also bear in mind the cost of maintenance and upkeep. Buying a home abroad is usually a good long-term investment, although in the late '80s and early '90s many people got their fingers burnt when property values plummeted in the wake of the world-wide recession.

Although agents will often tell you that there's never been a better time to buy a home abroad, it was actually true in the mid-'90s, when homes in resort areas in most countries were severely under-valued because of the recession in the early '90s. However, there was a huge surge in the sale of both holiday and permanent homes in popular resort and rural areas, e.g. in France and Italy, in the late '90s, which continued unabated into the 21st century. This resulted in spiralling prices, which doubled in just a few years in many popular areas. Although it seemed in late 2001 that a world-wide recession was possible in 2002, few believed that it would have a dramatic effect on house prices in most countries; this remains to be seen.

Note that in many countries, local inhabitants don't buy domestic property as an investment, but as a home for life. You shouldn't usually expect to make a quick profit when buying property abroad and should look upon it as a long-term investment. Most people buying a home abroad are buying into a lifestyle, e.g. guaranteed sunshine, unspoilt natural beauty, charming towns and villages, fine cuisine and wines, fascinating art and culture, and friendly neighbours, rather than simply making an investment.

In most countries, property values usually increase at an average of around 4 or 5 per cent a year (or in line with inflation), which means that you must usually own a home for at least three years simply to recover the costs associated with buying (usually paid by the buyer – see **Fees** below). House prices rise faster than average in some fashionable areas, although this is generally reflected in much higher purchase prices. The stable property market in most countries acts as a discouragement to speculators wishing to make a quick profit, particularly when a property requires a substantial investment in restoration or modernisation before it can be sold at a profit. Note that capital gains tax (see page 63) can easily wipe out a third of any profit made on the sale of a second home.

Although there's evidence of dual pricing in some countries, the practice of routinely quoting higher prices to foreigners is rare, and prices advertised locally are usually identical to those advertised abroad. However, local inhabitants in many countries are often astonished at the high prices foreigners are prepared to pay for nondescript homes in uninspiring areas (although they never complain about foreigners driving up prices when they're on the receiving end!). The French think that the British are particularly insane for buying up their tumbled-down farmhouses and crumbling *châteaux* (few foreigners share the British passion for spending their holidays and weekends up to their elbows in bricks and mortar).

Apart from obvious points such as size, quality and land area, the most important factor influencing the price of a house is its location. For example, a restored or modernised house in an unpopular region may be worth double or treble the price in an area that's popular with both local and foreign buyers. Similarly, the closer to the coast the higher the cost of property, with properties located on a fashionable coastline (such as the French or Italian Riviera) *very* expensive. You also pay a hefty premium for properties in ski resorts in all countries because of the high cost of land and the good (often year-round) letting potential.

Sellers generally expect buyers to haggle and rarely expect to receive the asking price for a property (although some vendors ask an unrealistic price and won't budge a cent). **In popular areas, asking prices may be unrealistically high particularly to snare the unsuspecting and ignorant foreign buyer.** Always compare prices and try to obtain a reduction, even if you think a property is a bargain. Try to find out how long a property has been on the market, as the longer it has been for sale, the more likely a lower offer will be accepted. The state of a property and its surrounds is usually a good indication of how long it has been empty. Generally the older the property, the more likely you are to get the price reduced (unless it's a period property in excellent condition).

If you're dealing with an agent, you should always discuss an offer with him. Don't, however, believe him when he tells you that a vendor won't drop his price (the agent wants the best price he can get, as it increases his commission). If you make a lower offer, you should indicate to the owner a few points of weakness (without being too critical) meriting a reduction in price. Note, however, that if you make too low an offer, an owner may feel insulted and refuse to do business with you. If a property has been realistically priced, you shouldn't expect to get more than a 5 or 10 per cent reduction. Cash buyers in some countries may be able to negotiate a considerable price reduction, e.g. 20 or 25 per cent, for a quick sale, depending on the state of the local property market. An offer should always be made in writing, as it's likely to be taken more seriously than a verbal offer. **Always be prepared to walk away from a deal rather than pay too high a price.**

To get an idea of property prices in different regions of a country, check the prices of properties advertised in English-language property magazines and local newspapers, magazines and property journals. **Before deciding on the price, make sure you know *exactly* what's included, as it isn't unusual for sellers in some countries to strip a house bare and take everything that isn't part of the structure.** Have fixtures and fittings that are included in a purchase listed in the contract and check that they're still there before signing the final contract.

THE FEES

A variety of fees (also called closing or settlement costs) are payable when you buy a home abroad, which vary considerably with the country, e.g. around 2 per cent in Britain, 5 per cent in the USA, 10 per cent in Spain, 12 per cent in Italy and some 15 per cent in France. Most fees are payable by the buyer and may include a lender's appraisal or valuation fee, title search and insurance, mortgage tax and insurance, notary's fees, VAT or transfer tax, land tax, property registration fees, legal fees, surveyor's or architect's fees, and utility connection and registration fees. **Before signing a purchase contract (even a preliminary contract) or paying any money, always check exactly what fees are payable and how much they will be, and have them confirmed in writing.**

In many countries a public official called a notary handles the completion of all property sales. He represents the government (not the seller or buyer) and his main task is to ensure that the documentation is in order and that all state taxes and fees are paid on completion of a sale. The notary is also required to withhold capital gains tax in some countries, e.g. France, while in others the buyer must deduct a percentage, e.g. 5 per cent in Spain, from the purchase price when the seller's a non-resident. All fees are payable on completion of a sale.

Land tax is payable in some countries, e.g. Spain, and is a municipal tax on the increase in the value of land since the last change of ownership. It's usually payable by the vendor as he's the one who has made the profit, although the purchase agreement may stipulate that the buyer pays. Value added tax is payable on new properties in many countries and is usually included in the purchase price when they're sold for the first time. In some countries, e.g. France, the fees payable when buying a new property, e.g. less than five years old, are much lower than when buying an 'old' property.

Note that an estate agent's fees (see page 101) may be paid by the vendor, the buyer or they may be shared, depending on the country, although it's usual for the vendor to pay in most countries. Always check in advance who pays the agent's fees. Note that prices may be quoted inclusive or exclusive of agency fees. Make sure you know whether *all* agents' fees are included in the price quoted and, if you negotiate a price reduction, check that the agent or vendor hasn't merely excluded some fees (which you must pay separately).

Declared Value: Most property fees are based on the 'declared' value of a property, which may be less than the purchase price or 'market' value. Never be tempted to evade tax in reducing the price declared to the authorities by an 'under the table' payment. It's possible when buying a property direct from the vendor that he may suggest this, particularly if he's selling a second home and he must pay capital gains tax on the profit. Obviously if the vendor can show a smaller profit, he pays less tax. **You should steer well clear of this practice, which is strictly illegal (although widespread in some countries).** If you're selling a property, you should also bear in mind that if the buyer refuses to pay the illicit payment after a contract has been signed, there's (legally) nothing that you can do about it.

In many countries the local authorities maintain tables to calculate the official or fiscal value of properties, which should be used when declaring the value of a property. In some countries, e.g. Spain, severe penalties have been introduced for gross under-valuation. Reviews of declared values are common in some countries and it can be risky to make a low declaration. If you grossly under-value a property, the authorities may also have the right to buy it within a specified period, e.g. two years, at the under-valued price.

Running Costs: In addition to the fees associated with buying a property you must also take into account the running costs. These include local property taxes (rates) and other fees which may include refuse collection tax, community fees (see page 85), building insurance (essential), utilities (electricity, water, gas), garden and pool maintenance, telephone, wealth tax, 'letting' tax, and a local fiscal representative's or tax consultant's fees. In most countries, annual running costs average around 2 to 3 per cent of the cost of a property.

CHOOSING THE LOCATION

The most important consideration when buying a home abroad is usually its location, or as the old adage goes, the *three* most important points are location, location and location! A property in reasonable condition in a popular area is likely to be a better investment than an exceptional property in a less attractive location. There's no point in buying a dream property in a terrible location. **Note that the wrong decision regarding location is one of the main causes of disenchantment among those buying property abroad.**

Where you buy a property will depend on a range of factors including your preferences, your financial resources and not least, whether you plan to work. If you've been offered a job abroad, the location of your home is likely to be determined by its proximity to your place of employment. However, if you intend to look for employment or start a business, you must live in an area that allows you the maximum opportunities. Unless you have reason to believe otherwise, you would be unwise to rely on finding employment in a particular area. If you don't speak the local language fluently you will find it extremely difficult to find a good job (or any sort of job) in some countries.

If, on the other hand, you're looking for a holiday or retirement home, the world is your oyster. In the latter case, don't be too influenced by where you've spent an enjoyable holiday or two, as a town or area that was acceptable for a short holiday may be totally unsuitable for a permanent home, particularly regarding the proximity to shops, medical services (e.g. doctors, hospitals), public transport, and sports and leisure facilities. A quiet spot in the country may be fine for a few weeks a year, but could you stand the seclusion and remoteness all year round? If you have little idea about where you wish to live, read as much as you can about the different regions of your chosen country and spend some time exploring your areas of interest.

Note that the climate, lifestyle and cost of living can vary considerably, even within a particular region. Before looking at properties it's important to have a good idea of the type of property you're looking for and the price you wish to pay, and to draw up a short list of the areas or towns of interest. If you don't do this, you're likely to be overwhelmed by the number of properties to be viewed. Estate agents usually expect serious buyers to know where they want to buy within a 30 to 40km (18 to 25mi) radius and some even expect clients to narrow their choice down to specific towns and villages.

The 'best' area in which to live depends on a range of considerations, including proximity to your place of work, schools, pub or bar, countryside, towns, shops, public transport, restaurants, sports facilities, swimming pool , etc. There are many excellent areas to choose from in most countries, most within easy travelling distance of a town or city. Don't, however, always believe the times and distances given in advertisements or stated by estate agents. According to most agents' blurb, every home is handy for an airport, railway station, motorway or market town, and none are stuck halfway up a mountain and accessible only by risking life and limb negotiating a poorly maintained, narrow track with a sheer drop into the valley below! When looking for a home, bear in mind travelling times (and the cost) to your place of work, shops and schools (and the local pub). If you buy a remote country property, the distance to local amenities and services could become a problem, particularly if you plan to retire there.

If possible, you should visit an area a few times over a period of a few weeks, both on weekdays and at weekends, morning and afternoon, to get a feel for the neighbourhood (don't just drive around, but walk). You should also visit an area at different times of the year, e.g. in both summer and winter, although this may be impractical. An area that may be wonderful in summer can be forbidding and inhospitable in winter (or vice versa if you don't like extreme heat). In any case you should view a property a number of times before deciding to buy it. If you're unfamiliar with an area, many experts recommend that you rent for a period before deciding to buy (see **Renting** on page 74). This is particularly important if you're planning to buy a permanent home in an unfamiliar area. Many people who don't do their homework change their minds after a period and it isn't unusual for families to move once or twice before settling down permanently.

If you'll be working abroad, obtain a map of the area and decide the maximum distance that you wish to travel to work, e.g. by drawing a circle with your workplace in the middle. Obtain a large scale map of the area where you're looking, if possible one showing individual buildings on which you can mark the places that you've seen. You could do this using a grading system to denote your impressions. If you use an agent, he'll usually drive you around and you can then return later to those you like best at your leisure (provided you've marked them on your map!).

There are many points to consider regarding the location of a home. These can roughly be divided into the immediate surroundings or neighbourhood, and the general area or region. Take into account the present and future needs of all members of your family, including the following:

Climate: For most people climate is the most important factor when buying a home abroad, particularly a holiday or retirement home. Do you want or need winter *and* summer sunshine? Bear in mind both the winter and summer climate, the position of the sun, the average amount of sunshine, plus rainfall and wind conditions. If you want morning or afternoon sun (or both), you must ensure that balconies, terraces and gardens are facing the right direction. Note that, although the winter climate is mild and pleasant in southern Europe and on most Mediterranean islands, it may seem quite cool if you're accustomed to the blazing heat of high summer (when air-conditioning is a blessed relief). If you're looking for a holiday home for winter sports, you will need to investigate the local snowfall record.

Natural Phenomena: Check whether an area is susceptible to natural disasters such as earthquakes, fires, floods, hurricanes, tornadoes or violent storms. Note that insurance against flood damage to homes situated close to the coast (or a river) or in a flood plain may be prohibitively expensive. You may also wish to check whether an area is susceptible to periodic (or prolonged) droughts. Some areas are liable to subsidence, radiation (which can cause cancer) and wood-boring insects such as termites. Because of the climate in some countries, infestations of cockroaches, ants, beetles, termites and other insects are common in many areas, even in fairly new buildings. If you're in any doubt, have a full structural survey (see page 86) carried out on a property that you're planning to buy.

Tourists: Bear in mind that, while a 'front-line' property on a beach or in a marina development sounds attractive and may be ideal for short holidays, it isn't always the best choice for permanent residents. If you buy a home in a popular tourist area, you will be inundated with tourists in summer (of which you may be one!). They will not only jam the roads and pack the beaches and shops, but may also occupy your favourite table at your local bar or restaurant (heaven forbid!). Many beaches are hopelessly crowded in the peak season, streets may be smelly from restaurants and fast food outlets, parking impossible, services stretched to breaking point, and the incessant noise may drive you crazy. You may also have to tolerate water shortages, power cuts and sewage problems in some countries. Some people prefer to move a little inland, perhaps to higher ground where it's cooler, less humid, quieter and you can enjoy panoramic views. On the other hand, getting to and from hillside properties is often difficult and the poorly maintained roads in some countries (often narrow and unguarded) are for sober, confident drivers only.

Noise: Noise can be a problem in some areas, e.g. Spain, particularly in summer. Although you cannot choose your neighbours, you can at least ensure that a property isn't located next to a busy road, industrial plant, commercial area, building site, discotheque, night club, bar or restaurant, where revelries may continue into the early hours. Look out for objectionable neighbouring properties that may be too close to the one you're considering and check whether nearby vacant land has been zoned for commercial activities. In community developments, e.g. apartment blocks, many properties are second homes and are let short-term, which means you may have to tolerate boisterous holiday-makers as neighbours throughout the year (or at least during the summer months). In towns, traffic noise, particularly from motorcycles, can continue all night!

Community: Do you wish to live in an area with many other expatriates from your home country or as far away from them as possible (practically impossible on many parts of the Mediterranean coast)? If you wish to integrate with the local community, avoid the foreign 'ghettos' and choose a village with mainly local inhabitants. However, unless you speak the local language fluently or intend to learn it, you should think twice before buying a property in a village (although foreigners who take the time and trouble to integrate into the local community are warmly welcomed in most countries).

On the other hand, if you wish to mix only with your compatriots and don't plan to learn the local language, then living in a predominantly foreign community is ideal. Note that properties in many developments and towns in popular tourist areas are mostly holiday homes, and the area is sparsely populated most of the year. In some areas, many amenities, businesses and shops close outside the main tourist season, when even local services such as public transport and mail collections may be severely curtailed.

Neighbours: If you're buying a permanent home, it's important to check your prospective neighbours, particularly when buying an apartment. For example, are they noisy, sociable or absent for long periods? Do you think you will get on with them? Good neighbours are invaluable, particularly when buying a second home in a village.

Environment: Do you wish to be in a town or do you prefer the countryside? Inland or on the coast? How about living on an island? Life on an island is more restricted and remote, e.g. you cannot jump into your car and pop over the border into a neighbouring country. Bear in mind that if you buy a property in the country you'll probably have to tolerate poor public transport, long travelling distances to a town of any size, and solitude. You won't be able to stroll along to the local baker for some fresh rolls or bread for breakfast, drop into the local bar for a glass of your favourite tipple with the locals, or have a choice of restaurants on your doorstep. In a town or large village, the weekly market and shops will be just around the corner, the doctor and pharmacy close to hand, and if you need help or run into any problems your neighbours are nearby.

On the other hand, in the country you will be closer to nature, will have more freedom, e.g. to make as much noise as you wish, and possibly complete privacy, e.g. to sunbathe or swim *au naturel*. Living in a remote area in the country will suit nature lovers looking for peace and quiet, who don't want to involve themselves in the 'hustle and bustle' of town life. If you're after a peaceful life, make sure that there isn't a busy road or railway line nearby or a church within 'donging' distance. Note, however, that many people who buy a remote country home find that the peace and tranquillity of the countryside palls after a time, and many yearn for the more exciting town or coastal night-life. If you've never lived in the country, you should rent before buying.

Garden: If you're planning to buy a country property with a large garden or plot of land, bear in mind the high cost and amount of work involved in its upkeep. If it's to be a second home, who will look after the house and garden when you're away? Do you want to spend your holidays gardening and cutting back the undergrowth? Do you want a home with a lot of outbuildings? What are you going to do with them? Can you afford to convert them into extra rooms or guest accommodation?

Employment: How secure is your job or business and are you likely to move to another area in the near future? Can you find other work in the same area, if necessary? If there's a possibility that you will need to move within a few years, you should rent or at least buy a property that will be relatively easy to sell and recoup the cost (or even make a profit!). Consider also your partner's job and children's job prospects.

Schools: What about your children's present and future schooling? What is the quality of local schools? Note that even if your family has no need or plans to use local schools, the value of a home may be influenced by the quality and location of schools.

Health Services: What local health and social services are provided? How far is the nearest hospital with an emergency department? Are there English-speaking doctors and dentists, and private clinics or hospitals in the area?

Shopping: What shopping facilities are provided in the neighbourhood? How far is it to the nearest town with good shopping facilities, e.g. a supermarket or hypermarket? How would you get there if your car was out of order? Note that many rural villages are dying and have few shops or facilities, so they aren't usually a good choice for a retirement home.

Sport & Entertainment: What is the range and quality of local leisure, sports, community and cultural facilities? What is the proximity to sports facilities such as beaches, golf courses, ski resorts or waterways? Bear in mind that properties in or close to coastal resorts are generally more expensive, although they also have the best letting potential. Note that marina properties can be noisy and the marina itself is often a tourist attraction, which creates additional problems such as parking.

Public Transport: Is the proximity to public transport, e.g. an international airport, port or railway station, or access to a motorway important? Don't believe all you're told about the distance or travelling times to the nearest airport, port, railway station, motorway junction, beach or town, but check for yourself.

Parking: If you're planning to buy in a town or city, is there adequate private or free on-street parking for your family and visitors? Is it safe to park in the street? Note that in cities it's important to have secure off-street parking if you value your car. Parking is a problem in cities and most large towns, where private garages or parking spaces are unobtainable or expensive. Traffic congestion is also a problem in many towns and tourist resorts, particularly during the high season. Bear in mind that an apartment or townhouse in a town or community development may be some distance from the nearest road or car park. How do you feel about carrying heavy shopping hundreds of metres to your home and possibly up several flights of stairs? If you're planning to buy an apartment above the ground floor, you may wish to ensure that the building has a lift.

Crime: What is the local crime rate? In many resort areas the incidence of housebreaking and burglary is high, which also results in more expensive home insurance. Check the crime rate in the local area, e.g. burglaries, housebreaking, stolen cars and crimes of violence. Is crime increasing or decreasing? Note that crooks love isolated houses, particularly those full of expensive furniture and other belongings that they can strip bare at their leisure. You're much less likely to be the victim of thieves if you live in a village, where crime is virtually unknown – strangers stand out like sore thumbs in villages, where their every move is monitored by the local populace.

Municipality: Is the local council well run? What are the views of other residents? If the municipality is efficiently run, you can usually rely on good local services and amenities and local property taxes may be lower. In areas where there are large numbers of foreign residents, the town hall may have a special 'foreigners' department'.

CONVEYANCING

Conveyancing (properly called 'conveyance') is the British legal term for processing the paperwork involved in buying and selling a property and transferring the deeds of ownership (a conveyance is a deed or legal document which conveys a house from the seller to the buyer, thereby transferring ownership). Conveyancing is carried out by a lawyer (or solicitor), a public notary and in some countries, e.g. Britain, a licensed conveyancer. It usually includes the following tasks:

- Verifying that a property belongs to the vendor or that he has legal authority from the owner to sell it.

- Checking that there are no pre-emption rights or restrictive covenants over a property (such as rights of way) and that there are no plans to construct anything which would adversely affect the value, enjoyment or use of the property such as roads, railway lines, airports, shops, factories or any other developments. In some countries, many people have had the enjoyment of their property (not to mention its value) diminished by unsightly developments. Check whether there's a zoning plan for the surrounding area and what (if anything) can be built there.

- Checking whether the land has been registered at the land registry, and ensuring that a new property has the necessary building permits and planning permission (and that they're genuine) and that a building was built in accordance with such plans. A newly completed building must usually have a 'habitation certificate', which confirms that it may be lived in. If any alterations or improvements have been made to a building, either internally or externally, they should also have the necessary planning permission.

- Checking that there are no encumbrances, e.g. mortgages or loans, against a property or any outstanding debts such as local taxes (rates), community charges, water, electricity, telephone or any other debts. **Note that in many countries all**

unpaid debts on a property are inherited by the buyer. If there's an outstanding loan or taxes on a property, the lender or local authority has first claim on the property and has the right to take possession and sell it to repay the debt. It's particularly important to check whether there's an outstanding loan against a property when buying from a builder or developer.

● Ensuring that a proper title is obtained and arranging the necessary registration of ownership. In some countries, e.g. the USA, it's essential (and often mandatory) to have title insurance to protect against a future claim on the title by a third party.

There are two main stages when a lawyer or notary usually becomes involved in a property purchase. The first is the signing of a preliminary contract and the second is the completion of the sale at the signing of the deed of sale. In many countries, conveyancing is performed by a public notary, who must follow a strict code of conduct and sign a personal insurance covering his professional responsibility and guaranteeing clients against any errors he may make. He also usually has a financial guarantee covering money temporarily held in his care.

However, he represents neither the seller nor the buyer but the government, and his main task is to ensure that the documents are in order and that all state taxes are paid on the completion of a sale. A notary may check only planned developments directly affecting the property itself and not those that might affect its value, such as a new railway line or motorway in the vicinity. Obviously a new motorway or railway that disturbs the peace of your home will be something of a disaster, although on the other hand, a new motorway junction or railway station within a few kilometres may enhance a property's value considerably.

Where applicable, a notary is responsible for ensuring that a sales contract is drawn up correctly and that the purchase price is paid to the vendor. He also witnesses the signing of the deed, arranges for its registration (in the name of the new owner) in the local property register and collects any fees or taxes due. **He doesn't verify or guarantee the accuracy of statements made in a contract or protect you against fraud.** Don't expect a notary to speak English or any language other than the local language (although some do) or to explain the intricacies of local property law. Even when a notary is involved in a purchase, it's wise to employ a lawyer specialising in local property law to safeguard your rights and oversee the notary's work. When the services of a notary are obligatory, you must pay a set fee for his services, irrespective of whether you employ your own lawyer.

In many countries, hiring an experienced lawyer for a property transaction is standard practice. Before hiring a lawyer, compare the fees charged by a number of practices and obtain quotations in writing. Always check what's included in the fees and whether the fee is 'full and binding' or just an estimate (a low basic rate may be supplemented by much more expensive 'extras'). A lawyer's fees may be calculated as an hourly rate or a percentage of the purchase price of a property, e.g. 1 to 2 per cent, and there may be a minimum fee of £500 or £1,000 ($750 or $1,500). **Note that complaints about high lawyers' fees and overcharging on property transactions involving foreigners are common in some countries.**

The cost of conveyancing for a home abroad depends on whether you employ a local or overseas lawyer, or both. If you employ a foreign-based lawyer, i.e. one who isn't based in the country where you're buying a home, you can expect to pay heavily for his services, e.g. around £100 ($150) per hour in Britain. **Note, however, that although engaging a lawyer based in your home country when buying a home abroad may provide added peace of mind, you won't usually receive any extra services and will simply pay more.** Many experts believe that when buying property abroad you should employ the services of an experienced local lawyer who speaks English or a language that you speak fluently.

Anyone buying (or selling) a home abroad shouldn't even think about doing it without obtaining expert, experienced, independent legal advice. You should certainly never sign anything or pay any money before obtaining legal advice. This shouldn't be seen as an optional extra – you simply cannot afford *not* to take legal advice! Your lawyer should also check that the notary does his job correctly, thus providing an extra safeguard. In some countries, estate agents will carry out the conveyancing checks (listed above) for you and pass the information to your lawyer, however, it's still wise to have your lawyer double-check. It isn't wise to use the seller's lawyer, even if this would save you money, as he's primarily concerned with protecting the interests of the seller and not the buyer. See also **Avoiding Problems** on page 72.

PURCHASE CONTRACTS

The first stage when buying a home abroad is usually the signing of a preliminary contract. Although it isn't always necessary to employ a lawyer before signing a preliminary contract, it's recommended, even when you're protected by local law. **Most experts believe that you should *always* have a preliminary contract checked by your legal adviser before signing it.** If necessary, obtain a translation of a contract before signing it, but bear in mind that translations are often so bad as to be misleading or meaningless (and they aren't usually legally binding).

Types of Contracts: The first thing to bear in mind is that property sales contracts vary greatly with the country and you should always be guided by your legal adviser. In most countries there are many different types of preliminary contract depending on whether you're buying a resale property or a property 'off plan', which has still to be built or is under construction. When buying a property off plan it's common to sign a reservation or option 'contract' and care should be taken that you aren't asked to sign a binding purchase contract. If there's any doubt about whether you can complete a sale in the specified time, you should always sign a contract with an option to purchase. Note, however, that you may not be able to dictate the type of contract used and it may vary with the country, the area or even the individual agent or developer.

Contract Conditions: In some countries, preliminary contracts, whether for resale or new properties, may contain certain conditional clauses detailing conditions that must be met to ensure the validity of the contract. Conditions usually apply to events out of control of the vendor or buyer. If any of the conditions aren't met, the contract can be suspended or declared null and void and the deposit returned. If you fail to go through with a purchase and aren't covered by a clause in the contract, you usually forfeit your deposit. On the other hand, if the vendor withdraws from the sale, he must reimburse your deposit and in many countries pay a penalty equal to the amount of the deposit. Note, however, that with some contracts the buyer can be legally compelled to go through with a sale (as can the vendor). A deposit paid on an option or reservation contract on a un-built property should be returnable if you don't proceed. **Always ensure that you know the terms regarding the forfeiture or reimbursement of a deposit.**

The most common conditional clause is that the buyer is released from the contract if he's unable to obtain a mortgage (this condition is compulsory for property purchases in some countries). You shouldn't give up your right to obtain a mortgage, even if you don't need one; if you change your mind and fail to obtain a mortgage, you will lose your deposit. You must usually make an application for a loan within a certain period after signing a contract and you have a limited time in which to secure it.

There are many other possible conditional clauses concerning matters such as obtaining government or local planning permission, proposed public works (road, railway, etc.), third-party rights of way or state pre-emption (compulsory purchase), dependence on the sale of another property, and fixtures and fittings included in the price. Note that in some countries if you don't include the bathroom suite, fitted kitchen or even the light fittings in the contract, you may find them missing when you take possession. Generally, anything that you agree with the vendor should be included as a condition in the preliminary contract. You should discuss whether conditional clauses are necessary with your legal adviser. **Note that in some countries the vendor remains responsible for any major hidden defects in a property for six months from the date of signing the deed of sale (although this is no consolation if he has 'disappeared').**

Buying 'Off Plan': When buying a new property off plan, it's normal to pay a reservation fee, which is usually forfeited if you back out of the purchase. Before paying any money you should ensure that a developer, builder or architect has the necessary financial bank guarantees (obligatory in many countries). If a property is still to be built or completed, payment is made in stages. The contract should include the purchase price, the payment of a deposit, the schedule for payment of the balance or stage payments, any extras that you've agreed to purchase, and the intended date of completion. Stage payments vary with the country, e.g. 10 per cent on signing the contract, 30 per cent within 30 days, 30 per cent on completion of the roof and the final 30 percent on completion.

If possible, you should have a clause inserted in the contract allowing you to withhold 5 or 10 per cent of the purchase price for up to six months as a guarantee against the builder not correcting any faults in the property. The completion of each stage should be verified by your own architect or representative abroad. Note that it's important to ensure that money is paid on time; if it isn't, you could lose your deposit or even lose the property to another buyer. See also **Avoiding Problems** on page 72.

Deposits: When you sign a preliminary contract, you must pay a deposit. Although the amount varies with the country and the type of property being purchased, it's usually 5 or 10 per cent of the purchase price or a fixed sum (e.g. £1,000/$1,500). The sum may be negotiable, particularly on expensive properties. Once you've paid the deposit, there's a legally binding agreement between you and the vendor. **Note that if you fail to complete the sale within the specified time limit, e.g. 60 to 90 days, you will lose your deposit.**

The safest and quickest method of paying a deposit is usually to make a direct transfer from your bank to that of the agent or notary who is handling the sale. Note, however, that in some countries estate agents don't have the legal authority to hold money on behalf of their clients. All deposits should be held in a separate bonded (escrow) account. Always ensure that you comply with any fiscal rules regarding the importation of money into a country, as this may be essential if you want to re-export the proceeds on the sale of the property. Note that a deposit is usually refundable only under strict conditions, notably relating to the conditional clauses mentioned above. **Make sure you know** *exactly* **what the conditions are regarding the return or forfeiture of a deposit.**

Completion: When all the necessary documents regarding a purchase have been acquired by the lawyer or official, e.g. notary, handling a sale, he will contact you directly and request the balance of the purchase price less the deposit. He will also send you a bill for his fees and all taxes, which must be paid on completion. At the same time, you should also receive a draft deed of sale, which should be complete without any blank spaces to be completed later. If you don't understand the deed of sale, you should have it checked by your legal adviser. Property is usually sold subject to the condition that it's accepted in the state that it's in on completion, so you should be aware of anything that occurs between signing the preliminary contract and completion.

Before signing the deed of sale, you should check that the property hasn't fallen down or been damaged in any way, e.g. by a storm or a fallen tree, and that the vendor hasn't absconded with anything that was included in the price (which should be listed in the contract). In some countries, e.g. the USA, it's common to do a final check or inventory when buying a property, usually one or two days before completion. You should list the fixtures and fittings and anything that was included in the contract or paid for separately, e.g. carpets, light fittings, curtains or kitchen appliances. This is particularly important if the furniture and furnishings (and major appliances) were included in the price.

Inheritance & Capital Gains Tax: Before registering the title deed, you should carefully consider the tax and inheritance consequences of the person(s) in whose name the deed will be registered. Property can usually be registered in one name, both names of a couple, joint buyers' names, the name or names of children giving a surviving parent sole use during his or her lifetime, or in the name of a local or offshore company. In most countries it's no longer possible to avoid capital gains and inheritance tax by registering a property in the name of an offshore company, although there are exceptions, e.g. Portugal. **Whatever you decide, it should be done at the time of purchase, as it can be difficult or expensive to make changes later and may even be impossible.** Consult a lawyer who is experienced in local inheritance law before signing a contract. See also **Capital Gains Tax** on page 63 and **Inheritance Tax** on page 64.

Signing the Deed of Sale: The final act of a purchase is the signing of the deed of sale, transferring legal ownership of a property, and the payment of the balance due. Non-resident purchasers in some countries must obtain a certificate from a local bank stating that the amount to be paid has been imported in a foreign currency, a copy of which is attached to the title deed. Before the deed of sale is signed, the notary checks that all the conditions contained in the preliminary contract have been fulfilled. It's usual for both parties to be present when the deed of sale is read, signed and witnessed, although you can give a representative abroad power of attorney. This is quite common among foreign buyers and will be arranged by your lawyer. If you don't understand the local language, you can have an interpreter present, although this shouldn't be necessary, as a copy of the deed of sale should have been scrutinised by your legal adviser beforehand.

In some countries there are no title deeds, and ownership is proven and guaranteed by registration of the property at the land registry. The land registry's stamp is placed on the deed of sale, a copy of which is usually sent to the buyer a few months after completion of a sale. If you require evidence of ownership, for example to import furniture and personal effects, ask your lawyer for an attestation that you're the owner of the property.

Registration: When the contract is signed by the official in charge, e.g. a notary, he will give you a certified copy of the deeds. A notarised copy is lodged at the property registry office and the new owner's name is entered on the registry deed. As noted above, you should ensure that the deed is registered *immediately* after signing it, if necessary by registering it yourself. **Registering ownership of a property is the most important act of buying property in most countries.** Until the property is registered in your name, even after you've signed the contract before a notary, charges can be registered against it or someone else can register ownership in his own name. **Only when the deed is registered do you become the legal owner of the property.** Following registration, the original deeds may be returned to you, usually after a number of months. See also **Avoiding Problems** on page 72 and **Conveyancing** on page 95.

ESTATE AGENTS

The vast majority of property sales in most countries are handled by estate agents (or brokers), particularly where foreign buyers are concerned. Estate agents (or real estate agents) in many countries advertise abroad, e.g. in the publications listed in **Appendix A**, and in local magazines and newspapers, including expatriate publications. In many countries, agents or their staff speak English and other foreign languages, so don't be discouraged if you don't speak the local language. If you want to find an agent in a particular town or area, look in the local Yellow Pages, which are often available at libraries.

Estate agents in most countries are regulated by law and must be professionally qualified and licensed and hold indemnity insurance. The rules for local estate agents also apply to foreign-based agents, who cannot usually sell property abroad without a local licence (although in some countries, some local agents are little more than sleeping partners in foreign-owned companies). You should choose an agent who is a member of a professional association, most of which insist that members have professional indemnity insurance and adhere to a code of ethics. If you pay a deposit to an agent, you should always ensure that he's licensed (bonded) and that all clients' money is deposited in a special bonded (escrow) account. There are unlicensed, 'cowboy' agents operating in many countries (particularly in resort areas) who should be avoided. Ask to see an agent's registration number and check it if you aren't convinced that it's genuine.

It's common for buyers in some countries, e.g. Britain, to use an agent in their home country who works in conjunction with agents and developers abroad. When two agents are involved in a sale the commission is shared, so buyers usually pay no more by using a foreign agent. **However, always check in advance whether this is the case and how much you're required to pay.** In most countries there are no controls on agents' fees, although they may be obliged to post them in their offices. Note that the agent's fee may be paid by the vendor, the buyer, or a combination of both (although in most countries it's normal for the vendor to pay). The buyer usually pays in any case, as agents' fees are generally included in the asking price. If you view a property with one agent, you aren't permitted to buy the property through another agent or direct from the vendor without paying the commission of the first agent.

It's wise to do some research and decide the area where you want to live, what sort of property you want, and your budget, *before* visiting agents abroad. Before travelling, obtain details and photographs of as many properties as possible that meet your requirements in your chosen area, and make a list of those you wish to view.

The quantity and quality of information provided by agents varies considerably but is usually sparse. Few agents provide detailed descriptions of properties and often there's no photograph (even when there is, it frequently doesn't do a property justice). Obviously with regard to an old property badly in need of renovation or restoration, there isn't a lot that can be said apart from stating the number and size of the buildings and the land area. However, agents advertising in foreign journals or working closely with overseas agents usually supply coloured photographs and a full description, particularly for expensive properties. Don't rely on an estate agent's room, patio or garden measurements, but check them yourself (this also applies to anything else that isn't immediately obvious). **Always check that a property is still for sale (and the price) before making a trip abroad to view it.**

It will come as no surprise to most people to learn that in most countries many homebuyers are overcharged by estate agents. Be particularly wary of agents who try to sell you something outside your price range or properties that don't match your specifications. If an agent tries to dictate to you or argue about an offer, go elsewhere. **Note that an agent usually represents the seller (the principal) and is trying to get the highest possible price for a property (and the highest possible commission for himself) and not the best deal for you the buyer.** Never tell an agent your highest price or how high you're willing to go on a particular property, as he may (by law) be required to pass this information on to the seller. If an agent offers to make a considerable reduction on the advertised price of a property, it will probably be because it's overpriced and has been on his books for a long time. In some countries, e.g. the USA, you can employ a buyer's broker to represent your interests.

Most agents expect customers to know where they want to buy within a 30 to 40km (18 to 25mi) radius and some even expect them to narrow their choice down to specific towns or villages. If you cannot define where and what you're looking for, at least tell the agent so that he will know you're undecided. If you're 'just looking', say so. Many agents will still be pleased to show you properties, as they're well aware that many people fall in love with a property and buy it on the spot. Note, however, that some agents are reluctant to drive 'sightseers' around.

In most countries, you're shown properties by agents and aren't given the keys (especially to furnished properties) or allowed to deal with tenants or vendors directly. One reason is that many properties are almost impossible to find if you don't know the area (in some countries it isn't unknown even for agents to get hopelessly lost when looking for properties). Many rural properties have no numbers, and street names are often virtually non-existent. You should always make an appointment to view properties, as most agents don't like people just turning up 'on spec'. **If you make an appointment, you should always keep it or call and cancel it.** If you're on holiday, it's acceptable to drop in unannounced to have a look at what's on offer, but don't expect an agent to show you properties without an appointment.

In many countries agents and developers arrange viewing trips with inexpensive or free accommodation for prospective buyers and will often refund the cost of travel if you buy a property. By all means take advantage of low-cost inspection flight offers, but don't allow yourself to be pressurised into buying on a viewing trip. Always allow yourself sufficient time to view and compare properties offered by a number of agents and developers (although some agents offering subsidised viewing trips will try to ensure that you have no free time to view properties offered by rivals). A long weekend isn't sufficient time to have a good look around, unless you already know exactly what you want to buy and where. Some market analysts advise buyers to travel independently and shop around a number of agents.

You should try to view as many properties as possible during the time available, but allow sufficient time to inspect each property thoroughly, to travel (and get lost) between houses, and to eat (it's *mandatory* to have a good lunch in many countries!). You should also avoid looking at properties during the hottest part of the day. Although it's important to see sufficient properties to form an accurate opinion of price and quality, don't see too many properties in one day, as it's easy to become confused as to the merits of each property. **If you're shown properties that don't meet your specifications, tell the agent immediately.**

You should make notes of both the good *and* bad features and take lots of photographs of the properties you like, so that you're able to compare them later at your leisure (but keep a record of which photos are of which house!). It's also wise to mark each property on a map, so that should you wish to return you can find them without getting lost (too often). **The more a property appeals to you, the more you should look for faults and negative points.** If you still like it after stressing all the negative points, it must have special appeal.

Many estate agents produce free newspapers and magazines containing details of both old and new homes and provide colour prospectuses for new developments. Most agents offer after-sales services and will help you to arrange legal advice, insurance, utility connections and interior decoration. Many also offer a full management and rental service for non-resident owners. Note, however, that agents often receive commissions for referrals and you may therefore not receive independent advice (you can always ask). In some countries, e.g. Britain, some agents are owned by or tied to companies such as banks and building societies, whose main business is providing loans and insurance for home buyers (which may not offer the best value).

RENOVATION & RESTORATION

In some countries, e.g. France and Italy, many properties purchased by foreigners, particularly homes in rural areas, are in need of restoration, renovation or modernisation. The most common examples are 18th and 19th century farmhouses and village houses that have been almost totally neglected since they were built (or abandoned) many years ago. A derelict building often needs a damp-proof course, timber treatment, new windows and doors, a new roof or extensive repairs, a modern kitchen and bathroom, re-wiring, central heating and decorating.

It's vitally important to ensure that a property has sound walls. Buildings that have walls with serious defects, e.g. bulging, are best avoided, as it's usually cheaper to knock them down and erect a totally new building! Almost any other problem can be fixed or overcome (at a price). A sound roof that doesn't leak is desirable. Don't believe a vendor or agent who tells you that a roof or anything else can be repaired or patched up, but obtain expert advice from a local builder. Electricity and water should already be connected, as they can be expensive to extend to a property situated in the middle of nowhere.

Note that rural properties in many countries get their water from a spring or well. This isn't usually a problem, although you should check the reliability of the water supply, as wells can run dry! The absence of a septic tank or other waste water system isn't usually a problem, provided the land allows for their installation. If a property doesn't have electricity, mains gas, mains water, or a telephone link, check the nearest connection points and the cost of extending the service to the property. **It can be very expensive!**

One of the first decisions you need to make regarding restoration or modernisation is whether to do all or some of the work yourself, have the work done by local tradesmen or employ foreign builders. A working knowledge of the local language is usually essential for DIY, especially the words relating to building materials and measurements (renovating a house abroad will also greatly improve your ability to swear in the local language!). Special dictionaries and books are available for DIY restorers in some countries.

In many countries the local inhabitants aren't too keen on DIY and building materials and tools may therefore be difficult to obtain and expensive. You shouldn't tackle jobs yourself or with friends unless you're certain that you're doing it right. In general, you should aim to retain as many of a property's original features as possible and stick to local building materials such as wood, stone and tiles, reflecting the style of the property (which may even be obligatory). When renovations and 'improvements' have been botched, there's often little that can be done except to start again from scratch. It's important not to over-modernise a property, so that too much of its natural charm and attraction is lost. If modernisation of an old building involves making external alterations, such as building an extension or installing larger windows or new doorways, you usually need planning permission and a building permit from the local authorities. **You should never start any building work before you have official permission (although it's a common practice in some countries).**

The cost of total renovation by professional builders is usually quoted per square metre (m^2) and depends on the type of work involved, the quality of materials used and the region. In most countries you should reckon on paying £200 to £300 per m^2, although the cost of renovating a ruin can be over £500 per m^2. As a rough guide, you should expect the cost of renovating an old 'habitable' building to be at least equal to its purchase price; if it's a 'ruin', you can pay up to three times as much. In some countries it's possible to obtain a mortgage which includes the cost of renovation, but you must obtain detailed written quotations for your lender.

How much you spend on restoring a property depends on your objective and the depth of your pockets. If you're restoring a property as an investment, it's easy to spend much more than you could ever hope to recoup when you sell the property. On the other hand, if you plan to use a property as a holiday home or live there permanently, there's no limit to what you can do and how much money you can spend. **Note that original estimates can escalate wildly and many buyers have been bankrupted by the cost of restoring an old property!**

When it's a choice between employing local or foreign builders, most experts recommend using local labour for a number of good reasons. Local artisans understand the materials and the traditional style of building, are familiar with local planning and building regulations, and usually do excellent work. Their quotations are usually binding and their prices reasonable because of low labour costs. In some countries, e.g. France, all work done by locally registered builders is insured for ten years, even if the builder goes out of business before the period has elapsed. Check whether this is the case before signing a contract. Building costs can usually be offset against income from renting or against capital gains tax when selling a property. Note that hiring foreign labour won't endear you to the local populace and may even create friction. You should never employ 'black' (i.e. unregistered) labour; apart from having no insurance, you can incur stiff penalties.

Although foreigners often complain about the length of time it takes to get work done abroad, most praise the quality and reasonable charges. However, if you aren't on the spot you should hire a 'clerk of works', e.g. an architect, to oversee a job or it could drag on for months (or years) or even be botched. You should expect to pay 7.5 to 10 per cent of the restoration costs to have someone manage a restoration. Some agents will handle a complete restoration using their own team of craftsmen and many estate agents act as managers. In some countries it's highly unlikely that your instructions will be followed if workers aren't closely supervised. Local 'work' practices are often notoriously erratic and sometimes workmen work for a few days and then disappear for weeks or months! Always obtain recommendations from local people you can trust, e.g. an estate agent, notary, local mayor or neighbours.

You should obtain written quotations from *at least* two builders before employing anyone. Note that for estimates to be accurate, you must describe in detail the work required, e.g. for electrical work this would include the number of lights, points and switches, and the quality of materials to be used. If you have only a vague idea of what you want, you will receive a vague and unreliable estimate. Make sure that an estimate includes everything you want done. You should expect to pay for a detailed written estimate, e.g. around £50, although the cost should be reimbursed by the builder who's awarded the contract. Be wary of any terms in an estimate allowing the price to be increased for inflation or any other reason, and check whether it's definitive or provisional, i.e. dependent on further exploratory work.

Note that in some countries, if you buy an old house and completely renovate it, e.g. retaining only the roof and external walls, thus transforming it into a 'new' house, you may be liable for VAT. Therefore you should, if possible, always retain a small part of the existing internal structure. Check with your financial adviser before starting work. Finally, before starting work and while work is in progress, most people find it worthwhile to keep a photographic record of their accomplishments, if only to justify the expense! See also **Buying an Old Property** on page 76, **Building** a **House** on page 80, **Survey** on page 86, **Water** on page 113 and **Heating & Air-conditioning** on page 115.

GARAGES & PARKING

A garage isn't usually provided when you buy an apartment or townhouse in most countries, particularly in towns and cities, although most new developments provide private parking spaces or a communal off-road parking area. Some developments have underground garage spaces and private lock-up garages, although these are usually in short supply. When available, private garages (or a space in an underground garage) can be rented or purchased, although the cost can be high, e.g. from around £5,000 ($7,500). Bear in mind that in a large development the nearest parking area may be some distance from your home. This may be an important consideration, particularly if you aren't up to carrying heavy shopping hundred of metres to your home (and possibly up several flights of stairs). Detached houses in most countries almost always have their own car port or garage.

Note that without a garage, parking can be a nightmare, particularly in cities or in summer in a busy resort town or development. Free street parking may be difficult or impossible to find in cities and large towns and in any case isn't recommended for anything but a wreck. A lock-up garage is important in areas with a high incidence of car theft and theft from cars, e.g. most cities and popular resorts, and is also useful to protect your car from climatic extremes.

It may be possible to rent a garage or parking space, although it can be prohibitively expensive in cities. Free on-street parking is difficult or impossible to find in many cities and large towns. In many towns, residents must obtain a permit for on-street parking, and in some it's prohibited.

SECURITY

Before (or soon after) moving into a new home it's wise to replace the locks or lock barrels and fit high security locks, as you have no idea how many keys are in circulation for the existing locks. At the same time you may wish to have an alarm system fitted, which is the best way to deter intruders and may also reduce your home contents insurance (see page 35). Many security companies provide security systems connected to a central 24-hour monitoring station. When a sensor, e.g. smoke or forced entry, detects an emergency or a panic button is pushed, a signal is automatically sent to the station (with some systems it's even possible to check properties remotely from another country via a computer link). Some local security companies guarantee to respond to an alarm within five or ten minutes.

External security lights (which switch on automatically when someone approaches), timed switches for internal lights, radio and television, dummy security cameras, and tapes that play barking dogs (triggered by a light switch) may also help deter burglars. Holiday homes are particularly vulnerable to thieves and in some countries are regularly ransacked. In many countries it's common for owners to fit two or three locks on external doors, alarm systems, grilles on doors and windows, window locks, security shutters and a safe for valuables. A dog can be useful to deter intruders, although it should be kept inside where it cannot be given poisoned food.

Irrespective of whether you actually have a dog, a warning sign with a picture of a fierce dog may act as a deterrent.

Many modern developments and communities have security gates and are patrolled by 24-hour security guards or local police cars, although they may have little influence on crime rates and may instil a false sense of security. If you own a holiday home abroad, your household insurance company (see page 34) may insist on extra security measures. In some countries, e.g. Spain, all ground-floor properties are fitted with iron grilles on all windows and glass doors, such as patio or terrace doors. The advantage of grilles is that they allow you to leave windows open without inviting criminals in (unless they're *very* slim). You can fit UPVC (toughened clear plastic) security windows and doors (which can survive an attack with a sledge-hammer without damage), and external steel security blinds (which can be electrically operated), although these are both expensive. Many people also use a metal clasp to secure their patio grilles and doors when a property is unoccupied. **Remember, prevention is better than cure, as stolen property is rarely recovered.**

However, no matter how secure your home, a thief can usually break in if he's determined enough, e.g. through the roof or by punching a hole in a wall in an isolated area! In secluded areas thieves can strip a house bare at their leisure and an alarm isn't much of a deterrent if there's nobody around to hear it. If you have a holiday home abroad, you shouldn't leave anything of value (monetary or sentimental) there. If you vacate a holiday or permanent home for an extended period, it may be obligatory to notify your caretaker or household insurance company, and leave a key with the caretaker in case of emergencies. In any case, it's wise to have someone make periodic checks on a property when it's unoccupied. If you have a break-in, you should report it immediately to your local police and make a statement. You will receive a copy, which is required by your household insurance company when you make a claim.

Another aspect of home security is your own safety. In some countries you should never open your front door automatically (especially late at night) and should have a spy-hole fitted so that you can check a caller's identity. Don't take identity cards at face value but verify the identity of an unexpected 'service' man with his company. Some apartment blocks are fitted with a security system, allowing residents to speak to callers before allowing them access to a building.

Finally, one of the most important aspects of home security is ensuring you have early warning of a fire, which is easily accomplished by installing smoke detectors (required by law in some countries). Battery-operated smoke detectors can be purchased for £5 to £10 in most countries (they should be tested regularly to ensure that the batteries aren't exhausted). You can also fit an electricity-powered gas detector that activates an alarm when a gas leak is detected. Keep the numbers of your local utility companies with those of the local police, fire and ambulance services (plus your doctor and local hospital) by your telephone.

UTILITIES

Electricity, gas and water supplies, collectively referred to as 'utilities' in most countries, may be owned and operated by private companies, local municipalities or the state or federal government (there are also co-operatives in some countries). In most countries, utility companies are monopolies and therefore services and prices are regulated by local and state governments. In some countries you may be billed for electricity and gas (and water) by the same utility company or by your municipality, although electricity and gas bills are always itemised separately.

Registration: Immediately after buying a property abroad you should apply to utility companies to have the electricity, gas and water services switched on or transferred to your name. You may need to apply in person and show proof of ownership and identification such as your passport or residence permit (take a good book, as queues can be long). If applicable, you should also take bills paid by the previous owner. Make sure that all previous bills have been paid and that the contract is registered in your name from the day you take over, or you may be liable for debts left by the previous owner. When registering, non-resident owners should also give their foreign address in case there are any problems requiring your attention, such as your bank refusing to pay a bill while you're abroad. If you wish to pay your bill by direct debit from a bank account (which is recommended), don't forget to provide your account details.

You may be required to pay a security deposit, depending on the country, your nationality, and whether you're a non-resident. This should be paid into an interest-earning account and is usually refunded after a period or offset against future bills. A registration fee is usually payable to be connected to the service and have the meter read, which is included in your first bill. In most European countries you need to sign a contract for electricity specifying the power supply installed and the tariff required (see below). You must contact your electricity, gas and water companies (well in advance in some countries) to obtain a final meter reading and bill when vacating a property.

Meter Reading: In most countries all homes, whether apartments or detached houses, have their own electricity, gas and water meters. They're usually located in the basement, in a special meter 'cupboard' (particularly in apartment blocks or townhouse developments) or in a box on an outside wall of a detached house, where they can be read by utility company employees when you aren't at home. You should have free access to your meter and should be able read it (some meters don't have windows to allow you to read the consumption). If your meter isn't accessible, or a house isn't permanently occupied, you will need to leave the keys with a neighbour or make arrangements to have your meter read. **A property, whether detached or part of a community, should always have its own meters (if it doesn't it may indicate serious problems, such as the building not having a 'habitation' or other official certificate).**

To ensure that your electricity, gas and water supply is connected and that you don't pay the previous owner's bills, you should contact your local utility office and ask them to read the meter before taking over a property. Meters are read periodically, e.g. bi-monthly or quarterly, although this varies with the country. If the meter reader is unable to read your meter, you will receive an estimated bill (which will be indicated on the bill). In some countries a utility company will send out a revised bill based on a meter reading provided by the householder, although a utility company is usually required to make a number of actual readings a year, e.g. two.

Bills: You're billed by your utility company periodically, e.g. from monthly or bi-annually, depending on the country and the company. Electricity and gas bills are usually payable every two or three months, while water bills may be payable bi-annually. The billing period is shown on bills. A number of bills received throughout the year, e.g. alternate bills, are usually estimated. Bills include a standing (service) charge, sales or value added tax, and possibly local taxes. All your utility bills (plus telephone) can be paid by direct debit from a bank or post office account. It's also possible in many countries to pay a fixed amount each month by standing order based on your estimated usage (sometimes called a budget account). At the end of the year you receive a bill for the amount owing or a rebate of the amount overpaid. These methods of payment are preferable, particularly if you spend a lot of time away from your home or you own a holiday home. If your bills aren't paid on time, your utility company may not hesitate to cut your service. If you're a non-resident, you may be able to have your bills sent to an address abroad or have a copy of your bill sent to a local relative, friend or organisation.

You're usually given around 14 days to pay a bill before it becomes overdue. If your payment arrives after the due date, you may be charged a late payment penalty. If you don't pay a utility bill, you will eventually receive a 'notice of discontinuation of service', when you should pay the bill within the period stated, even if you dispute the amount. In most countries utility companies are required by law to give adequate notice and a hearing before they can terminate the service. If your electricity, gas or water supply is cut off because of non-payment of a bill, you must pay the outstanding bill, a reconnection fee and possibly a deposit before it will be reconnected.

Most utility companies publish useful booklets explaining their services and tariffs and how to conserve energy or water (and thus reduce your bills). In some countries, utility and private companies will perform a home energy conservation survey of your home. Always check the identity of anyone claiming to be a utility employee (or any kind of 'serviceman') by asking to see a photo identity card.

Electricity

Power cuts are fairly frequent in some countries, particularly during thunderstorms, and it's wise to keep torches, candles or a gas or oil lamp handy. Power fluctuations and momentary drops are common in many countries (indicated by flickering lights) and often last just long enough to crash your computer! If you live in an area with an unstable electricity supply, you can buy a power stabiliser or an uninterrupted power supply (UPS) with a battery backup, which allows you time to save your work and shut down your computer after a power failure. **Even more important than a battery backup is a power surge protector for appliances such as TVs, computers and fax machines, without which you risk having your equipment damaged or destroyed.** In remote areas of some countries cuts are more frequent and if you rely on electricity for your livelihood, e.g. for operating a computer, fax machine and other equipment, you may need to install a backup generator. In some remote rural areas you *must* install a generator if you want electricity, as there's no mains electricity, although many people make do with gas and oil lamps (and without television and modern conveniences).

Wiring: In most countries modern properties, e.g. less than 20 years old, have adequate or good electrical installations. However, if you buy an old property you should ensure that the electricity system is in good order well in advance of moving house, as it can take some time to get a new meter installed or obtain a re-connection. If a property has inadequate electrical installations, an electricity company can demand that it's rewired to conform with the latest safety regulations (standards also change periodically, which may entail re-wiring). Bear in mind that the cost of completely rewiring a property can be expensive, e.g. £5,000 ($7,500) or more.

If you buy an old rural property in some countries, you may find that it has no electricity supply. If you buy an old property without electricity (or build a new property) there are usually public guarantees of essential services such as electricity (plus water, sewage, roads and telephone) and you aren't obliged to pay for the installation of electricity lines or transformers, only the connection to your property. However, the connection can be expensive for remote properties. Obtain a quotation in advance from the local electricity company. If you build your own home or rewire an old home, your electrician or builder must provide a certificate for the electricity company stating that your electricity installation meets the required standard.

In some countries the electrical system in older properties is often eccentric and may even be dangerous, with exposed sockets and bare wires. One of the most important tasks on taking over any property is to check that the electrical system is in good condition and adequate to meet your needs (see **Power Supply** on page 111). Make sure that you have sufficient power points installed, as even in new properties in some countries it's common for builders not to fit enough power points. You should use a qualified electrician for all electrical work. Apart from the danger of electrocuting yourself, wiring methods often vary from country to country. In most countries, only a qualified electrician is permitted to install electrical wiring and fittings, particularly in connection with fuse boxes. In some countries, electricity companies will service your major electrical appliances, e.g. heating or air-conditioning systems, and some provide service contracts.

Plugs & Sockets: Depending on your home country, you may need new plugs or a lot of adapters, e.g. most countries use a different system (there are over 20 plug configurations in Europe alone) and even in individual homes there may be different types of plugs and sockets. Plug adapters for imported lamps and other electrical apparatus may be difficult to obtain in some countries, so it's wise to bring some with you, plus extension cords and multi-plug extensions that can be fitted with a local plug. Electrical appliances in most countries are fitted with a moulded plug.

Note that in many countries, small low-wattage electrical appliances up to six amps, such as table lamps, small TVs and computers, don't require an earth. However, plugs with an earth must always be used for high-wattage appliances such as fires, kettles, washing machines, refrigerators and cookers. In some countries, all sockets aren't earthed and many electrical appliances are operated without an earth, with the notable exception of washing machines, dishwashers and dryers. Plugs in most countries aren't fitted with fuses (Britain is one of the few exceptions). Electrical appliances that are earthed have a three-core wire and must *never* be used with a two-pin plug without an earth connection. Note that the colour codes for wires aren't the same in all countries. For example, in most European countries the code is blue (neutral), brown or red (live) and green and yellow (earth), while in the USA it's usually white (neutral), black (live) and green (earth). **Always make sure that a plug is correctly and securely wired, as bad wiring can prove fatal.**

Fuses: Most apartments and all houses have their own fuse boxes. Fuses can be of various types. In some countries the electrical system in old houses may still use fuse wire, which has different ratings (before replacing the fuse wire, turn off the mains switch), while in others fuses have a coloured disk, which *when not displayed*, indicates that the fuse has blown. These fuses, which have different amp ratings, can be purchased in most electrical stores and supermarkets. In modern homes, fuses are of the resetting pop-out type or earth trip system. When there's a short circuit or the system has been overloaded, a circuit breaker is tripped and the power supply is cut. The fuse usually consists of a simple switch, which when a circuit is overloaded, trips to the OFF position. It may be necessary to switch off the main switch before opening the circuit breaker box. Before switching the fuse back to the ON position, locate and remedy the cause of the overload (if possible). If the power repeatedly trips off, switch off high-power appliances, as the system may be overloaded (see **Power Supply** below). Make sure that you know where fuses or trip switches are located and keep a torch handy so that you can find them in the dark.

Bulbs: Electric light bulbs in most countries are of the Edison type with a screw fitting, although in some countries, e.g. France, there are screw *and* bayonet fittings. Note that bulbs with a bayonet fitting are unavailable in some countries, although you can buy adapters to convert from bayonet to screw or vice versa. Bulbs for non-standard electrical appliances (i.e. appliances not made for the local market) such as refrigerators, sewing machines and lamps, may not be available abroad, so you should bring some spares with you.

Converters & Transformers: The electricity supply in most of Europe is 220/240 volts AC with a frequency of 50 Hertz (cycles), while in the USA and some other countries (including some older building in some European countries) it's 110/120 volts AC, with a frequency of 60 Hertz. Electrical equipment rated at 110 volts (for example from the USA) requires a converter or a transformer to convert it to 240 volts, although some electrical appliances, electric razors and hair dryers, are fitted with a 110/240 volt switch. Check for the switch, which may be inside the casing, and make sure it's switched to the correct voltage *before* connecting it to the power supply. Converters can be used for heating appliances, but transformers are required for motorised appliances. Total the wattage of the devices you intend to connect to a transformer and make sure that its power rating *exceeds* this sum. Generally all small, high-wattage, electrical appliances (e.g. kettles, toasters, heaters and irons) need large transformers.

Motors in large appliances such as cookers, refrigerators, washing machines, dryers and dishwashers, will need replacing or fitting with a large transformer. In most cases it's simpler to buy new appliances locally, which in most countries are of good quality and reasonably priced. If you buy a home in the USA (or another country) with a 110 volt system, it's possible to operate electrical equipment rated at 240 volts with a converter or a step-up transformer to convert it to 110 volts, although generally it isn't worthwhile taking electrical appliances that aren't rated at 110 (or 110/220) volts. Note also that the dimensions of imported cookers, microwave ovens, refrigerators, washing machines, dryers and dishwashers, may differ from those sold locally, and imported appliances won't fit into a standard kitchen in many countries.

Frequency: An additional problem with some electrical equipment is the frequency rating, which in some countries, e.g. the USA, is designed to run at 60 Hertz (Hz) and not Europe's 50Hz. Electrical equipment *without* a motor is generally unaffected by the drop in frequency to 50Hz (except TVs). Equipment with a motor may run but with a 20 per cent drop in speed, however, automatic washing machines, cookers, electric clocks, record players and tape recorders are unusable if they aren't designed for 50Hz operation. To find out, check the label on the back of the equipment. If it says 50/60Hz, it should be okay. If it says 60Hz, you might try it anyway, **but first ensure that the voltage is correct as described above.** Bear in mind that the transformers and motors of electrical equipment designed to run at 60Hz will run hotter at 50Hz, so ensure that equipment has sufficient space for cooling.

Power Supply: If the power keeps tripping off when you attempt to use a number of high-power appliances simultaneously, it probably means that the power supply of your property is too low to operate all the appliances simultaneously. This is a common problem in many countries, particularly in holiday homes, where the power supply rating is deliberately kept low to reduce costs. If this is the case you must contact your electricity company and ask them to uprate the power supply to your property, which is usually shown on your meter (and on your bill). It can also be downgraded if the power supply is more than you require.

The power supply increases by increments e.g. 3, 6, 9 and 12 kilowatts (KW), and you usually need a power supply of at least 12KW to operate an electrical heating system. In some countries it can take weeks or months to get your power supply changed, so check the power supply when buying a home and if required apply to have it uprated as soon as possible. To calculate the power supply required, list all the electrical appliances you have (plus any you intend installing, such as an electric shower or dishwasher) and the power consumption of each item. Add the power consumption of all the appliances you're likely to operate simultaneously to obtain the total kilowatt power supply required. If you have appliances such as a washing machine, dishwasher, water heater and electric heating in an average size house, e.g. two to three bedrooms, you may need an 18KW supply. Your standing (service) charge depends on the power rating of your supply, which is why most owners tend to keep it as low as possible.

Tariffs: In most countries, electricity companies offer different tariffs, which usually apply at different times of the day and different seasons (usually summer and winter). In order to use certain tariffs a special meter must be installed. With the normal tariff all electricity consumed is charged at the same rate, with no difference between day and night rates. This is the most expensive rate and is for those who use only a small amount of electricity. Most electricity companies offer a reduced tariff, which usually applies overnight (but may also be valid for a limited period during the day), which is generally used to heat hot water and charge night storage heaters. It's also a good time to run your washing machine, drier or dishwasher and some companies will install relays to automatically switch on appliances during the cheap period. In some countries, e.g. France, there's a special tariff designed to encourage users to conserve electricity during severe cold weather when demand is at its highest. It allows you to use electricity at a reduced tariff throughout the year with the exception of peak demand days. This is the best choice for anyone owning a holiday home that will be unoccupied most of the time.

Gas

Mains gas is available in cities and large towns in most countries, although modern houses are often all electric and mains gas is rarely available in rural and remote areas. If you buy a property without a mains gas supply, you may be able to have it connected, but it could be prohibitively expensive. As with electricity, you can choose the gas tariff that best suits your requirements. The cubic metres of gas consumed may be converted to kilowatt hours for invoicing (although in the USA you're charged by the cubic calorific foot or therm (which is equal to 100 cubic feet). In some countries, in apartment buildings where gas is used for cooking only, a standard charge for gas may be included in your community fees. As with heating and hot water charges, this isn't ideal if you own a holiday home.

In some countries, homes use bottled gas for cooking, hot-water and heating, particularly in rural areas. You can have a combined gas hot-water and heating system (providing background heat) installed, which is relatively inexpensive to install and cheap to run. In many countries, cookers often have a combination of electric and (bottled) gas rings (you can choose the mix). If your gas rings are sparked by electricity, keep some matches handy for use during power cuts. Check when moving into a property that the gas bottle isn't empty. Keep a spare bottle or two handy and make sure you know how to change bottles (get the previous owner or the estate agent to show you). A bottle used only for cooking will last an average family six to eight weeks. Note that the rubber cover over the gas outlet may turn clockwise, in contrast to most other threaded devices.

The cost of bottled gas varies considerably: in some countries it's much cheaper than mains gas, while in others it's more expensive. In some countries, e.g. Spain, gas bottles are delivered to homes by the gas company, for which a contract is required (which may be approved only after a safety inspection has been made of the property where the gas appliance is to be used). In some countries you can also buy bottled gas at petrol stations, supermarkets and hypermarkets, but you should always trade in an empty bottle for a new one, otherwise it's much more expensive. If you need to buy new gas bottles, a retailer will ask you to register and pay a bottle deposit. Some village shops also sell bottled gas. Some houses keep their gas bottles outside, often under a lean-to. If this is so, you must buy propane gas rather than butane, as it can withstand a greater range of temperatures than butane, which is for internal use only. **Bear in mind that gas bottles are very heavy and inconvenient to use.**

Gas central heating is common in some countries, although in rural areas the gas supply comes from a gas tank installed on the property, rather than a mains supply. Some gas suppliers will install a tank free of charge in return for a contract to provide gas for a fixed period. Note that having a gas tank on your property may increase your insurance premiums. You should have gas appliances serviced periodically and checked for leaks, particularly in the rubber tubing. Gas leaks are extremely rare and explosions caused by leaks even rarer (although spectacular and therefore widely reported). You can install an electrically-operated gas detector that activates an alarm when a gas leak is detected.

Water

The quality and reliability of the water supply is a *very* important consideration when buying a home in some countries, and should always be thoroughly investigated in advance. In some countries the quality of tap water is poor and drinking and cooking water may need to be filtered, while in others (particularly some areas of Italy and Spain) there are critical water shortages and cuts are frequent. Water shortages are exacerbated in resort areas in summer, when the local population may swell tenfold and coincides with the hottest and driest period of the year.

Restrictions: During water shortages, local municipalities restrict the water consumption or cut off supplies altogether for hours or even days at a time. Restrictions can be severe and householders may be limited to as little as three cubic metres a month, which is sufficient for around 10 baths or 20 showers. You can forget about watering the garden or washing your car unless you have a private water supply. During severe droughts, cuts are usually scheduled to take place at the same time each day. If a water company needs to cut your supply, e.g. to carry out maintenance work on pipes and other installations, they will usually notify you in advance so that you can store water for cooking.

Before moving into a new home you should enquire where the main stop-valve or stopcock is, so that you can turn off the water supply in an emergency. If the water stops flowing for any reason you should ensure that all the taps are turned off to prevent flooding when the supply starts again. Note that in community properties, the tap to turn the water on or off is usually located outside the building. If your water goes off suddenly, check that someone hasn't switched it off by mistake. In countries and regions where water shortages are common, water tankers deliver water to homes. Some properties don't have a mains water supply, but a storage tank that's filled from a tanker (customers are charged by the litre plus a delivery charge). Note that in some areas, water shortages create low water pressure, resulting in insufficient water to take a shower.

Check the Supply: One of the most important tasks before buying a home abroad is to investigate the reliability of the local water supply (over a number of years) and the cost. Ask your prospective neighbours and other local residents for information. In most countries supplies are adequate, although there may be cuts in summer in some areas. It's unwise to buy a community property where the water supply is controlled by the developer, as some developers charge many times the actual cost or charge owners for a minimum daily quantity, even when they're non-residents.

Some properties have their own well, spring or water channel, particularly in rural areas. Note, however, that a well containing water in winter may be bone dry in summer and you may have no rights to extract water from a water channel running alongside your land. If a property takes its water from a well or spring (possibly on a neighbour's land), make sure that there's no dispute about its ownership and your rights to use it, e.g. that it cannot be stopped or drained away by your neighbours. Although rare, in some countries people in remote areas need to spend a small fortune to ensure a reliable, year-round, water supply, which may need to be piped from many kilometres away. You don't pay water charges for well water or for water from a stream or river running through your property.

Storage Tanks: If you own a detached house or villa, you can reduce your water costs by collecting and storing rain water and installing a storage tank. Tanks can be both roof-mounted or installed underground, which are cheaper and can be any size but require an electric pump. Check whether a property has a water storage tank or whether you can install one. Many modern properties have storage tanks which are usually large enough, e.g. 500 litres, to last a family of four for around a week or even longer with careful use. It's also possible to use recycled water from baths, showers, kitchen and apparatus such as washing machines and dish washers, to flush your toilets or water your garden. Note that in recent years it has become common in some countries to have a storage tank installed that refills automatically when the water supply is restored after having been cut off.

Hot Water: Water heating in apartments may be provided by a central heating source for the whole building, although in most countries apartments have their own water heaters. If you need to install a hot water boiler and immersion heater, make sure it's large enough for the size of the property. Many holiday homes have quite small water boilers, which are often inadequate for more than two people. If you need to install a water heater or a larger water heater, you should consider the merits of both electric and bottled gas heaters. An electric water boiler with a capacity of 75 litres (sufficient for two people) usually takes between 75 to 125 minutes (in winter) to heat water to 40°C.

A gas flow-through water heater is more expensive to purchase and install than an electric water boiler, but you get unlimited hot water immediately whenever you want it and there are no standing charges. A gas heater should have a capacity of 10 to 16 litres per minute if it's to be used for a shower. Note that there's usually little difference in quality between the cheaper and more expensive heaters, although a gas water heater with a permanent flame may use up to 50 per cent more gas than one without. A resident family with a constant consumption is usually better off with an electric heater operating on a reduced tariff, while non-residents using a property for short periods will find a self-igniting gas heater more economical. If you own a home in a hot country, solar energy is a viable option and the local authorities may provide a grant for its installation.

Connection Costs & Standing Charges: Water is a local matter in many countries and is controlled by local municipalities, many of which have their own springs or wells. If you own a property without mains water in or near a village, you may be able to have it connected to the mains water system. Note, however, that connection can be expensive as you must usually pay for the installation of pipes. Obtain a quotation from the local water company for the connection of the supply and the installation of a water meter. In most areas there's a standing quarterly charge or a monthly charge for a minimum consumption, even if you don't use any water during the billing period (water shortages don't stop municipalities from levying high standing charges for water consumption that's sometimes non-existent).

Water Rates: The price of water varies considerably according to the country and its availability. In most countries, homes are metered, where you pay only for the water you use, plus a rental charge for the meter if it's owned by the water company. The cost of water has risen dramatically in many countries in recent years, particularly in areas where water is in short supply, e.g. in most resort areas in Spain. In some areas, tariffs start with a low basic charge per cubic metre, but become prohibitively expensive after a certain consumption. In some countries the cost of water in apartment blocks may be divided among apartments according to their size. Hot water may be charged by adding an amount per cubic metre consumed by each apartment to cover the cost of heating water or may be shared among apartments in proportion to their size. It's even possible (although rare) in some countries that you won't receive a water bill at all, as the cost is included in local property taxes.

Water Quality: Water is supposedly safe to drink in most countries, although it's often of poor quality, perhaps brown or rust coloured, full of chemicals and tastes awful. In some countries people fit cold-water taps with filters, which are used for drinking or cooking water. Many people find the taste of water or the purifying chemicals, e.g. chloride and fluoride, unpleasant and prefer to drink bottled water (when not drinking something stronger!). In rural areas, water may be extracted from mountain springs and taste excellent, although the quality standards applied in cities may be absent and water may be of poor quality.

You shouldn't drink water from rivers, wells, and streams, unless you know it's okay, as it may be polluted. In rural areas, water may be contaminated by fertilisers used in farming and in some coastal areas drinking water is contaminated by salt water. If you're in any doubt about the quality of your water you should have it analysed. You can install filtering, cleansing and softening equipment to improve its quality. Obtain expert advice before installing a system, as not all equipment is equally effective. **Note that while boiling water will kill any bacteria, it won't remove any toxic substances contained in it.**

In many countries water is hard and it's common for home owners to install a filter to prevent the furring of pipes, radiators and appliances. In some countries, water contains lime which leaves a deposit in pipes and appliances. This problem can be overcome by installing a water softening unit and changing the filter system regularly.

HEATING & AIR-CONDITIONING

When buying a home abroad you will need to consider whether heating and air-conditioning are necessary, which may depend on whether it's to be a permanent or holiday home, or the time(s) of the year when you will be resident. In most southern European and Mediterranean countries, some form of heating is necessary in winter and air-conditioning is a blessed relief in summer, while in the USA's sunbelt states (particularly Florida) air-conditioning is considered mandatory at any time of the year. In some countries the weather fluctuates between boiling hot and freezing cold, when both central heating and air-conditioning are essential.

Heating: Central heating, double glazing and good insulation are common in new houses in northern Europe, where they're considered essential. In the USA, most modern homes have a combined heating and cooling (air-conditioning) system which is thermostatically controlled. However, in southern Europe where winter temperatures are higher, central heating is usually found only in 'luxury' apartments and villas, and heating is usually provided by open fires, and portable gas and electric heaters. If you're used to central heating and like a warm house, you will almost certainly miss it in winter, even in many 'hot' countries. Note that in hot countries, homes are designed to exclude the heat and stay cool in summer, and most have marble, tile or stone floors. This means they're much cooler in winter than (for example) a home with wooden floors and fitted carpets. If your home has stone floors you'll usually find carpets and rugs and some form of heating necessary in winter.

Central heating systems may be powered by oil, gas, electricity, solid fuel (usually wood) or even solar power. Whatever form of heating you use, it's essential to have good insulation, without which up to 60 per cent of heating goes straight through the walls and roof. In rural areas in many countries, many homes have open wood-burning fireplaces and stoves, which may be combined with a central heating system and also provide hot water. In most countries people burn wood rather than coal, which is a relatively cheap fuel, particularly if you buy it uncut (it's sold by the cubic metre in most European countries).

Electric Heating: Electric central heating isn't common in many countries as it's too expensive and requires good insulation and a permanent system of ventilation. Most stand-alone electric heaters are also expensive to run and are best suited to holiday homes, although night-storage heaters operating on a reduced night tariff can be economical. Note that if you have electric central heating (or air-conditioning), you may need to uprate your electricity supply (see **Power Supply** on page 111). Many people find that electric fan heaters suffice in the south of Spain.

Gas Heating: Stand-alone gas heaters using standard gas bottles are an economical way to provide heating in areas with mild winters. Note that gas heaters must be used only in rooms with adequate ventilation and it can be dangerous to have too large a difference between indoor and outdoor temperatures. The filters of gas heaters must be cleaned regularly and heaters must be periodically serviced and checked for leaks. Gas poisoning due to faulty ventilation ducts for water gas heaters isn't uncommon in some countries.

Solar Heating: If you own a house in a hot country, solar heating may be a viable option and the local authorities may provide a grant for its installation. Although it's most commonly used to provide hot water, dual solar hot water and heating systems (with a hot-air solar radiator) are available. These are usually combined with an electrical or gas heating system, as solar energy cannot be relied upon year-round for hot water and heating requirements (although advances in solar cell technology are expected to increase the efficiency and reduce the cost dramatically in the next few decades).

In some countries, apartment blocks may have a centrally-controlled heating system which provides heating (and possible air-conditioning) to a whole block, with the cost included in community fees (see page 85). Heating is turned on in the autumn and off in the spring and you may have no control over room temperatures, apart from turning individual radiators on or off (although radiators may have a gauge with low, medium and high settings). If you're a non-resident or absent for long periods, you should choose an apartment with it's own heating (and cooling) system rather than a central system, otherwise you will be contributing towards your neighbours' bills.

Air-conditioning: In European and Mediterranean countries, air-conditioning is rare, even in the hottest areas, and it's usually confined to luxury properties. However, you won't consider it a luxury when the temperature soars above 40°C (104°F)! You can choose between a huge variety of air-conditioners, fixed or moveable, indoor or outdoor installations, with high or low power. An air-conditioning system with a heat pump provides cooling in summer and economical heating in winter. Some air-conditioners are noisy, so always check before buying one.

Most window-mounted, air-conditioning units have a choice of fan speeds and the fan can usually be switched on separately from the cooling system. The cooling system can be adjusted for temperature and units often have a vent that can be opened to allow air into the room when they aren't in use. When using air-conditioning, all windows and outside doors should obviously be closed. Note that if you suffer from asthma or respiratory problems, air-conditioning can cause negative health effects. In many countries, homes have ceiling fans for extra cooling in the summer.

PROPERTY INCOME

Many people buying a home abroad are interested in owning a property that will provide them with an income, e.g. from holiday letting. **If this is your intention, it's important to ensure that letting, particularly short-term holiday letting, is permitted before buying a property.** For example, in Cyprus, holiday letting by non-resident home owners is forbidden, in Malta it's limited to villas with a swimming pool, and in some states in the USA short-term rentals (generally less than 30 days, but possibly less than six months) are prohibited. Rentals are restricted to protect local hotels (and others offering permanent tourist accommodation) and also because many permanent residents don't wish to live in a community or development where short-term rentals are commonplace. In some countries you may be required to notify the 'community of owners' or management committee before letting a home in a community development (see page 84). You may also be required to notify your household insurance company if you let a property.

If you're planning on holiday lets, don't overestimate the length of the season, which varies with the country and region. In some countries, the holiday letting season is as long as 16 weeks, while in others it's ten weeks or less. In countries with a warm climate throughout the year, properties have year-round letting potential and this usually also applies to homes in cities and winter holiday resorts. One of the main points to bear in mind when buying a property for letting is access, which is of paramount importance. A rental property should usually be located as close as possible to the main attractions and/or a beach, and be suitably furnished and professionally managed.

If you let a property, don't fill it with expensive furnishings or valuable personal belongings. While theft is rare, items will certainly get damaged or broken over a period of time. To maximise rental income, a swimming pool (which could be shared with other properties) is obligatory, as a property with a pool is much easier to rent than one without (unless it's situated close to a beach). You can also charge a higher rent for a property with a pool and may be able to extend the rental season further by installing a heated or indoor pool. Some rental agencies won't handle properties without a pool.

In some countries, many people let their vacation homes for most of the year and many developers offer a rental management package. Don't always believe an agent's or developer's rental and occupancy rates, which are sometimes highly exaggerated. Some agents or developers offer a rental income guarantee, although this is illegal in some countries. You should always err on the conservative side when estimating rental income and bear in mind that in some countries a home may need to be available to let for 40 weeks a year (80 per cent occupancy) to cover your mortgage and other costs. **Note that most estate agents advise people not to buy a property if they need to rely on rental income to pay the mortgage.**

If you're planning to let a second home, one of the most important decisions is whether to let it yourself or use an agent or management company. Generally you're better off using an agent, who takes care of everything and saves you the considerable expense of advertising. If you want your property to appear in an agent's catalogue, you must usually contact him the summer before you wish to let it (i.e. one year in advance). Some letting contracts don't permit owners to use a property during the peak letting season, e.g. June to August, and may also restrict their use at other times of the year. **Take care when selecting a letting agent, as in some countries many have gone bankrupt in recent years, some owing owners an entire season's income! Make sure that your letting income is secured in a special account and paid to you regularly.** In some countries dishonest letting agents are endemic. If you suspect your agent isn't declaring all lets, get a friend to enquire when your home is available in order to confirm whether it has been let surreptitiously.

Letting agents usually charge 10 to 30 per cent of the rental income for their services, which may include full personal insurance and a complete management service, e.g. cleaning, gardening, laundry, reading meters, organising repairs, replacing damaged equipment, and dealing with tenants' problems on the spot. With holiday letting someone must be on hand to provide the keys, check that everything is in order, clean the property in between lets and provide clean linen, and be available to deal with equipment breakdowns and emergencies.

Some owners prefer to let a property only to family, friends and colleagues, which allows them more control (and *hopefully* the property will be better looked after). If you wish to let a property yourself, there's a wide range of local and foreign newspapers and magazines in which you can advertise. There are also companies producing catalogues of properties let directly by owners, e.g. *Holiday Villas*, *Private Villas* and *Vacances en Campagne* in Britain (all available from newsagents). National and regional tourist agencies can also provide details of local letting agents.

To get an idea of the rent you should charge, simply ring a few letting agents and ask them what the rent would be for a property such as yours in the relevant months. they're likely to quote the highest possible rent you can charge. You should also check the advertisements in newspapers and magazines. In most countries it's usual to include all utilities and the cost of cleaning in the rent, although they're sometimes charged separately. Heating in winter is usually charged extra in European countries for long-term lets, e.g. one month or longer. Set a realistic rent as there's usually a lot of competition. If you want to impress your guests you could arrange for a welcome card, fresh flowers, fruit and a good bottle of wine (not cheap plonk) to greet them on their arrival, as personal touches like this ensure repeat business and recommendations. Note that properties may need to be better equipped for long-term rentals than for short-term, holiday letting. Some up-market letting agents (with glossy brochures and high prices) insist on a high quality of furnishings and level of equipment and reject many homes.

Bed & Breakfast: If you're a permanent resident abroad, you may wish to offer bed and breakfast or self-catering accommodation in a self-contained apartment or cottage adjoining (or in the grounds) of your family home. This is a common form of property income for many home owners abroad, particularly in France. If you're buying a property with the intention of establishing self-catering holiday accommodation, you should ensure that permission will be granted before buying or make it a condition of the purchase.

Running Costs: Running costs when letting a property may include electricity, water/sewage, cleaning, cable or satellite TV, telephone line rental, pest control, pool service, management fees and lawn/garden care. Maintenance fees are payable for the common elements of a community property and if communal facilities are provided there may also be an 'amenities' fee. It's easy to spend £100 or more a month on electricity in some countries, particularly when you're running air-conditioning 24-hours a day (in some countries air-conditioning must be left on for part of the year to prevent mildew, even when a home is unoccupied). When letting a three-bedroom home with a swimming pool, your monthly running costs may be around £400 (although costs could be reduced by around half by an owner-occupier). To this must be added mortgage costs (if applicable), insurance and taxes. If you employ a management company, check all charges in your statements and query anything that you think is too high or incorrect.

Taxes: Rental income earned by non-residents is taxable in most countries, often at a fixed rate, e.g. 25 or 30 per cent. In some countries, e.g. Spain, non-resident home owners must pay an imputed 'letting' tax based on the value of their property, irrespective of whether or not it's let. Other taxes may also be payable such as value added tax, or in the USA, e.g. Florida, sales and 'tourist development' taxes. Non-residents with a property income must usually file an annual tax return (joint property owners may need to file separately). Note that if you fail to declare rental income to the local tax authorities, you could be liable for a large assessment and possibly a fine, and your future declarations will be under close scrutiny.

Generally all property-related expenses such as repairs and maintenance, cleaning costs, mortgage interest, management expenses, business trips abroad in connection with property ownership, and possibly an allowance to cover depreciation and insurance, can be deducted from your property income. It's possible for owners in some countries, e.g. Britain, to offset the interest paid on a mortgage secured on an overseas property against the income received from that property.

The taxation of rental income is a complicated subject and you should obtain professional advice from an experienced accountant or tax specialist. If possible, this should be done before buying in order to determine the best method of ownership (which may be through a trust or offshore company).

SELLING A HOME

Although this book is primarily concerned with buying a home abroad, you may wish to sell your home at some time in the future. Before offering a property for sale, whether in your home country or abroad, you should investigate the state of the property market. For example, unless you're forced to sell, it definitely isn't wise to do so during a property slump when prices are severely depressed. It may be wiser to let your home long-term and wait until the market has recovered. Having decided to sell, your first decision will be whether to sell a home yourself (or try) or use the services of a estate agent. In most countries, the vast majority of homes are sold through estate agents, although in some countries it's common for owners to sell their own homes.

Selling Your Home Yourself: While certainly not for everyone, selling a home yourself is a viable option for many people and is particularly recommended when you're selling an attractive home at a *realistic* price in a favourable market. It may allow you to offer it at a more appealing price, which could be an important factor if you're seeking a quick sale. How you market your home will depend on the type of home, the price, and the country or area from where you expect your buyer to come. For example, if your property isn't of a particular type or style and in an area desirable to local inhabitants, it's usually a waste of time advertising in the local press (but it could be advertised in the expatriate press).

The first step in many countries is to erect a professional looking 'for sale' sign in your garden or post a sign in a window with your telephone number. Do some market research into the best newspapers and magazines for advertising your property, and place an advertisement in those that look most promising. You could also have a leaflet printed extolling the virtues of your property, which you could then drop into local letter boxes or have distributed by a local newspaper (in some countries the majority of buyers buy a new home in the immediate vicinity of their present home). When selling a modest holiday home in some countries, e.g. Spain, it's common to include the furniture and fittings (plus major appliances) in the sale, particularly when selling a relatively inexpensive property with modest furnishings.

You could also offer a finders fee, e.g. £500, for anyone who finds you a buyer. Don't omit to market your home around local companies, schools, etc., particularly if they have a lot of itinerant, e.g. foreign, employees. Unless you're in a hurry to sell, set yourself a realistic time limit for success, after which you can try an estate agent. If you have an unusual property such as a period building or a converted barn or mill, you could try selling it at auction, which may increase the price (although you must pay the auctioneer's commission). Finally, you can also advertise your home on the Internet with many companies.

Using an Agent: If you're selling a holiday home, you may prefer to use the services of an estate agent, either in the country where the property is situated or in your home country. If you purchased the property through an agent, it's often wise to use the same agent when selling, as he will already be familiar with it and will have the details on file. You should take particular care when selecting an agent as they vary considerably in their professionalism, expertise and experience (the best way to investigate an agent is by posing as a buyer). Note that in many countries, agents cover a relatively small local area, so you should take care to choose an agent who regularly sells properties in your area and price range. If you own a property in an area popular with foreign buyers, your best course of action may be to use an overseas agent or advertise in foreign newspapers and magazines, such as the English-language property publications listed in **Appendix A**.

Before offering a property for sale, an agent must have a signed authorisation from the owner or his legal representative. There are usually two types of contract, an ordinary or non-exclusive contract (also called 'multiple agency/listing'), which means that you reserve the right to deal with other agents and to negotiate directly with private individuals. The other type of contract is an exclusive contract, which gives a single agent the exclusive right to sell a property, although you can reserve the right to find a private buyer. **Note that if you sign an exclusive contract without the right to find your own buyer, you must still pay the agent's commission even if**

you sell your home yourself. Most people find that it's best to place a property with a number of agents, i.e. non-exclusive, where the agent who sells the property receives the commission.

Contracts are always for a limited period, e.g. three to six months, and state the agent's commission, what it includes, and most importantly, who must pay it. With an exclusive contract an agent may provide a 'for sale' board, photographs, information leaflets and may also include some advertising other than in his office window, although advertising is usually charged separately. **Generally you shouldn't pay any fees (other than the normal agent's fees) unless you require extra services, and you should never pay any fees before a sale is completed.** Check the contract and make sure you understand what you're signing.

Agents' fees vary considerably according to the country, the area, the local property market, the price of a property and the agency arrangement, and can be anywhere between 2 and 10 per cent of the sale price. The cheaper the property, generally the higher the fee as a percentage of the sale price. On more expensive properties, e.g. over £200,000, an agent's fee may be negotiable. Fees are *usually* paid by the vendor, although in some countries an agent's fee may be paid by the buyer or shared between the vendor and buyer. An agent usually receives a lower commission when he's acting as the sole or exclusive agent. In some countries an agent will sell your home for a fixed fee, although this is unusual. The fee is usually non-returnable and you must pay it regardless of whether the agent sells your property. Shop around for the best deal as there's fierce competition among agents in some countries and many 'tout' for properties to sell, e.g. by advertising in the expatriate press. An agent's commission is usually included in the sale price of a property.

It's important to bear in mind that (like everything) property has a market price and the best way of ensuring a quick sale (or any sale) is to ask a realistic price. During the recession in the '90s, prices plummeted and buyers all but disappeared in many countries. During this period many properties remained on the market for a number of years, mainly because owners asked prices that didn't take account of the changed marketplace. An agent should always act in the best interests of the seller and obtain the highest price he can for a property. However, you should never tell an agent the lowest price you will accept, as he may pass it on to a buyer in the hope of making a quick sale.

As when buying a home abroad, you must be very, very careful whom you deal with when selling a home. Make sure that you're paid with a certified banker's draft before signing over your property to a buyer, as once the deed of sale has been signed the property belongs to the buyer, whether you've been paid or not. Although rare, sellers in some countries occasionally end up with no property *and* no money! Sales should always be conducted through a lawyer. Note that when selling a second home abroad, you must usually pay capital gains tax and a percentage of the price may need to be retained (by law) by the buyer in lieu of capital gains tax. See also **Purchase Contracts** on page 97, **Estate Agents** on page 100 and **Capital Gains Tax** on page 63.

5.

MOVING HOUSE & SETTLING IN ABROAD

One of the most important tasks for anyone moving to a new home abroad is to ship your household and personal effects, and to ensure that everyone necessary is notified of your move. In addition to information concerning moving house and customs, this chapter also contains a checklist of tasks to be completed before, or soon after, arrival and includes suggestions for finding local help and information.

MOVING HOUSE

After buying a permanent home abroad you will probably want to transport the contents of your present home or, if you're buying a holiday home, you may wish to ship some spare furniture and personal effects abroad. However, before planning to move your belongings you should consider whether it's worthwhile taking all your furniture and household appliances with you. For example, it's pointless shipping obsolete items such as incompatible electrical appliances, televisions and video players (see page 48), wardrobes (when they're already built-in) and items that aren't suitable for the climate abroad.

Often people find that it's best to sell (or store) their present furniture, which in many cases isn't suitable, and buy new furniture and furnishings locally. A wide range of reasonably-priced furniture (see page 40) is available in most countries, and holiday homes in resort areas are often sold fully furnished. You can also save money by buying new or second-hand furniture abroad, particularly when you consider the money saved on shipping costs. On the other hand, it may pay you to buy certain household items before you leave, some of which will be much more expensive abroad. Note, however, that you may need to have owned and used articles for six months to import them into most countries tax and duty free.

Moving house requires a great deal of organisation and planning and isn't something to be undertaken lightly (for many people it can be as stressful as a divorce or losing your job!). Before shipping household effects abroad you should enquire about customs formalities well in advance; if you break the rules you can encounter numerous problems and delays, and may be charged duty or even fined. Usually a number of forms (often available from embassies) need to be completed, which may depend on whether your home abroad will be your main residence or a holiday home. Shipping companies usually take care of the paperwork and ensure that the right documents are provided and correctly completed (but confirm this yourself). Usually a complete inventory must be provided (possibly in the local language).

When selecting a shipping company, you should choose one that's a member of an international organisation such as the International Federation of Furniture Removers (FIDI) or the Overseas Moving Network International (OMNI), who usually subscribe to an advance payment scheme providing a guarantee. If a member company fails to fulfil its commitments to a customer, the move is completed at the agreed cost by another company or your money is refunded. You should use a shipping company experienced in making shipments to the country where you have your home, which can usually be verified by asking for a company's fact sheet or information package. Some shipping companies have subsidiaries or affiliates abroad, which can be useful if you encounter problems or need to make an insurance claim. Make sure that a shipping company guarantees delivery to your door and not just to a depot abroad.

Obtain at least three written quotations before choosing a company, but don't assume that the lowest price is the best. The cost will vary considerably according to the company, what you're shipping and the countries concerned. If you have a flexible delivery date most shipping companies will quote a lower fee based on a 'part load', where the cost is shared with other shipments. This can result in a saving of 50 per cent or more compared with a 'special' delivery. Most companies charge by the cubic metre and will pack your belongings and provide packing cases and special containers, although this is naturally more expensive than packing yourself. Ask how they pack fragile and valuable items, and whether the cost of packing cases, materials and insurance (see below) are included in the quotation. If you're packing yourself, most shipping companies will provide packing crates and boxes.

Make a complete list of everything to be shipped and give a copy to the shipping company. Don't include anything illegal (guns, bombs, drugs, pornography, etc.) with your belongings, as customs checks can be rigorous and penalties severe. Give the shipping company *detailed* instructions how to find your home abroad from the nearest motorway or main road and a telephone number where you can be contacted.

Make sure you fully insure your belongings with a well established insurance company. You should compare the insurance policy provided by the shipping company with independent insurance companies, as it may limit the shipping company's liability to a paltry sum. Insurance premiums are usually 1 or 2 per cent of the declared value of your goods, depending on the type of cover chosen. It's wise to make a photographic or video record of valuables for insurance purposes. Most insurance policies cover for 'all-risks' on a replacement value basis. Note that china, glass and other breakables are usually excluded from an 'all-risks' policy unless they're packed by the shipping company. If you will be living abroad for a limited period only, it's wise to leave your most valued possessions at home, e.g. with relatives or friends, particularly if their insured value wouldn't provide adequate compensation for their loss.

If there are any breakages or damaged items, these must be noted and listed before signing the delivery note. If you need to make a claim, be sure to read the small print, as some companies require you to make claims within a few days, although seven is usual. Send a claim by registered mail. Some insurance companies apply an 'excess' (deductible) of around 1 per cent of the total shipment value when assessing claims. This means that if your shipment is valued at £20,000 ($30,000) and you make a claim for less than £200 ($300), you won't receive anything. If you're unable to ship your belongings directly abroad, most shipping companies will put them into storage and some allow a limited free storage period prior to shipment, e.g. 14 days. **Note that if you need to put your household effects into storage it's imperative to have them fully insured as warehouses have been known to burn down.**

If you plan to transport your belongings abroad personally, check the customs requirements in all the countries you will pass through. If you're transporting household goods between European countries, it's possible to hire a self-drive van and do it yourself. Many transport companies sell packing boxes in various sizes and rent or sell equipment (trolleys, straps, etc.) for those who feel up to doing their own move. However, most people find it isn't wise unless it's a simple job, e.g. personal effects only. It's certainly no fun heaving beds and wardrobes up stairs and squeezing them into impossible spaces. If you're taking pets with you, you may need to ask your vet to tranquillise them, as many animals are frightened (even more than people) by the chaos and stress of moving house.

Bear in mind when moving house that everything that can go wrong often does, so allow plenty of time and try not to arrange your move from your old home on the same day as the new owner is moving in. That's just asking for trouble! Last but not least, buy a house allowing access to a large truck. If it has lousy access don't tell the shipping company! Note, however, that if your home is in an awkward location or difficult to access, e.g. where furniture must be brought in through an upstairs window or terrace, you may be required to pay an additional fee.

Checklist

When moving house, whether within a country or internationally, there are many things to be considered and a 'million' people to be informed. The checklists contained below are designed to make the task easier and hopefully help prevent an ulcer or a nervous breakdown - provided of course you don't leave everything to the last minute. The following items must be considered for both a domestic and an international move:

- If you live in rented accommodation you must give your landlord notice (the period will depend on your contract). If you don't give your landlord sufficient notice, you'll be required to pay rent until the end of your contract or for the full notice period. This also applies if you have a separate contract for a garage or other rented property, e.g. a holiday home. Make sure that you get your deposit returned (if applicable).
- If you own your home, arrange to sell or let it well in advance of your move.
- Inform the following:
  - Your employer.
  - Your local town hall or municipality. You may be entitled to a refund of your local taxes.
  - In some countries it's necessary for foreigners to register with the police. If so, you should inform them of your new address (or that you're moving abroad) and re-register at the nearest police station in your new area.
  - Your electricity, gas, telephone and water companies.
  - Your insurance companies (for example health, car, home contents and private pension), banks, post office (if you have a post office account), stockbroker and other financial institutions, credit card, charge card and hire purchase companies, lawyer and accountant, and local businesses where you have accounts.
  - Your family doctor, dentist and other health practitioners. Health records should be transferred to your new doctor and dentist, if applicable.
  - Your children's schools. If applicable, arrange for schooling in your new area or country. Try to give a term's notice and obtain a copy of any relevant school reports or records from your children's current schools.

- All regular correspondents, subscriptions, social and sports clubs, professional and trade journals, and friends and relatives. Give or send them your new address and telephone number. Arrange to have your mail redirected by the post office.
- If you have a driving licence or car you will need to give the local vehicle registration office your new address or, in some countries, return your car's registration plates.
- Your local consulate or embassy if you're registered with them.

● Return any library books or anything borrowed.

● Arrange shipment of your furniture and belongings by booking a shipping company well in advance. If you have only a few items of furniture to move, you may prefer to do your own move, in which case you may need to hire a van.

● Arrange for a cleaning and/or decorating company to renovate a rented property, if applicable.

If you're leaving a country permanently or for an indefinite period, the following items should be considered *in addition* to those listed above:

● Give notice to your employer, if applicable.

● **Check that your own and your family's passports are valid.**

● Check whether there are any special requirements, e.g. visas, permits or inoculations, for entry into your country of destination by contacting the local embassy or consulate in your present country of residence. An exit visa or permit is required to leave some countries.

● Book a shipping company well in advance. Major international shipping companies can usually provide a wealth of information and can advise on a wide range of matters concerning an international relocation. Find out the exact procedure for shipping your belongings to your country of destination from the local embassy or consulate of the country you're moving to. Special forms may need to be completed before your arrival.

● Arrange to sell anything you aren't taking with you, e.g. house, car and furniture. If you've been living in a country for less than a year, you're usually required to export all personal effects, including furniture and vehicles, that were imported tax and duty free.

● If you have a car that you're exporting permanently, you need to complete the relevant paperwork in the country where it's currently registered and to re-register it in your new country of residence after arrival. Contact the local embassy or consulate of the country to which you're moving for information.

● Depending on your destination, your pets may require special inoculations or may need to go into quarantine for a period (see page 44).

● You may qualify for a rebate on your tax and social security contributions. If you're leaving a country permanently and have been a member of a company or state pension scheme, you may be entitled to a refund or may be able to continue payments in order to qualify for a full (or larger) pension when you retire. Contact your company personnel office, local tax office, or pension company for information.

- Contact your telephone company well in advance, particularly if you need to get a deposit refunded.

- Arrange health, travel and other insurance as necessary (see page 31).

- Depending on your destination, you may wish to arrange health, dental and optical checks for your family before leaving. Obtain a copy of all health records and a statement from your private health insurance company stating your present level of cover.

- Terminate any outstanding loan, lease or hire purchase contracts and pay all bills (allow plenty of time as some companies are slow to respond).

- Check whether you're entitled to a rebate on your road tax, car and other insurance. Obtain a letter from your motor insurance company stating your no-claims discount.

- Obtain expert legal advice regarding the sale of a home or business, as you may be able to save tax by establishing a trust or other legal entity. If you own more than one property you may have to pay capital gains tax on any profits from the sale of a second home.

- Check whether you need an international driving licence or a translation of your current or foreign driving licence(s) for your country of destination or any countries that you will pass through.

- Give friends and business associates a temporary address and telephone number where you can be contacted abroad.

- If you will be living abroad for an extended period, you may wish to give someone 'power of attorney' over your financial affairs in your home country so that they can act for you in your absence. This can be for a fixed period or open-ended and can be for a specific purpose only. **You should always take expert legal advice before doing this!**

- If you're travelling by air, allow plenty of time to get to the airport, register your luggage, and clear security and immigration.

- Buy a copy of *Living and Working in* ******** before leaving. If we haven't published it yet, drop us a line and we'll get started right away!

ARRIVAL ABROAD

On arrival in the country where you've purchased a home, your first task will be to negotiate immigration and customs. Fortunately this presents few problems for most people, particularly for citizens of a European Union (EU) country going to another EU country. Non-EU nationals arriving in an EU country for any purpose other than as a visitor may require a visa. If you're travelling by road, you should bear in mind that not all border posts may be open 24-hours a day. Some of the smaller posts open from early morning until late in the evening only (or have more restricted hours) and times may vary with the season. So if you plan to enter a country using a minor border post, check the opening times in advance.

CUSTOMS

Customs regulations vary considerably according to the country, your nationality, and whether your home country has a customs agreement with the country where you own a home or is a member of a 'trading block' such as the European Union (EU) or NAFTA. The rules regarding the importation of furniture and personal effects usually also vary according to whether you're a temporary or permanent resident abroad. Before making any plans to ship goods to any country, check the latest regulations with a local embassy or consulate in your home country.

European Union (EU) Nationals: The Single European Act, which came into effect in 1993, created a single trading market and changed the rules regarding customs for EU nationals shipping goods or household effects to another EU country. The shipment of personal (household) effects from one EU country to another isn't subject to customs formalities, although an inventory must be provided. Note, however, that all those arriving in an EU country (including EU citizens) are still subject to customs checks and limitations on what may be imported duty-free. There are no restrictions on the import or export of local or foreign banknotes or securities within the EU, although if you enter or leave a country with more than a certain amount in cash or negotiable instruments (see **Importing & Exporting Money** on page 54), you must make a customs declaration.

Primary or Secondary Residence: European Union (EU) nationals planning to take up permanent or temporary residence in another EU country are permitted to import their household and personal effects free of duty or taxes, provided they were purchased tax-paid within the EU or have been owned for at least six-months. Non-EU nationals must have owned and used all goods for at least six months to qualify for duty-free import into an EU country. You may need a special application form (available from local embassies), depending on whether you intend to set up a primary or secondary residence, plus a detailed inventory of the items to be imported and their estimated value in local currency. All items to be imported should be included on the list, even if some are to be imported at a later date. Customs' documents may need to be signed and presented to an embassy or consulate abroad with your passport.

It's necessary to show proof of purchase of a home, and in some countries you may need to pay a deposit or obtain a bank guarantee equal to the value (or a percentage) of the personal effects to be imported. The deposit is returned after a specified period, e.g. one or two years, or when the goods are exported or you've obtained a residence permit. Belongings imported duty-free mustn't be sold within a certain period, e.g. one or two years, and, if you leave the country within this period, everything imported duty-free must be exported or duty paid.

If you use a shipping company to transport your belongings they will usually provide all the necessary forms and complete the paperwork. Always keep a copy of all forms and communications with customs officials, both with those abroad and in your 'home' country. Note that if the paperwork isn't in order your belongings may end up incarcerated in a customs storage depot for a number of months. If you personally import your belongings, you may need to employ a customs agent at the point of entry to clear them. You should have an official record of the export of valuables in case you wish to export them later.

Prohibited & Restricted Goods: Certain goods are subject to special regulations in all countries and in some cases their import and export is prohibited or restricted. These may include the following:

- animal products;
- plants;
- wild fauna and flora and products derived from them;
- live animals;
- medicines and medical products (except for prescribed drugs and medicines);
- firearms and ammunition;
- certain goods and technologies with a dual civil/military purpose;
- works of art and collectors' items.

If you're unsure whether anything you're importing falls into the above categories, check with the local customs authorities. If you're planning to import sporting guns you may require a certificate from an embassy or consulate abroad, which is usually issued on production of a local firearm's licence. Those travelling to western European countries and North America from 'exotic' regions, e.g. Africa, South America, and the Middle and Far East, may find themselves under close scrutiny from customs and security officials looking for illegal drugs.

Car Importation: Car importation is a popular topic among expatriates in many countries, where importing a car often involves a long, drawn out battle with the local authorities. The process has been simplified in recent years for European Union (EU) citizens moving between EU countries, although it still involves completing a mountain of forms and can take a number of months. Most countries allow residents to import a car that has been owned for a limited period, e.g. six months. In most countries a permanent resident isn't permitted to operate a car on foreign registration plates and must import it and operate it on local plates. Note that a vehicle must be de-registered in its original country after it has been re-registered abroad. A vehicle that's imported tax and duty free mustn't usually be sold, rented or transferred within one year of its registration. Note that the registration of a right-hand drive vehicle in a country where traffic drives on the right may be prohibited. In many countries, e.g. Britain, you can buy a tax-free car and operate it for six months before exporting it, which may help reduce your tax liability.

An imported vehicle must comply with certain safety and other requirements (called homologation) before it can be registered, although this isn't necessary when taking a car from one EU country to another. When necessary, homologation can be expensive in some countries. Local taxes must usually be paid when importing a car, depending on its year of manufacturer, where it was manufactured and its current registration. These may include value added tax, sales tax, registration or car tax, and import duty. The amount payable is usually based on the vehicle's original price with a reduction for each year of its age. The procedure for the importation of a boat, caravan or motorcycle (with an engine capacity over 50cc) is usually the same as for a car. Mopeds with engines below 50cc can be freely imported into many countries as part of your personal possessions and require no special paperwork.

Non-residents: Non-residents can operate a foreign-registered vehicle in most countries for up to six months in a calendar year without paying local taxes and may be permitted to keep a foreign-registered vehicle permanently at a holiday home abroad. The vehicle must be road-legal in its home country, meaning that it must be inspected (for roadworthiness) and taxed each year in its country of registration, and must be insured for local use. Non-residents can operate a car on tax-free (or 'tourist') plates in some countries. **Note that anyone who illegally operates a vehicle on foreign or tax-free plates can be fined and the vehicle confiscated.**

RESIDENCE

Foreigners (legally) residing in a country for longer than 90 days must usually either obtain an extension as a visitor or apply to become a resident. Note that if you don't have a regular income or adequate financial resources, your application may be refused. Failure to apply for a residence card within the specified time is a serious offence and can result in a heavy fine and deportation.

Note that residence in a country may depend on your nationality and reciprocal agreements between your home country and the country where you own a home, and may be impossible.

EMBASSY REGISTRATION

Nationals of some countries are required to register with their local embassy or consulate after taking up residence abroad. Registration isn't usually mandatory, although most embassies like to keep a record of their country's citizens abroad. Many countries maintain a number of consulates in certain countries, e.g. most major European countries have consulates in main cities in North America and parts of Europe popular with their nationals. Consulates are an important source of local information for residents and can often provide useful contacts.

FINDING HELP

One of the major problems facing new arrivals in a foreign country is where to get help with day-to-day problems. How successful you are at finding local help depends on the town or area where you live (e.g. residents in resort areas are far better served than those living in rural areas), your nationality, your language proficiency and your gender (women are usually better catered for than men through various women's clubs). There's often an abundance of information available in the local language, but little in English and other foreign languages. An additional problem is that much of the available information isn't intended for foreigners and their particular needs. You may find that your friends, neighbours and colleagues can help as they can often offer advice based on their own experiences and mistakes. **But take care!** Although they mean well, you're likely to receive as much false and conflicting information as accurate (it may not necessarily be wrong, but often won't apply to your particular situation).

Your local town hall may be a good source of information, but you usually need to speak the local language to benefit and may still be sent on a wild goose chase from department to department. However, town halls in some countries, e.g. Spain, in towns where there are many foreign residents, may have a foreigners' department where staff speak English and other foreign languages.

A wealth of valuable information is available in major cities and resort towns, where foreigners are well-served by resident associations, property owners' organisations, associations of foreign business owners, English-speaking clubs and a variety of expatriate organisations. Contacts can also be found through expatriate magazines and newspapers. Most consulates provide their nationals with local information including details of lawyers, translators, doctors, dentists, schools, and social and expatriate organisations.

HOME HELP

If you spend long periods in a home abroad or live abroad permanently, you may wish to employ someone to help around the home such as a cleaner, housekeeper, maid, nanny, cook, gardener, chauffeur, nurse or baby-sitter. If you have young children, you can also employ an au pair in many countries. If you need or wish to hire a full-time employee there are a number of important points to take into consideration. These may include work and residence permits, employment contracts, working conditions, minimum wages, holidays and time off, income tax and social security, room and board, dismissal, redundancy payments, and accident and health insurance.

In most countries there are strict regulations concerning the employment of full-time domestic staff including minimum salaries, time off and paid vacation. Minimum salaries may vary considerably with the nationality, age and experience of an employee. You may need to apply for a work or residence permit and pay an employee's pension, accident and health insurance (or part). It may also be necessary to deduct tax at source from your employee's income (including lodging and meals, if part of his salary) and complete all the associated official paper work. In many countries, an employer and a domestic employee must have a written contract of employment, and if there's no written contract the law may assume that there's a verbal agreement for a minimum period, e.g. one year. If you break the law regarding the hiring and firing of employees, an employee may have redress to a labour court, which can result in a substantial compensation award.

Most regulations apply to full-time staff only and not to temporary staff employed for less than a specified number of hours per week, e.g. 15 or 20. In many countries you should ensure that employees are covered by social security, as you can be held responsible should they have an accident on your property. Always ask to see an employee's social security card and obtain legal advice if you're unsure of your obligations under the law. Note that if you're found to be employing someone who isn't paying social security (and income tax), you can be heavily fined and may have to pay any unpaid social security payments.

In some countries you should ask for a written quotation from temporary staff stating the work to be done and the cost, as this will then make them legally responsible for their own insurance and social security. Note that although there are statutory minimum wages in many countries for full-time employees, you may need to pay a higher rate for temporary employees, who are employed by the hour, half-day or day. Enquire among your neighbours and friends to find out the going rate – if you pay too much you could find yourself unpopular! If you need to hire someone who speaks English or another 'foreign' (non-local) language, you may need to pay a premium.

CHECKLISTS

The following checklists are mainly designed for permanent residents, although some points also apply to temporary residents and visitors.

Before Arrival

The following checklist contains a summary of the tasks that should (if possible) be completed before your arrive abroad:

- If necessary, obtain a visa for all your family members. Obviously this *must* be done before arrival.
- If applicable, arrange local schooling for your children.
- Arrange for shipment of your furniture and personal effects.
- Arrange to ship your car or to hire or buy a car abroad. If you purchase a car abroad, register it and arrange local insurance.
- Arrange health insurance for yourself and your family (see page 32). This is essential if you won't be covered by a local public health scheme or an employer on your arrival.
- Open a bank account and transfer funds (you may be able to do this while abroad). It's best to obtain some local currency before you arrive as this will save having to change money on arrival.
- Obtain an international driver's licence, if necessary.
- Obtain an international credit or charge card, which will be invaluable during your first few months abroad.
- Compile and update your personal records, including those relating to your family's medical, dental, educational (schools), insurance (e.g. car insurance), professional and employment history.

Don't forget to take all your family's official documents with you including birth certificates, driver's licences, marriage certificate, divorce papers, death certificate (if a widow or widower), educational diplomas and professional certificates, employment references, student ID cards, medical and dental records, bank account and credit card details, insurance policies, and receipts for any valuables. If applicable, you will also need the documents necessary to obtain a residence card or work permit plus certified copies, official translations and numerous passport-size photographs.

After Arrival

The following checklist contains a summary of tasks to be completed after arrival abroad (if not done before you arrive):

- On arrival at the airport or port, have your visa cancelled and passport stamped, as applicable.
- If you don't own a car, you may wish to rent one for a week or two until you buy one locally. Note that it's practically impossible to get around in rural areas in most countries without a car.
- Apply for a residence card at your local town hall.
- Register with your local consulate.
- Do the following within the next few weeks:
  - register with your local social security office;
  - open a bank account;
  - arrange schooling for your children;
  - find a local doctor and dentist;
  - arrange whatever insurance is necessary, e.g. health insurance (see page 32), car insurance (see page 24) household insurance (see page 34) and third-party liability insurance (see page 38).
- Break out the champagne and invite the neighbours for a house-warming party!

6.

COUNTRY PROFILES

This chapter contains profiles of the most popular countries for those seeking a holiday home or planning to retire abroad. Property prices are shown in local currency and are intended as a rough guide only. Exchange rates and interest rates shown are official rates (at October 2001) and mortgage rates are usually one or two percentage points higher than interest rates. Note that for all the euro-zone countries the interest rate is the same, namely the rate set by the Central Bank of Europe.

ANDORRA

Background Information

Capital: Andorra la Vella.
Population: 63,500.
Foreign Community: Only some 15,000 of the population are native born Andorrans. The remainder are foreigners comprising mostly Spanish, Portuguese and French, plus various other nationalities including some 1,000 Britons. Except in special cases, foreign residents can obtain Andorran nationality only after official residence of 25 years.
Area: 486km² (188mi²).
Geography: Andorra is a landlocked mountainous country in the eastern Pyrenees, with France to the north (Toulouse 190km/118mi) and Spain to the south (Barcelona 206km/128mi). The maximum distance is 32km from east to west and 25km from north to south. Andorra is one of the smallest countries in Europe, although larger than Liechtenstein and Monaco. The lowest point is Sant Juliá de Lória (980m/3,215ft) in the south, while the highest mountain peaks reach over 3,000m (9,840ft).
Climate: Andorra has a dry Mediterranean climate with an average minimum temperature of -2°C/28°F and an average maximum of 24°C/75°F. Annual rainfall is between 70 and 110cm (27.5 to 43in), which occurs mainly between October and May. During winter there are regular snowfalls at higher altitudes, although most days are sunny. Spring is usually warm but variable with snow or rain showers. Summer is mainly dry and hot with low humidity, and autumn is clear and fresh.
Language: The official language is Catalan, with Spanish and French also widely spoken. English is spoken in tourist areas.
Political Stability: Excellent. Andorra is a co-principality (since 1278) with the President of France and the Bishop of the Spanish town of La Seu d'Urgell as joint sovereigns, although they have only limited powers. In 1993, the Andorran people voted for their own constitution and Andorra is now a sovereign state which makes its own foreign policy and has its own democratically elected parliament (*Consell-General*).

Finance

Currency: Andorra has no currency of its own (except for *diners*, which are used for commemorative collectors' coins only). The euro (€) is the official currency as from January 2002. Since there are no exchange controls, any currency is acceptable for financial or property transactions.

Exchange Rate: £1 = €1.60.
Exchange Controls: None.
Interest Rate: 3.75 per cent.
Cost/Standard of Living: Similar to Spain and France. Many imported items such as alcohol, cigarettes and luxury goods (e.g. jewellery, perfume, cosmetics, high fashion, stereo and electrical goods) are inexpensive due to low import duties. Andorrans generally enjoy a high standard of living and a relatively low cost of living, due to the low level of taxes.
Income Tax: Andorra is one of the world's principal tax havens and has no income tax. Foreign residents must make an interest-free deposit, which is returnable on leaving the country (see Residence Permits below).
Capital Gains Tax (CGT): None.
Wealth Tax: None.
Inheritance & Gift Tax: None.
Value Added Tax (VAT): There's no VAT in Andorra. The primary source of government income is import duty (*Impost de Mercaderies Indirecte/IMI*) which is imposed on all goods imported for resale. The standard rate is 4 per cent with other rates of 1 per cent (agricultural products), 7 per cent (e.g. TVs, VCRs, computers, vehicles, consumer electronics) and a luxury rate of 12 per cent (e.g. jewellery). VAT paid on goods purchased in a European Union country can be reclaimed when goods are officially imported and IMI paid.

Property

Market: Andorra is most popular with winter sports fans and has a good snow record. The majority of foreign buyers purchase apartments and let them for tax-free income when they aren't in residence. There's an active rental market in winter and summer, especially July and August. Andorra is an excellent location for summer holiday homes, particularly for outdoor enthusiasts such as hikers, and there's an increasing demand for permanent tax-free residence. The property market was badly hit by the world-wide recession in the early '90s, during which prices fell by around 20 per cent, but it has since recovered to well above the '80s boom levels.
Areas: The most popular areas for foreign buyers are centred on three of the five main ski resorts of Arinsal, Soldeu/El Tarter and Pas del la Casa/Grau Roig (Arcalís/Ordino and Pal don't have adjacent ski villages), although buyers here should note that no freehold property is available. The strategically placed towns of La Massana and Ordino, with their satellite villages of Anyós, Erts, Pal and Sispony are favourites with the international and residential foreign community, and the mountains above the southern border of St. Julià de Lória (where nordic skiing is available) also have a strong following. Property in the central urban parishes of Andorra La Vella (the capital) and Escaldes is the most expensive.
Cost: Because only 8 per cent of Andorra's small land area can be built on, the average cost of property in Andorra is higher than in many other parts of Europe (although property in ski resorts is good value when compared with the Alps). Prices in a ski resort range from around €63,000 for a studio, €70,000 for a one-bedroom apartment, from €81,000 for a two-bedroom apartment, €135,000 for a three-bedroom apartment, from €156,250 for a three-bedroom townhouse and from €33,500 for a

three-bedroom detached villa (*xalet*). Underground parking spaces or garages are usually extra and cost between €16,000 and €28,000 new. Most modern properties are relatively small and cost between €1,140 and €1,260 per m² for resale apartments, and from €1,440 per m² for new apartments and detached properties (plus the cost of land, which is an average of €390 per m² for a minimum plot size of 400m²). Old village houses in need of restoration (or already restored) can be obtained and make desirable homes, but can be expensive to buy and run.

Local Mortgages: Mortgages are available from all Andorran banks, usually in pesetas or French francs, but banks will quote in any major currency. Maximum mortgages for non-residents are 60 per cent over 10 years, but better deals can sometimes be arranged.

Property Taxes: Annual property taxes are low and are between £150 and £250, depending on the parish and the size of a property.

Purchase Procedure: A deposit (usually 10 per cent) is payable and is forfeited if the buyer doesn't complete the purchase. Government approval (*súplica*) is required, after which the purchase contract is signed before a notary, the balance of the purchase price paid and the title deeds (*escritura*) issued. All transfers are with clear title and properties with outstanding debts cannot be sold or transferred. The purchase procedure usually takes between four and eight weeks.

Fees: An acquisition tax is payable in each parish (*común*), of which there are seven, and may be a percentage of the purchase price (maximum 2 per cent) or a fee per m². Notary fees are payable according to price bands and average less than 1 per cent of the purchase price. There's a €150 fee for preparation of the *súplica* (see above). There's no stamp duty and no land registry fee in Andorra. Estate agent's fees are usually included in the price.

Holiday Letting: No restrictions. Short winter lets are common and lets are also available throughout the year from a few agents. There's a small communal tax (average around 2.5 per cent) on rental income, although it's mainly paid only on long-term rentals and is handled by the letting agent.

Restrictions on Foreign Ownership: Foreigners may own one property, i.e. one dwelling or plot of land not exceeding 1,000m². A husband and wife may own only one unit between them, but a child aged over 18 may buy a property in his own name.

Building Standards: Excellent for new buildings, which usually contain many 'luxury' features as standard. Kitchens are usually fully fitted with all major appliances. Older and restored buildings vary in quality.

Personal Effects: Can be imported without any restrictions, provided there's no intention to resell.

General Information

Crime Rate: Very low and one of the lowest in Europe, with serious crime virtually unknown.

Medical Facilities: Very Good. Andorra has a new state-of-the-art hospital with a full staff of specialists (many English-speaking), which is supplemented by a number of private clinics. A social security health plan is available to working residents, but for others private insurance is necessary.

Pets: No quarantine but dogs need a rabies vaccination.

Residence Permits: Permanent residence permits, known as 'passive' residence permits (some 200 are granted annually) are available in principle to anyone of any nationality, although nationals of certain countries may be viewed with caution. Applicants for passive residence must own or rent a property and are supposed to spend 183 days a year in Andorra. Applicants must have a (future) pension entitlement, private health insurance and must satisfy an income requirement of €24,000 per initial permit and €6,000 for each other family member. Passive residents must make an interest-free deposit of €24,000 for the first person and €6,000 for each family member. Deposits, less any outstanding debts, can be reclaimed on leaving Andorra. Permits are initially issued for one year and are renewable thereafter every three years.

Work Permits: Work permits are difficult to obtain, but possible in trading businesses or tourism, although you should note that foreigners cannot be self-employed. Preference is given to nationals of western European countries, although others who are 'highly qualified' are also accepted. To obtain a permit you must have a firm offer of employment from an Andorran company.

Reference

Useful Addresses

Andorra Delegation, 63 Westover Road, London SW18 2RF, UK (☎ 020-8874 4806).

Servissim, Edifici Areny, Baixos, Carretera General, Arinsal, La Massana, Andorra (☎ 837836, ✉ servissim@andorra.ad). Relocation advisers, property services and management, rentals, multilingual negotiation, and information and assistance services.

Syndicat d'Iniciativa de les Valls d'Andorra, Carrer Dr Vilanova, Andorra la Vella, Andorra (☎ 820214).

AUSTRALIA

Background Information

Capital: Canberra.
Population: 19 million.
Foreign Community: Australia is largely a nation of migrants and has assimilated some 4 million people since World War II. It's an extremely cosmopolitan country and although the bulk of post-war immigrants have come (and still come) from Britain and other European countries, many now come from Asia.
Area: 7,682,300km² (2,966,368mi²).
Geography: Australia is the world's largest island, with an area equal to continental USA and a coastline of 36,755km (22,827mi). It's around 25 times the size of the British Isles and almost twice the combined area of India and Pakistan. The average elevation in Australia is less than 300m (984ft), compared with a world-wide average of around 700m (2,297ft). The highest point is Mount Kosciusko (2,228m/7,310ft) in

the Australian Alps in the south-east of the country. Australia is one of the oldest and driest land masses in the world, with vast uninhabitable arid and semi-desert areas. However, Australia is a land of great contrasts with rain forests and vast plains in the north, desert in the centr, fertile croplands in the east, south and south-west; and snowfields in the south-east. On its western coast is the Indian Ocean and on its east the Coral and Tasman seas of the South Pacific Ocean.

Climate: Australia's climate ranges from tropical in the northern 40 per cent of the country (above the Tropic of Capricorn) to temperate in the rest of the country. It's less subject to climatic extremes than other regions of comparable size because it's surrounded by oceans and has no high mountain ranges. Clear skies and low rainfall are characteristic of the weather in most of the continent. Coastal regions generally enjoy an excellent year-round climate, with no state capital averaging less than 5.5 hours of sunshine per day. Australia's seasons are the opposite of the northern hemisphere, e.g. summer is from December to February and winter from June to August. In mid-summer (January) average temperatures range from 29°C/84°F in the north to 17°C/63°F in the south, and in mid-winter (July) from 25°C/77°F in the north to 8°C/46°F in the south. Average annual rainfall is 46.5cm (18in), although rainfall varies considerably according to the region from less than 15cm (6in) in the centre to over 2m (79in) in parts of the tropics and western Tasmania. The wettest cities are Darwin, Sydney, Brisbane and Perth. Adelaide, Canberra, Hobart and Melbourne receive around half the rainfall of Sydney. The northern (tropical) region experiences heavy rainfall and oppressive temperatures between November and March.

Language: English is the national language, although there are some regional variations in pronunciation and phraseology.

Political Stability: Australia's system of government is based on the British parliamentary model and is very stable. It consists of three tiers: commonwealth, state and local governments. Australia is a member of the British Commonwealth, although 45 per cent of Australians voted for a republic in a referendum in 1999 and Australia is expected to become a republic in the near future.

Finance

Currency: Australian dollar (A$).
Exchange Rate: £1 = A$2.80.
Exchange Controls: None.
Interest Rate: 4.5 per cent.
Cost/Standard of Living: Living costs vary from state to state and even within states, and much depends on the actual area where you live and your lifestyle. Overall it's similar to most northern European countries. Prices are relatively low for essentials such as food, drink and clothes, however, manufactured goods are generally expensive as many are imported. Car prices are around 25 per cent higher than in most western European countries and up to twice those in the USA (imported cars are particularly expensive). Australians enjoy a high standard of living.
Income Tax: Australia has a PAYG (pay as you go) scheme with the basic rate starting at 17 per cent on incomes of A$6,000 to A$20,000 and rising to 47 per cent on incomes above A$60,000.

Capital Gains Tax (CGT): There's no CGT on the sale of a taxpayer's principal residence. CGT is 33 per cent on gains on property by non-residents, although gains are indexed to allow for inflation. Capital gains made by residents are taxed as income in the tax year in which they were realised.

Inheritance & Gift Tax: None.

Value Added Tax (VAT): Australia introduced a Goods and Service Tax (GST) in July 2000, which is levied at a flat rate of 10 per cent on most goods and services. Basic food items and certain medical aids are exempt.

Property

Market: Australia has a flourishing property market and around 80 per cent of Australians own their own homes, one of the highest rates in the world. A huge choice of homes is available including apartments, townhouses and a wide range of standard and individually-designed, detached homes. Apartments (called 'units' or 'home units') are common in inner cities and coastal areas, and townhouses are common in the suburbs of the major cities. Outside the major cities most people have a home built to a standard (or their own) design on their own plot of land. Package deals including a plot of land and a house are common. Waterfront homes are in short supply and are considered a good investment. Magazines are published by local property associations in major cities and states.

Areas: Australia is a highly urbanised society with over 70 per cent of the population living in the main cities situated on the coast, i.e. Adelaide, Brisbane, Darwin, Hobart, Melbourne, Perth and Sydney, all of which have their own character and particular attractions. Only some 15 per cent of Australians live in rural areas.

Cost: Property prices vary considerably throughout the country and in the various suburbs of the major cities. Not surprisingly, the further you are from a town or city the lower the price of land and property. Two-bedroom apartments (of around 75m²) start at around A\$80,000 in city suburbs and rise to over double this in a central or popular beach location. A two or three-bedroom single-storey home in most city suburbs costs between A\$60,000 and A\$100,000, and four-bedroom, two-storey homes cost from around A\$80,000 to A\$200,000. Sydney has the most expensive property, where a reasonable two-bedroom apartment in a nice building with water views costs around A\$500,000.

Land prices reduce considerably from around 15km outside a city and are at their lowest around 25km from cities. The cost of land varies from as little as A\$25,000 for an average size suburban plot over 25km from cities such as Adelaide, Hobart and Perth to over A\$200,000 for a plot within 15km of central Sydney. The cost of building a home varies according to location, quality and materials used, e.g. brick (most expensive), brick veneer, weatherboard and fibre cement (cheapest). Brick veneer is the most popular and costs from around A\$550 to A\$650 per metre, depending on the location. For up-to-date prices obtain a copy of the *Cost of Living and Housing Survey Book* published by the Commonwealth Bank of Australia.

Local Mortgages: Mortgages are available from a large number of banks and building societies. they're usually for a maximum of 75 or 80 per cent of the value, although loans of up to 100 per cent are available. The maximum term is 30 years, although the repayment period is usually between 15 and 25 years. Both variable and fixed-rate loans are available.

Property Taxes: Property taxes vary considerably depending on the municipality.

Purchase Procedure: Most land and property in Australia is owned freehold, the only exception being the Australian Capital Territory (ACT) or Canberra, where all land is sold on a 99-year lease.

Fees: Fees usually total 4 to 5 per cent of the purchase price. The main fees are stamp duty and legal fees. Stamp duty varies depending on the state and is lowest in New South Wales and highest in the Northern Territory and Victoria. Some states waive or reduce stamp duty for first time buyers. Legal fees are usually 1 to 2 per cent of the purchase price, but costs may be based on the actual work involved. Land transfer registration is imposed by each state and may be a flat or variable fee.

Restrictions on Foreign Ownership: All proposed acquisitions of urban property by non-resident foreigners must be approved by the Australian authorities. There are no restrictions for residents.

Building Standards: Generally excellent. Construction varies from brick to brick veneer (a timber inner frame lined with plasterboard), weatherboard and fibre cement.

Personal Effects: Personal effects can be imported duty-free, but must have been owned for a minimum of one year. Immigrants can import a car, but duty and sales tax are payable on its value. The duty rate on cars is 15 per cent plus 10 per cent GST, and there's a 25 per cent tax on vehicles valued at more than A$55,134.

General Information

Crime Rate: Violent crime in Australia is rare, although car and house crime is common in the major cities.

Medical Facilities: Excellent. Australia has a contributory (1.5 per cent of taxable income) national health scheme called Medicare. It pays for 85 per cent of medical costs (the scheduled fee) and provides free hospital treatment. Private health insurance is necessary for non-residents and retirees who aren't covered by Medicare. The cost of health insurance starts at A$500 annually, depending on the cover required. Reciprocal agreements cover visitors from many countries, but not the UK.

Pets: Australia has strict quarantine laws to protect its unique wildlife and livestock. To import a pet (e.g. a cat or dog) you must obtain a permit from the Australian Quarantine and Inspection Service, GPO Box 858, Canberra ACT 2601, Australia (☎ 1800-020504; 🖥 www.aqis.gov.au).

Residence Permits: Australia has a permanent programme of immigration with an annual quota, e.g. 85,000 in 2001/2002. Immigration is decided on a selective policy based on a points system, with preference given to those with special skills that are in demand and those wishing to start a business. Retirees must be aged 55 or over and need to transfer at least $A650,000 or $A200,000 with an annual pension or income of at least $A45,000. An initial permit is granted for four years and extensions may be granted. Everyone except New Zealand passport holders requires a visa to enter Australia.

Work Permits: Authorisation is required from an Australian Consulate under the points system mentioned above.

Reference

Further Reading

LIVING & WORKING IN AUSTRALIA, David Hampshire (Survival Books).
Everything you need to know about living and working in Australia.
Australia (Australian Government Publishing Service).
Australia's Foreign Investment Policy: A Guide for Investors (Australian Government Publishing Service).
Australian News, 1 Commercial Road, Eastbourne, East Sussex BN21 3XQ, UK (☎ 01323-726040; 🖳 www.outbound-newspapers.com).
Australian Outlook, 3 Buckhurst Road, Bexhill-on-Sea, East Sussex TN40 1QF, UK (☎ 01424-223111; 🖳 www.consylpublishing.co.uk).
The Cost of Living and Housing Survey Book (Commonwealth Bank of Australia).

Useful Addresses

Australian Embassy, 1601 Massachusetts Ave., NW, Washington, DC 20036, USA (☎ 202-797 3000, 🖳 www.ausemb.org).
Australian High Commission, Australia House, Strand, London WC2B 4LA, UK (☎ 020-7438 4334, 🖳 www.australia.org.uk).
Australian Tourist Commission, 1st Floor, Gemini House, 10-18 Putney Hill, London SW15 6AA, UK (☎ 020-8780 2227, 🖳 www.australia.com).
Foreign Investment Review Board, Department of the Treasury, Parkes Place, Parkes, ACT 2600, Australia (☎ 02-6263 3795, 🖳 www.firb.gov.au). Provides information about buying property in Australia for non-residents and retirees.

AUSTRIA

Background Information

Capital: Vienna.
Population: 8.1 million.
Foreign Community: Mostly consists of Germans and Italians. There are relatively few American or British residents.
Area: 83,855km² (32,367mi²).
Geography: Austria is a landlocked, mountainous country situated in central Europe in the eastern Alps. Some two-thirds of its territory and less than a third of its population are in the eastern Alps, which extend on a series of longitudinal ridges from the Swiss border in the west almost to Vienna in the east. The valleys between the ridges are home to most of the Alpine population. Austria is even more Alpine than Switzerland and has a wide range of vegetation, with over 35 per cent of its landscape forested.
Climate: Austria has a moderate central European climate with an Atlantic influence in the west and a continental influence in the east. It consists of three distinct climatic zones: east continental Pannonian, central Alpine and European. Temperatures vary

considerably depending on the area, altitude and geographical situation. In the coldest winter months (December/January) the temperature ranges from a maximum of 2°C/36°F to a minimum of -6°C/20°F in Salzburg and the Tyrol. In summer (July) in Salzburg and the Tyrol the temperature reaches a maximum of 25°C/77°F and a minimum of 13°C/55°F. The winter sports season extends from December to March (or May in the higher resorts).

Language: The national language is German, spoken by some 98 per cent of the population. The other 2 per cent speak Italian. English is widely spoken, particularly in the major cities and resort areas.

Political Stability: Austria is a federal republic and since 1945 has been one of the most stable countries in Europe. Austria is neutral (enshrined in the constitution since 1955), although this doesn't prevent it from taking sides on certain international issues. Formerly a member of the European Free Trade Association (EFTA), Austria joined the European Union on 1st January 1995. The general elections in 2000 resulted in a majority for the extreme right with racist and xenophobic policies, which resulted in diplomatic sanctions from the EU. Sanctions were lifted after reassurances of moderation from the Austrian government.

Finance

Currency: Euro (€).
Exchange Rate: £1 = €1.60.
Exchange Controls: None.
Interest Rate: 3.75 per cent.
Cost/Standard of Living: The cost of living in Austria is relatively high, although Austrians enjoy a high standard of living. Membership of the EU should reduce the cost of many imported goods and lower the cost of living.
Income Tax: Austria has a PAYE income tax system with progressive rates from 10 to 50 per cent.
Capital Gains Tax (CGT): Capital gains made by residents are taxed at a flat rate of 25 per cent. Principal residences are exempt after five years ownership.
Wealth Tax: None.
Inheritance & Gift Tax: Inheritance tax is levied at between 14 and 60 per cent, depending on the relationship between the donor and donee and the amount.
Value Added Tax (VAT): VAT rates are from 10 per cent on food to 34 per cent on cars.

Property

Market: Austria has a stable property market which is largely unaffected by outside influences such as international recessions. Property is expensive and scarce, although cheaper than Switzerland. All Austrian provinces impose strict regulations on the purchase of property by non-Austrians and purchases must be approved by state governments. In some areas of the country it's virtually impossible for a foreigner to buy property.
Areas: The most popular areas with foreign buyers are usually in ski resorts (subject to the restrictions on foreigners buying homes). Austria is also an excellent choice for

a summer holiday home, particularly for those who are keen on outdoor pursuits such as hiking. In recent years Saltzburg has been increasingly popular among foreigners buying property in Europe.

Cost: Prices vary depending on the area, but you can expect to pay from €55,000 for a studio apartment, from €90,000 for a one-bedroom apartment, from €125,000 for a two-bedroom apartment and from €320,000 for a luxury flat. Detached four or five-bedroom chalets cost from €800,000.

Local Mortgages: Mortgages are available from Austrian banks for both residents and non-residents.

Property Taxes: Property tax is 0.5 per cent and property tax around 0.8 per cent of the assessed value of a property, which is much lower than the market price. Both are payable annually.

Purchase Procedure: Property sales are handled by a lawyer who usually acts for both parties. A deposit of 10 per cent may be payable (deposits aren't always necessary), which is refunded if a sale falls through due to a defective title or failure to obtain registration. The purchase agreement is written in German (a translation is provided if required) and the documents can be signed before an official at an Austrian embassy abroad. The funds, payable when the deed is signed, are deposited in a trustee (escrow) account until completion takes place. The title is registered in the land registry (*grundbuch*) which usually takes between four and six months, after which the taxes and fees are paid by the lawyer and the purchase price paid to the vendor.

Fees: Fees total around 8 to 9 per cent of the purchase price. They include property transfer tax (3.5 per cent); notary fees (3 to 4 per cent); title registration (1 per cent); stamp duty (0.5 to 1 per cent); and the land registry court fee (€150 to €300).

Holiday Letting: No restrictions.

Restrictions on Foreign Ownership: Permission to buy property is required from the relevant provincial government office (*Amt der Landesregierung*). Foreigners aren't permitted to buy holiday homes in certain provinces, e.g. the Tirol.

Building Standards: Excellent.

Personal Effects: Personal effects can be imported duty free, although an inventory is required.

General Information

Crime Rate: Very low. One of the safest countries in the world.

Medical Facilities: Excellent. Austria has a national health service, administered by the provinces, which is available to all who pay social security. Austria has reciprocal health agreements with some countries. Visitors or residents who aren't covered by social security or a reciprocal agreement need private health insurance.

Pets: Austria has no quarantine, but cats and dogs need a rabies vaccination not less than 30 days or more than one year before arrival.

Residence Permits: A formality for EU nationals, although non-working residents must have sufficient income to maintain themselves. EU nationals must apply for a resident permit on arrival.

Work Permits: Not necessary for EU nationals, but difficult for others to obtain.

Reference

Useful Addresses

Austrian Embassy, 3524 International Court, NW, Washington, DC 20008, USA
(☎ 202-895 6700, 💻 www.austria-emb.org).
Austrian Embassy, 18 Belgrave Mews West, London SW1X 8HU, UK
(☎ 020-7235 3731).
Austrian National Tourist Office, 30 St. George Street, London W1R 0AL, UK
(☎ 020-7629 0461, 💻 www.austria-tourism.at).

BRITAIN

Background Information

Capital: London.
Population: 58 million.
Foreign Community: Around 5 per cent of the British population is made up of immigrants from British Commonwealth countries and their descendents. There's also a large foreign population from throughout the world, particularly in London, the world's most ethnically diverse city.
Area: 242,432km² (93,600 mi²).
Climate: Britain has a generally mild and temperate climate, although it's extremely changeable and usually damp at any time of the year. Because of the prevailing south-westerly winds, the weather is variable and is affected mainly by depressions moving eastwards across the Atlantic Ocean (which make British weather reports depressing!). This maritime influence means that the west of the country tends to have wetter, but also milder weather than the east. The amount of rainfall also increases with altitude and the high areas of the north and west have more rain (160cm/63in annually) than the lowlands of the south and east, where the average is 80cm/31in. Rain is fairly evenly distributed throughout the year in all areas, but the driest months are usually March to June and the wettest September to January.

In winter (December to February), it's often cold, wet and windy, although temperatures are higher in the south and west than in the east. Winters are often harsh in Scotland and on high ground in Wales and northern England, where snow is usual. Although winter temperatures drop below freezing at night, it's rarely below freezing during the day and the average temperature is 4°C/39°F. For many, spring is the most pleasant time of year, although early spring is often wet, particularly in Scotland.
Language: English.
Political Stability: Excellent. One of the most politically stable countries in the world.

Finance

Currency: Pound sterling (£).
Exchange Controls: None.
Interest Rate: 4.5 per cent.

Cost/Standard of Living: Britain has a high cost of living, particularly food and consumer goods, making it one of the most expensive places to live in the world, although there's a huge disparity between the wealthy, expensive south and the relatively 'poor' (and less expensive) north of England, Scotland, Wales and Northern Ireland. Duty and taxes on cars, petrol, alcohol and tobacco are high. London is one of the world's most expensive cities although this is largely due to the high cost of property.

Income Tax: Britain has three income tax rates: a lower rate of 10 per cent on the first £1,500, a basic rate of 23 per cent on income from £1,501 to £28,000, and a higher rate tax of 40 per cent on taxable income above £28,000 a year.

Capital Gains Tax (CGT): Anything you sell (from a second home to shares or antiques) which reap profits above £7,100 a year (2001/02) is liable to CGT. Net gains over £7,100 are taxed at 20 per cent where the aggregate of income and gains is less than the basic rate limit, and at 40 per cent where they exceed that limit. There's no CGT on a profit made on your primary residence.

Wealth Tax: None.

Inheritance & Gift Tax: Inheritance tax of 40 per cent is payable on any bequests over £231,000, if left to anyone other than your spouse or a registered charity. You're permitted to give away up to £3,000 a year, which can be carried over for one year without paying gift tax. Note that inheritance and gift tax is complicated and professional advice should be sought.

Value Added Tax (VAT): 17.5 per cent (8 per cent on domestic fuels). Most food, new buildings, young children's clothes and footwear, books and newspapers are exempt.

Property

Market: Home ownership in Britain is around 65 per cent and among the highest in the European Union. During the recession in the early 1990s there was an unprecedented collapse in the value of property, although the market has now fully recovered in most areas and prices are at an all-time high. There's a flourishing market for homes in central London, where property prices are among the highest in the world, and many areas in the south of England are enjoying a mini-boom. If you want a property for an investment, then the best buy is usually a character, period property or a waterfront home.

Areas: The areas most favoured by second home owners include the Lake District (in the northwest of England), the West Country (e.g. Cornwall and Devon), Wales, East Anglia (on the coast or the Norfolk Broads) and the Chilterns. Most foreign residents tend to live in the cities or the southeast of England, where property is the most expensive. Property in central London is among the most expensive in the world, although it remains popular with foreign buyers and is a good long-term investment (particularly properties at the top end of the market). The most popular areas among overseas buyers in central London include Belgravia, Kensington, Knightsbridge, Mayfair and St. Johns Wood.

Cost: House prices vary considerably depending on the region and whether a property is located in a town or the country. A three-bedroom semi-detached house costing £70,000 in the north of England or Scotland, will usually cost at least 50 per cent more in the southeast of England. The average price of a house in Britain in 2001 was around £85,000, with the cheapest homes in Northern Ireland and the most expensive in London. Older, cheaper houses are available in some areas, but most have been snapped up and modernised years ago, and those that are left are no longer bargains. Most semi-detached and detached houses have single or double garages included in the price, although they're rare in cities.

Local Mortgages: Mortgage repayments are relatively low in Britain due to the long repayment period, typically 25 to 30 years. Mortgages of up to 95 per cent are widely available and discounts are provided for first-time buyers and those switching lenders, with interest rates up to two percentage points lower than the standard rate for a number of years. The availability and terms of mortgages mean that it's usually cheaper to buy a home than rent one.

Property Taxes: There's no property tax in Britain but instead residents pay 'council tax', which is calculated according to the value of the property, the number of people who live there and the area where the property is situated. Annual rates range from £400 in a rural area to £900 in a major city. Payment can be made in installments.

Purchase Procedure: Most property in Britain is sold freehold, although there's also a system of leasehold for apartments (flats) where buyers buy a lease, e.g. from 99 to 999 years (when the lease expires the property reverts to the original owner, i.e. the freeholder). When buying property in England, Wales or Northern Ireland, prospective buyers make an offer subject to survey and contract. Either side can amend or withdraw from a sale at any time before the exchange of contracts (when a sale is legally binding). In Scotland neither side can pull out once an offer has been made and accepted.

Fees: Fees total around 3 to 5 per cent of the purchase price and include legal fees, land registry fees and stamp duty. Stamp duty is 1 to 4 per cent depending on the purchase price (properties below £60,000 are exempt). There are various fees associated with obtaining a mortgage including a valuation fee, indemnity insurance and an arrangement or acceptance fee. Survey fees are optional, but are common on older resale properties. The fees for buying a property in Britain are among the lowest in the world.

Precautions: There are few special precautions that need to be taken when buying property in Britain apart from using an experienced solicitor (lawyer) or conveyancer. It's unwise, however, to use the legal adviser or conveyancer who's acting for the seller, in order to avoid potential conflicts of interest. When a property is owned jointly you must ensure that the sales contract is signed by all the co-owners. In some areas (and with some properties) there are problems such as woodworm, subsidence, landslip, overhead electricity cables or sub-stations, and radiation (in areas with a high concentration of radon). All these problems (if they exist) should be exposed by a survey, which is highly recommended on older properties. Buyers should be wary of buying an apartment in an 'old' apartment block, however much of a bargain it may appear, as many have serious problems (which in some cases cost owners more to rectify than the value of their property).

Holiday Letting: No restrictions.

Restrictions on Foreign Ownership: None.

Building Standards: Generally excellent.

Personal Effects: Household goods purchased within the European Union can be imported duty-free and don't need to be retained for a minimum period. However, goods (including vehicles) purchased outside the EU must have been owned for at least six months and cannot be sold for 12 months after importation.

General Information

Crime Rate: The crime rate in Britain is low in most areas, although it has increased considerably in recent years, particularly in inner cities. Drug-related violent crime is an increasing problem and car crime, burglary and house-breaking are widespread.

Medical Facilities: Excellent. Employees and retirees from many countries are covered by the National Health System (NHS). All visitors are provided with free emergency treatment and many countries have reciprocal agreements with Britain. If you aren't covered by the NHS, private health insurance is necessary and may be mandatory for foreign residents.

Pets: Animals imported into Britain from Western Europe and North America must be micro-chipped and have a veterinary certificate of vaccination, including rabies, and a pet 'passport' certifying that the animal is free from rabies. Animals without the necessary documents or imported from other countries are subject to the toughest quarantine regulations in the world and must spend six months in quarantine on arrival in Britain.

Residence Permits: Residence permits are a formality for EU nationals, although non-working residents must have sufficient income to maintain themselves. Visitors may remain for up to six months. Nationals of most non-EU countries require a visa to work or reside permanently in Britain. Non-EU retirees and persons of independent means must have a minimum of £200,000 in disposable capital or an annual income of at least £25,000, and must be able to prove that they're able to support and accommodate themselves and their dependants indefinitely without working, and without recourse to public funds. Applicants must also show that they have a 'close connection' with Britain through either family or employment.

Work Permits: No restrictions for EU nationals, but difficult for others to obtain.

Reference

Further Reading

BUYING A HOME IN BRITAIN, David Hampshire (Survival Books). *Everything you need to know about buying a property in Britain.*
LIVING & WORKING IN BRITAIN, David Hampshire (Survival Books). *Everything you need to know about living and working in Britain.*
LIVING & WORKING IN LONDON, Claire O'Brien (Survival Books). *Everything you need to know about living and working in London.*
How to Buy a House, Council of Mortgage Lenders, 3 Saville Row, London W1S 3PB, UK, 🖥 www.cml.org.uk. Free booklet downloadable from the website.
Top Towns (Guinness Publishing).
Which? Way to Buy, Sell and Move House (Which? Books).

Useful Addresses

The Association of Relocation Agents, PO Box 189, Diss, IP22 1PE, UK
(☎ 08700-737475, 🖳 www.relocationagents.com).
The British Association of Removers (BAR), 3 Churchill Court, 58 Station Road,
North Harrow, London HA2 7SA, UK (☎ 020-8861 3331, 🖳 www.barmovers.com).
British Embassy, 3100 Massachusetts Ave, NW, Washington, DC 20008, USA
(☎ 202-588 6500, 🖳 www.britainusa.com).
British Tourist Authority (BTA), Thames Tower, Black's Road, Hammersmith,
London W6 9EL, UK (☎ 020-8846 9000, 🖳 www.visitbritain.com or www.bta.
org.uk).
National Association of Estate Agents (NAEA), Arbon House, 21 Jury Street,
Warwick CV34 4EH, UK (☎ 01926-496800, 🖳 www.naea.co.uk).
Americans in Britain (🖳 www.britain-info.org). Website providing a comprehensive
set of fact sheets regarding living and working in Britain.

CANADA

Background Information

Capital: Ottawa.
Population: 30 million.
Foreign Community: Canada is a cosmopolitan country due to the large number of
immigrants (Toronto and Vancouver are among the most multi-racial cities in the
world). Over 40 per cent of the population is of British origin and 30 per cent of
French origin, and the country also has large German, Dutch and Ukranian
communities. There has been a large influx of Asian immigrants in the last decade,
particularly from Hong Kong. Most new immigrants come from Asia, Africa and
Latin America.
Area: 9,976,185km² (3,852,106 mi²).
Geography: Canada is the largest country in the world with an area equal to that of
Europe (40 times that of the UK and 18 times the size of France) and a coastline of
250,000km (155,000mi). Sparsely populated, Canada has huge areas of wilderness
including mountains, forests (one third of the country), tundra, prairies, and polar
desert in the north and west. Almost 8 per cent of the country consists of inland fresh
water, including four of the world's largest lakes (Huron, Superior, Great Bear and
Great Slave). In the east are the maritime provinces of Newfoundland, Nova Scotia,
New Brunswick and Prince Edward Island, and the predominantly French-speaking
province of Québec. The central province of Ontario borders the Great Lakes,
extending north across the shield to Hudson Bay. Further to the west are the prairie
provinces of Manitoba, Saskatchewan and Alberta, with fertile farmlands to the south
and lake-strewn forest on the sub-arctic wastelands in the north. Southwestern Alberta
contains a substantial part of the Rocky Mountains with peaks rising to over
4,000m/13,120ft. The western-most province of British Columbia is mountainous
with forests, lakes and sheltered valleys with rich farmland. The vast, largely
unpopulated, northern areas include the Yukon Territory bordering Alaska and the
extensive Northwest Territories.

Climate: The Canadian climate is noted for its extremes of hot and cold weather, which are more pronounced inland than on the coast. Regional climates vary enormously. The Pacific coast (e.g. Vancouver) is warm and fairly dry in summer and mild, cloudy and wet in winter. Inland conditions are more extreme, depending on the altitude. The region from the Great Lakes to the Rocky Mountains experiences cold winters and warm summers with low rainfall. The southern areas of central Canada are humid with hot summers and cold winters and rain throughout the year, while the Atlantic regions have a humid but temperate climate. The northern regions, comprising some 40 per cent of the county's area, experience arctic conditions with temperatures below freezing for most of the year and falling as low as -40°C in winter. Average daily temperatures are around 21°C/69°F in summer (July) in Montreal and Toronto, falling to between -7 and -10°C/14 to 20°F in winter (January). In Vancouver, average temperatures are around 17°C/63°F in July and 2.5°C/36°F in January.

Language: Canada has two official languages, English and French (spoken mostly in Québec), which enjoy equal status. English is spoken by some 65 per cent of the population and French by 25 per cent, although only around 15 per cent are fluent in both languages. Chinese is Canada's third most widely-spoken language due to the large number of Asian immigrants in recent years.

Political Stability: Canada is one of the most politically stable countries in the world, although tensions have been running high for some years between Québec and the rest of Canada, due to the agitation of the separatist *Parti Québécois* for independence, an issue still unresolved. Canada has two tiers of government, federal and provincial, with the provinces having considerable autonomy. Canada is a member of the North American Free Trade Association (NAFTA), with the USA and Mexico, NATO and the British Commonwealth.

Finance

Currency: Canadian dollar (C$).
Exchange Rate: £1 = C$2.25.
Exchange Controls: None.
Interest Rate: 3.5 per cent.
Cost/Standard of Living: Canada enjoys one of the highest standards of living in the world. It has a relatively low cost of living (lower than most western European countries) with low inflation and high salaries. The economy was hard hit by the recession in the early 1990s when unemployment soared, although it has since fallen back. The quality of life in Canada has been rated the highest in the world by the United Nations.

Income Tax: Residents in Canada must pay both federal and provincial income tax. Federal income tax rates range from 17 per cent on earnings up to C$29,590 to 29 per cent on earnings above C$59,180. Provincial income tax rates depend on the province and are calculated on the percentages of federal income tax payable and range from around 42 to 70 per cent.

Capital Gains Tax (CGT): CGT is levied on the sale or purchase of any asset excluding your principal residence. The taxable portion of capital gains and the deductible portion of capital losses are each 75 per cent. Non-resident property owners must also pay CGT on the sale of property in Canada.

Inheritance & Gift Tax: None, although beneficiaries may be required to pay income tax on a bequest.

Value Added Tax (VAT): An 8 per cent Goods and Services Tax (GST) is levied by the federal government on most goods and services. Most provinces also levy a direct Provincial Sales Tax on retail sales, which varies depending on the province from 6 to 12 per cent. Note that in all provinces except Alberta, sales tax isn't shown in ticket prices, but is added at the checkout.

Property

Market: Canada has a flourishing housing market. In common with most of Europe, prices peaked in the late '80s and have since fallen some 10 to 30 per cent in most areas. The more expensive properties (C$150,000 plus) have fallen the furthest. There's a huge variety of property for sale from apartments (condominiums) to large detached properties with a substantial plot of land. Condominiums (apartments) usually have communal garages and sports facilities.

Areas: Apart from buying a home in the major cities such as Montreal, Toronto and Vancouver, many foreign buyers seek a holiday home for winter skiing or summer 'wilderness' holidays (or both). The most popular ski resorts include Banff, Jasper, Lake Louise, Okanagan Valley, Whistler, Kananaskis, Blue Mountain Resort and various resorts in Québec.

Cost: Average prices vary considerably with the province, e.g. from under C$100,000 in Saskatchewan to around C$285,000 in Vancouver (British Columbia) for a three-bedroom detached property. The average price for a three-bedroom detached home in a major city is around C$175,000, although cheaper properties are available in many suburbs and rural areas. Co-operative apartments and condominiums are common in cities and start at around C$110,000 for a small one-bedroom apartment. Small studio apartments in major ski resorts start from around C$75,500. Building plots in remote areas cost from as little as C$7,500 for those who wish to get 'back to nature'.

Local Mortgages: Mortgages of up to the legal maximum of 75 per cent of the purchase price are available from local banks and other financial institutions. The rate is traditionally for 25 to 30 years although shorter terms are available. New residents in Canada may find getting a mortgage difficult as you must provide proof of a perfect credit record (preferably in Canada) to obtain one.

Property Taxes: Property taxes are levied by local municipalities and vary considerably. Those living in apartments also pay monthly community fees.

Purchase Procedure: Buying a home in Canada is generally very safe and there are few traps for the unwary. However, it's advisable to engage a buyer's broker who acts solely for you and has your best interests in mind.

Fees: The fees associated with buying a home in Canada total just 2 to 3 per cent of the purchase price and include an appraisal, survey, legal costs, land transfer tax, title registration and a compliance certificate. Legal fees are usually 0.75 to 1 per cent and land transfer tax is from 0.5 to 2 per cent of the purchase price. New houses are subject to GST and in some provinces Provincial Sales Tax is also levied.

Precautions: It's important to have a structural survey completed before buying a resale home, which should include a termite inspection, particularly when homes are located near water.

Holiday Letting: No restrictions.
Restrictions on Foreign Ownership: None.
Building Standards: Excellent. Buildings have a high degree of insulation due to the extremely cold winters in most regions.
Personal Effects: Can be imported duty-free, but must have been owned and used prior to entry and must be retained for a minimum of one year. A detailed list of all items to be imported must be provided.

General Information

Crime Rate: The crime rate in Canada is low. Canada has strict gun control laws and a low murder rate, which is similar to most western European countries.
Medical Facilities: Excellent, although treatment is very expensive. There's a government-sponsored health scheme for residents which provides most medical services 'free' of charge. Private health insurance is vital for anyone who isn't covered by the government scheme.
Pets: All animals are subject to a veterinary inspection at the port of entry. Some (e.g. birds) are required to undergo a period of quarantine. Domestic animals such as cats and dogs can be imported from rabies-free countries (e.g. Britain) without a rabies vaccination or a quarantine period. Pets from countries with rabies must have a rabies vaccination at least one month prior to their importation.
Residence Permits: Resident permits are difficult to obtain unless you qualify for a work permit or start a business in Canada (see below). It isn't possible for retirees to emigrate to Canada even if they own property there unless they're sponsored by a 'very close' relative, e.g. by a son or daughter.
Work Permits: Canada has a permanent programme of immigration with an annual quota of around 180,000 immigrants, one of the highest quotas in the world. It operates a selective policy based on a points system, with preference given to those with special skills that are in demand, those wishing to start a business, those with family ties and refugees. Being bi-lingual (English/French) is an advantage for employees.

Reference

Further Reading

LIVING & WORKING IN CANADA, David Hampshire (Survival Books).
Everything you need to know about living and working in Canada.
Canada News, 1 Commercial Road, Eastbourne, East Sussex BN21 3XQ, UK (☎ 01323-726040, 🖳 www.outbound-newspapers.com).
The Canadian Immigration Handbook, M. J. Bjarnason (How To Books).
Immigrating to Canada, Gary L. Segal.
Live and Work in Canada (Grant Dawson).
Living in Canada (Canadian Ministry of Employment and Immigration).

Useful Addresses

Canadian High Commission, 501 Pennsylvania Ave., NW, Washington, DC 20001, USA (☎ 202-682 1740, 💻 www.cdnemb-washdc.org).
Canadian High Commission, Macdonald House, 1 Grosvenor Street, London W1X 0AB, UK (☎ 020-7258 6600, 💻 www.canada.org.uk).
Canadian Real Estate Association, 334 Slater St., Suite 1600, Canada Building, Ottawa, ON K1R 743, Canada (☎ 613-237 7111, 💻 http://crea.ca).
Canada Customs & Revenue Agency, International Taxation Office, 2204 Walkley Road, Ottawa, ON K1A 1A8, Canada (☎ 613-952 3741, 💻 www.ccra-adr.gc.ca).
The Visit Canada Centre, PO Box 5396, Northampton, NN1 2FA, UK (☎ 0870-161 5151, ✉ visitcanada@dial.pipex.com).

THE CARIBBEAN

Background Information

Countries: The Caribbean Sea region contains two major chains of islands: the Greater Antilles (which comprise almost 90 per cent of the region's total land area) and the Lesser Antilles (made up of the Leeward Islands in the north and the Windward Islands in the south). The Caribbean islands extend almost 4,000km (2,500mi) in a wide arc from the Bahamas 100km (60mi) off the east coast of Florida to Trinidad 24km (15mi) off the coast of Venezuela. Most of the major islands are independent countries, although retaining close ties with their former colonial rulers, and some remain colonies or dependent territories of Britain, France, the Netherlands or the USA. The countries which attract most foreign property buyers include those listed below.

Population: The populations of the Caribbean countries most favoured by foreign home buyers are: Antigua & Barbuda (77,000), Bahamas (285,000), Barbados (260,000), Bermuda (60,000), Cayman Islands (33,000), Dominica (75,000), Guadeloupe (350,000), Jamaica (2.4 million), Martinique (345,000), Montserrat (13,000), Puerto Rico (3.6 million), St. Christopher (St. Kitts) & Nevis (45,000), St. Lucia (150,000), St. Vincent & The Grenadines (115,000), Trinidad & Tobago (1.25 million), the Turks & Caicos Islands (10,000), the British Virgin Islands (13,000) and the US Virgin Islands (117,000). The majority of inhabitants are of African descent, their ancestors having been shipped to the Caribbean as slaves and indentured servants. Some islands also have a large Indian population whose forebears were brought to the Caribbean as indentured labourers by the British. The population of many islands swells considerably in the winter, when many visitors stay for the whole season.

Foreign Community: There's a significant foreign community in most of the Caribbean islands, mainly consisting of British and American retirees, and expatriate workers engaged in the financial services and tourist industries. Many visitors spend up to half the year in the Caribbean.

Area: The areas of the most popular countries among foreign home buyers are: Antigua & Barbuda (442km^2/179mi^2), the Bahamas (13,938km^2/5,382mi^2), Barbados (430km^2/166mi^2), Bermuda (53km^2/20mi^2), Cayman Islands (259km^2/100mi^2),

Dominica (748km²/289mi²), Guadeloupe (1,710km²/66mi²), Jamaica (10,990km²/ 4,243mi²), Martinique (1,100km²/425mi²), Montserrat (102km²/39mi²), Puerto Rico (8,897km²/3,435mi²), St. Christopher & Nevis (360km²/139mi²), St. Lucia (622km²/ 240mi²), St. Vincent & The Grenadines (388km²/150mi²), Trinidad & Tobago (5,130km²/1,981mi²), Turks & Caicos Islands (430km²/166mi²), British Virgin Islands (153km²/59mi²) and the US Virgin Islands (340km²/130mi²).

Geography: The Caribbean islands comprise a total land area of 234,000km² (90,350mi²) and with the exception of the Bahamas lie between latitude 10° north and the Tropic of Cancer (23°27' north). There are literally thousands of tropical islands and cays (the Bahamas alone comprises some 700), the vast majority of which are tiny and uninhabited. The islands are noted for their dazzling, white sandy beaches (some of the finest in the world) and fine coral reefs, warm clear seas, lush vegetation and exotic flora and fauna (rainforests, tropical plants and flowers), mountains, rivers and waterfalls, and cloudless blue skies. Some islands have live volcanoes, including Guadeloupe, Martinique, St. Vincent and Montserrat, which was devastated in 1997 when its Soufriere Hills volcano erupted, spewing ash and lava over half the island and burying the capital Plymouth.

Climate: The Caribbean islands enjoy a tropical or sub-tropical (in the northern Bahamas) climate, which is one of the healthiest in the world, with 3,000 hours (some 300 days) of sunshine a year. However, the climate differs considerably between the islands as a result of their different topography. In most islands, daytime temperatures rarely drop below 16°C/61°F or rise above 32°C/90°F and the average annual temperature is around 25°C/77°F. In winter the weather is usually pleasant with temperatures between around 18 to 25°C/64 to 77°F. The difference between the highest and lowest temperature varies throughout the year by just 3°C/5.5°F in the southern Antilles to 6°C/11°F in the Bahamas. Average sea temperatures range from around 28°C/82°F in the warmest months to 25°C/77°F in the coolest (in the sub-tropical Bahamas the temperature is a few degrees lower). Many islands experience high humidity, particularly during the summer months, although the heat is tempered by cooling trade winds. Annual rainfall varies considerably, but in most islands is between 1m and 1.5m (39 to 59in), with the wettest months between May and November and the driest from December to April, although on some islands rainfall is more or less constant throughout the year. The region is susceptible to violent storms and hurricanes between June and November, and most islands experience severe tropical storms around every ten years (hurricanes less frequently). During the northern hemisphere's winter, the Caribbean is the world's cruise centre.

Language: The official language is English (or American), French, Dutch or Spanish, depending on an island's former (or current) colonial allegiance. On the majority of islands the official language is English, while many also have their own colloquial languages such as Creole and Papiamento, the *patois* spoken in the former British possessions.

Political Stability: Political stability varies according to the island, but is generally good to excellent. Many islands are colonies or dependent territories (by choice) and are therefore very stable. Most ex-British colonies have a system of government based on the British parliamentary model. Some governments have been involved in corruption scandals in recent years, although this is the exception.

Finance

Currency: Various, many of which are tied to the US$ at a fixed exchange rate. Some islands share a currency, such as the Eastern Caribbean dollar (EC$). US$ banknotes and travellers' cheques are widely accepted (the US$ is the *de facto* currency in the Caribbean) and the US$ is the official currency on some islands. Many islands are popular tax havens, particularly the Bahamas and the Cayman Islands.

Exchange Controls: None on most islands, although some have limited restrictions. On some islands, the export of local currency is subject to severe restrictions and sometimes totally prohibited. Some islands require foreign currency to be declared on entry and exit, and only imported currency can be exported.

Interest Rate: 5.75 per cent (Bahamas).

Cost/Standard of Living: The cost of food and essential services is reasonably low on most islands, although imported goods (including most consumer durables) are expensive. Cars, clothing and appliances are comparatively expensive, while items such as jewellery, perfumes and alcohol are generally inexpensive. The cost of living is similar to most western European countries, but higher than the USA and Canada.

Income Tax: There's no income tax on many Caribbean islands and where there is, it's relatively low. Retired foreign nationals may be exempt from paying income tax on income earned abroad.

Capital Gains Tax (CGT): Most Caribbean countries have no capital gains tax.

Wealth Tax: None.

Inheritance & Gift Tax: None.

Value Added Tax (VAT): A few islands have a value added or sales tax, e.g. 15 per cent in Trinidad and Tobago. The main source of income for most governments is import duties, which are levied on most imported goods. Some islands have special taxes, such as a tax on hotel bills.

Property

Market: There's a buoyant market in luxury homes on most islands, although prices are comparatively high. Beach front properties are in particularly high demand. Many new homes are built mostly of wood and older wooden cottages are also available on many islands. Detached homes usually have their own swimming pools. New developments usually provide a wide range of amenities which may include restaurants, bars, shops, tennis courts, swimming pools, water sports facilities, private beaches, boat docks and on-site management offices. Most developers provide a management and letting service.

Cost: Homes on most islands are expensive on account of the high cost of land and because most building materials and fixtures and fitting must be imported. On the most popular islands, apartments start at around US$300,000 and detached villas at US$500,000, although cheaper property is available on some islands. Property is cheaper on the smaller, less developed islands, although these are generally for those seeking almost complete solitude. Prices have risen considerably in the last decade and beach front properties are prohibitively expensive on many islands. Most new developments comprise luxury condominiums (apartments) or luxury detached homes. Prices are usually quoted in US$.

Local Mortgages: Mortgages are available from local banks on most islands. Maximum loans are usually 50 to 60 per cent on second homes with repayment over a maximum of 15 years. A small duty may be imposed on mortgages. Loans are available in the local currency or US$, which usually offers a lower interest rate. Lenders generally insist that properties are insured for their full value and borrowers may also require life insurance.

Property Taxes: Property taxes are levied on most islands and are based on the market or rentable value. Taxes are usually low, e.g. in the Bahamas they're 1 per cent of the market value up to B$500,000 and 2 per cent of the market value above B$500,000 for non-residents (taxes are slightly lower for permanent residents). There may be an annual fee for refuse collection.

Purchase Procedure: It's usual to retain a local lawyer to complete the formalities. Foreign buyers may require police clearance from their country of residence and must usually produce evidence of their funds. The purchase procedure on most islands is based on the British model (see page 150). Most islands have an efficient and safe legal system and problems are rare.

Fees: Most countries levy duty and/or transfer tax on property purchases at between 5 and 10 per cent, e.g. 7 per cent on properties costing over B$100,000 in the Bahamas and 10 per cent in Antigua/Barbuda and Barbados. Estate agents' fees are usually between 5 and 10 per cent for developed property. Legal (conveyance) fees are usually 2.5 to 3 per cent of the sale price.

Precautions: Before buying building land, you must ensure that you have planning permission (or that it will be approved) for the size and type of property you plan to build, and that services will be provided. In view of the occasional severe storms (and erupting volcanoes!) it's important that a home is insured for the full cost of rebuilding.

Holiday Letting: No restrictions.

Restrictions on Foreign Ownership: Official government permission is usually required for foreigners to purchase land or property, although this is a formality and may be required only for properties above a certain land area, e.g. 2 hectares (5 acres) in the Bahamas. The amount of land that can be purchased for residential purposes without a permit is usually limited to between 1 and 5 acres.

Building Standards: Generally excellent for new properties. The quality of older properties is variable. Homes are usually built in the local style employing local materials (e.g. wood) whenever possible.

Personal Effects: Can be freely imported without any restrictions, although duty is payable on some large items (such as motor vehicles) and can be high. In some cases, items of high value such as photographic equipment, portable computers, electronics apparatus and sports equipment must be declared.

General Information

Crime Rate: Low on most islands, although crime has risen considerably on many islands in recent years and you should always keep an eye on your belongings. Violent and serious crime is relatively low, but increasing. Some areas on some islands are to avoided, particularly at night. Organised crimes such as drug trafficking and money laundering are a problem on some islands.

Medical Facilities: Good on most islands, although some facilities aren't available on the smaller islands. In the less developed islands, you will need to be flown out as soon as possible if you fall seriously ill. Private international health insurance is highly recommended, as the best hospitals are often private and it may be necessary to be evacuated to the USA or a neighbouring country to be treated for certain serious health problems (which must be covered by your insurance).

Pets: There's no quarantine for pets on most islands, but check before buying a home. All animals require a current vaccination certificate including rabies.

Residence Permits: Usually a formality, provided you have adequate means of financial support and own a property (or have made an investment) above a certain minimum amount, e.g. B$250,000 in the Bahamas. In most cases a temporary (e.g. annual) or permanent residence certificate must be obtained, for which there are high fees, e.g. up to B$10,000 in the Bahamas. On some islands the fee for a residence certificate is based on the value of your property, e.g. 5 per cent of a property's value in Antigua and Barbuda. Note that some islands also levy high fees for those wishing to become tax residents. Citizenship based on investment is also available on some islands.

Work Permits: Difficult to obtain unless you plan to start a business and create employment, when there are minimum levels of investment. Employers must usually show that there isn't a similarly qualified local resident available to fill a position.

Reference

Further Reading

Baedeker Caribbean (AA/Baedeker).

Useful Addresses

High Commission for Antigua and Barbuda, Antigua House, 15 Thayer Street, London W1M 5LD, UK (☎ 020-7486 7073/5, 💻 www.antigua-barbuda.com).

The High Commission of the Commonwealth of the Bahamas, Bahamas House, 10 Chesterfield Street, London W1X 8AH, UK (☎ 020-7408 4488).

The High Commission for Barbados, 1 Great Russell Street, London WC1B 3JY, UK (☎ 020-7631 4975).

Office of the High Commission of the Commonwealth of Dominica, 1 Collingham Gardens, London SW5 0HW, UK (☎ 020-7370 5194/5, 💻 www.dominica.co.uk).

High Commission of the Republic of Trinidad and Tobago, 42 Belgrave Square, London SW1X 8NT, UK (☎ 020-7245 9351).

Embassy of Antigua & Barbuda, 3216 New Mexico Ave, NW, Washington, DC 20016, USA (☎ 202-362 5122).

Embassy of The Commonwealth of The Bahamas, 2220 Massachusetts Ave, NW Washington, DC 20008, USA (☎ 202-319 2660).

Embassy of Barbados, 2144 Wyoming Ave, NW, Washington, DC 20008, USA (☎ 202-939 9200/2).

Embassy of The Commonwealth of Dominica, 3216 New Mexico Ave, NW, Washington, DC 20016, USA (☎ 202-3643 6781/2).

Embassy of Grenada, 1701 New Hampshire Ave, NW, Washington, DC 20009, USA (☎ 202-265 2561).
Embassy of Jamaica, 1520 New Hampshire Ave, NW, Washington, DC 20036, USA (☎ 202-452 0660, ⌨ www.emjam-usa.org).
Embassy of St. Kitts and Nevis, 3216 New Mexico Ave, NW, Washington, DC 20016, USA (☎ 202-686 2636, ⌨ www.stkittsnevis.org).
Embassy of St. Lucia, 3216 New Mexico Ave, NW, Washington, DC 20016, USA (☎ 202-364 6792/93).
Embassy of St. Vincent and the Grenadines, 3216 New Mexico Ave, NW, Washington, DC 20016, USA (☎ 202-364 6730).
Embassy of the Republic of Trinidad and Tobago, 1708 Massachusetts Ave, NW, Washington, DC 20036, USA (☎ 202-467 6490).

CYPRUS

Background Information

Capital: Nicosia (Lefkosia).
Population: 665,000.
Foreign Community: The population of Cyprus is 78 per cent Greek, 18 per cent Turkish and 4 per cent other nationalities. There's a large foreign community, including some 5,000 British residents concentrated mainly in resort areas.
Area: 9,250km^2 (3,572mi^2).
Geography: Cyprus is situated at the eastern end of the Mediterranean 64km (40mi) from Turkey and 122km (76mi) from Syria. It's 240km (149mi) in length and 96km (60mi) wide, with a coastline of 782km (486mi). The northern coast is backed by the long limestone range of Kyrenia. The central plain between Morphou and Famagusta is fertile and well irrigated, and produces fruit, flowers and early vegetables.
Climate: Cyprus is the sunniest island in the Mediterranean with over 300 days of sunshine a year and long, hot, dry summers and mild winters. Most rain falls between November and March. August is the hottest month, when temperatures are between 21 and 40°C/70 and 104°F, and January the coldest with temperatures between 6 and 13°C/43 and 55°F. Sea temperatures range from 16°C/61°F in January to 32°C/90°F in August. In winter it's possible to ski on Mount Olympus in the Troodos mountains. Cyprus suffered an earthquake in 1995 measuring 5.2 on the Richter scale, which damaged around 700 homes in 50 villages. However, modern homes are generally built to withstand the occasional earth tremors.
Language: National languages are Greek and Turkish, although most Turkish Cypriots now live in the self-declared Turkish Republic of Northern Cyprus. English is spoken by some 90 per cent of Greek Cypriots.
Political Stability: Cyprus has had a turbulent history since the 1950s and was partitioned in 1974 when Turkish forces invaded the north. The northern part of Cyprus (40 per cent of the island) remains under the jurisdiction of the Turkish Cypriots backed by the Turkish army, with the capital Nicosia partitioned. The Turkish cypriots have declared a Turkish Republic of Northern Cyprus, a pariah 'state' recognised only by Turkey. There's little communication between the Greek

and Turkish Cypriot communities. Today, at least as far as most foreigners are concerned, Cyprus effectively consists of the southern region governed by the Greek Cypriots, and the information in this section refers exclusively to this area. It should be noted that partition is of little or no consequence to foreigners living in the southern part of Cyprus. Cyprus is a member of the British Commonwealth and is expected to join the European Union in 2004.

Finance

Currency: Cyprus pound (C£).
Exchange Rate: £ = C£0.95.
Exchange Controls: Yes. Funds imported to buy a property should be officially documented so that when it's sold the proceeds can be repatriated.
Interest Rate: 6 per cent.
Cost/Standard of Living: The cost of living is low by European standards, but it has increased considerably in recent years, although Cyprus remains one of the cheapest countries in Europe. Some imported items are expensive, although car prices are as much as 50 per cent lower than in some northern European countries. Residents can import a new car tax and duty-free.
Income Tax: Income tax is levied on income remitted to Cyprus. The rate is just 5 per cent on pensions and investment income remitted to Cyprus by residents (the first C£4,000 is exempt for a single person or C£8,000 for a couple). After deducting their allowances, a retired couple would pay only around C£600 tax on C£15,000 remitted to Cyprus. For resident employees there's a PAYE system with progressive tax rates from 20 to 40 per cent (on earnings above C£5,000).
Capital Gains Tax (CGT): Gains from the sale of property in Cyprus are taxed at 20 per cent, although there's a lifetime exemption (i.e. once only) of between C£10,000 and C£50,000 depending on the type of property.You can export the initial purchase price plus C£50,000 profit, but any balance can be exported only at the rate of C£50,000 a year (plus interest), commencing the year following the sale.
Wealth Tax: None.
Inheritance & Gift Tax: Inheritance tax ranges from 10 to 30 per cent and is payable on estates in excess of C£20,000, although there are generous allowances for spouses and children. Inheritance tax must be paid on the world-wide assets of someone who was domiciled in Cyprus. However, if he purchased a property there after 1st January 1976 while resident abroad and with imported funds, the estate isn't taxable. Inheritance tax is payable by non-residents on property owned in Cyprus. There's no gift tax.
Value Added Tax (VAT): VAT is levied at a standard rate of 10 per cent and a reduced rate of 5 per cent, which applies to hotel and restaurant bills, and alcohol. Certain essential goods and services are zero-rated or exempt (including most food, medicines and financial transactions).

Property

Market: Cyprus has a flourishing property market and it's traditionally a popular location for both holiday and retirement homes. A wide range of properties is available, both new and old, including restored and unrestored old village houses. New developments abound, although many are uninspiring and few have swimming pools or sports facilities such as tennis courts, and there's just one golf course on the island (in Paphos). Over-development and mass-market tourism has ruined many coastal areas with the notable exception of Paphos, where there are strict building regulations. Most inland villages are unspoilt and full of character.

Areas: The most popular locations for foreign buyers are in and around the coastal towns of Ayia Napa, Limassol, Larnaka and Paphos. The Troodos mountains and the capital Nicosia are also popular.

Cost: A wide choice of properties is available, including apartments, townhouses and villas. Prices vary according to location, size and quality. One-bedroom apartments cost from around C£25,000, two-bedroom apartments from C£35,000, two-bedroom townhouses from C£45,000, and two-bedroom detached bungalows and villas from around C£60,000. Beach front properties attract a premium of around 20 per cent. Resale properties are often sold furnished. The cost of building land varies considerably with the area, from around C£50 to C£300 per m^2.

Local Mortgages: Mortgages of 70 or 75 per cent are available from local banks over five to ten years. There's a mortgage registration fee of at least 1 per cent of the amount borrowed. Some new properties are sold on 'hire purchase' terms by developers, e.g. a 25 per cent deposit with the balance payable in monthly instalments over two to five years. Other schemes require one third on signing, one third during construction and the remaining third to be paid in monthly instalments over two or three years.

Property Taxes: A local authority tax of between C£30 and C£100 a year is payable for services such as refuse collection and street lighting. There's also an annual tax based on a property's value: 2 per cent on properties valued at C£101,000 to C£250,000; 3 per cent between C£250,001 and C£500,000; 3.5 per cent C£500,000.

Purchase Procedure: Foreign currency must be imported to pay for property and an Import of Foreign Currency certificate is required by the Land Registry office. The purchase procedure is based on the British legal system. Both parties sign a preliminary contract which binds them to the transaction on mutually agreed terms. Contracts are subject to good title and any necessary government permits. A deposit is lodged with a lawyer or notary, and searches are carried out to ensure that the vendor has good title to a property. An application to purchase a property must be made to the Council of Ministers, although it's only a formality. When the searches have been completed and the permits approved, a final contract is drawn up and lodged with the land registry.

Offshore Companies: Offshore companies may be used to purchase property in Cyprus, in which case exchange controls don't affect the sale of a property and full repatriation of funds is possible. In addition no land registry fees are payable, which can make a large saving.

Fees: Fees total around 10 per cent of the purchase price. Lawyer's fees are between C£200 and C£500 or 1 per cent of the purchase price up to C£75,000. Stamp duty is C£1.50 per C£1,000 of value up to C£100,000 and C£2 per C£1,000 above this amount. The application to the Council of Ministers costs around C£200. A land registry fee or transfer tax is levied at between 3 and 8 per cent, depending on the value of the property. When a couple are buying a property together as co-owners, they can split the transfer tax between them.

Precautions: Buyers should engage a local lawyer, although it isn't required by law. Always ensure that the deeds are produced as required in the contract and make this a condition of a sale. Note that the signing of a contract and payment of a deposit can lead to a buyer being irrevocably committed, even if the title is defective or there are flaws in the contract.

Holiday Letting: Holiday letting isn't permitted by foreign property owners in Cyprus, although it isn't strictly enforced and many foreigners let their properties.

Restrictions on Foreign Ownership: Foreigners are permitted to own only one property or building plot at a time and the maximum plot size is usually two 'donums', i.e. $2,675m^2/28,800ft^2$ or approximately two thirds of an acre. In certain cases foreigners can own up to three donums (1 acre).

Building Standards: The design of new properties and developments has improved greatly in recent years, although it still lacks inspiration, and the construction quality of new properties is generally high. The quality of older resale properties is variable and a survey is recommended on older detached properties.

Personal Effects: Personal effects can be imported duty-free including vehicles (retirees are permitted to import two duty-free cars). Non-residents are allowed to import a car and use it for three months. Household effects must have been owned and used for 12 months, and must be imported within 12 months of taking up residence. A government levy, known as the Temporary Refugee Levy (TRL), applies to all imported goods, whether new or used. The rate is 1.7 per cent of the declared value and you can expect to pay between C£75 and C£150 for a typical shipment.

General Information

Crime Rate: Cyprus has one of the world's lowest crime rates, and both serious crime and crime against property are relatively low.

Medical Facilities: Very good. Many doctors are trained in the UK or USA, and inexpensive health services are provided at government hospitals. Private health insurance is necessary for retirees.

Pets: Pets must be vaccinated against echinoochus and have an import licence issued by the Department of Veterinary Services. A dog or cat must be quarantined for six months, although this may be at your own home. Dogs aren't permitted to roam freely and must be kept in an enclosed area (e.g. with a fence) or on a lead.

Residence Permits: Property owners with an adequate income can obtain a residence permit and foreign retirees are encouraged to take up residence. The annual income requirements in 2001 were C£7,000 for a single person and C£10,000 for a couple without children.

Work Permits: Work permits are difficult to obtain and a government permit is required under the Alien Immigration Law.

Reference

Further Reading

BUYING A HOME IN GREECE & CYPRUS, Joanna Styles (Survival Books).
Everything you need to know about buying a home in Greece and Cyprus.

Cyprus Magazine, PO Box 45Y, London W1 45Y, UK. Bi-monthly magazine.
Cyprus Daily/Weekly, PO Box 21144, 1502 Nicosia, Cyprus (🖳 www.cynews.com).

Useful Addresses

Centre for Overseas Retirement Studies, PO Box 3293, P Lordos Centre, 1st Floor, Block B, Byron Street, Limassol, Cyprus (☎ 05-354371).
Cyprus Embassy, 2210 R St, NW, Washington, DC 20008, USA (☎ 202-462 5772).
Cyprus High Commission, 93 Park Street, London W1Y 4ET, UK (☎ 020-7499 8272).
Cyprus Real Estate Agents Association, PO Box 1455, Nicosia, Cyprus (☎ 02-449500).
Cyprus Tourism Organisation, PO Box 24535, 1390 Nicosia (☎ 02-337715, 🖳 www.cyprustourism.org).
Ministry of the Interior, Migration Officer, Department of Aliens and Immigration, D. Severis Ave, Nicosia, Cyprus (☎ 02-804533).

FRANCE

Background Information

Capital: Paris.
Population: 58.8 million.
Foreign Community: France has a large foreign community in its major cities and some rural areas (e.g. Dordogne) have a large number of British and other foreign residents.
Area: 543,965km² (210,025mi²).
Geography: France is one of the largest countries in Europe, stretching 1,050km (650mi) from north to south and almost the same distance from West to East (from the tip of Brittany to Strasbourg). Its land and sea border extends for 4,800km (3,000mi) and includes 2,700km (2,175mi) of coastline. France also incorporates the Mediterranean island of Corsica (*Corse*) situated 160km (99mi) from France and 80km (50mi) from Italy, covering 8,721km² (3,367mi²) and with a coastline of 1,000km (620mi). France is bordered by Andorra, Belgium, Germany, Italy, Luxembourg, Spain and Switzerland, and the opening of the Channel Tunnel in 1994 connected it with Britain (by rail only).
Climate: France is the only country in Europe that experiences three distinct climates: continental, maritime and Mediterranean. It isn't easy to generalise about French weather, as many regions are influenced by mountains, forests and other geographical features, and have their own micro-climates. Generally the Loire river is considered to be the point where the cooler northern European climate begins to change to the warmer southern climate. Spring and autumn are usually fine throughout France, although the length of the seasons varies according to the region and altitude.

In Paris, it's rare for the temperature to fall below -5°C/41°F in winter or to rise above 30°C/86°F in summer. However, the capital receives its fair share of rain. The west and north-west (e.g. Brittany and Normandy) have a maritime climate tempered by the Atlantic and the Gulf Stream, with mild winters and warm summers, and most rainfall in spring and autumn. Many people consider the western Atlantic coast has the best summer climate in France, with the heat tempered by cool sea breezes. The Massif Central (which acts as a weather barrier between north and south) and eastern France have a moderate continental climate with cold winters and hot and stormy summers. However, the centre and eastern upland areas have an extreme continental climate, with freezing winters and sweltering summers.

The Midi, stretching from the Pyrenees to the Alps, is hot and dry except for early spring, when there's usually heavy rainfall. The Cévennes region is the wettest in France, with some 200cm of rain per year. Languedoc has hot dry summers and much colder winters than the Côte d'Azur, with snow often remaining until May in the mountainous inland areas. The South of France enjoys a Mediterranean climate of mild winters (daytime temperatures rarely drop below 10°C/50°F) and humid, hot summers, with the temperature often above 30°C/86°F. The average sunshine on the Côte d'Azur is five hours in January and 12 hours in July.

Language: French. France also has a number of regional languages including Alsatian (spoken in the Alsace), Basque (Pyrenees), Breton (Brittany), Catalan (Roussillon), Corsican (Corsica) and Occitan (Languedoc). Local dialects (*patois*) are also common in many areas.

Political Stability: Extremely stable, although periodically shaken by national strikes and riots. After many years of Socialist rule, a conservative coalition of the *Rassemblement pour la République* (RPR) and the Union for a Democratic France (*Union pour la Démocratie Française*/UDF) won the general election in 1993 but lost to a Socialist/Communist coalition in 1997. President Jacques Chirac runs for re-election in 2002. France is a founder member of the European Union.

Finance

Currency: Euro (€).
Exchange Rate: £1 = €1.60.
Exchange Controls: None.
Interest Rate: 3.75 per cent.
Cost/Standard of Living: Salaries are generally high in France and the French enjoy a high standard of living. With the exception of Paris, where the higher cost of living is offset by higher salaries, the cost of living in France is lower than the EU average, particularly in rural areas.
Income Tax: Income tax for most people in France is below the average for EU countries, particularly for large families. However, if the high social security contributions (regarded as a form of taxation in France) and other taxes are added, French taxes are among the highest in the European Union. Tax rates range from 10.5 to 54 per cent.
Capital Gains Tax (CGT): Gains on profits made on the sale of a second home in France that has been owned for less than two years are taxed at 33.3 per cent. On properties owned for more than two years, the difference between the purchase and selling price is reduced by 5 per cent for the third and subsequent years up to 22 years, multiplied by an index-linked multiplier of the sale price. CGT isn't payable on a profit made on the sale of a principal residence in France, provided it has been occupied since

its purchase or for a minimum of five years. CGT at 7 per cent is payable on articles such as antiques, art and jewellery, and at 19.4 per cent on securities.

Wealth Tax: A tax of between 0.5 and 1.8 per cent is levied on French residents with world-wide assets valued at over €760,000.

Inheritance & Gift Tax: Inheritance tax in France is paid by individual beneficiaries, irrespective of where they're domiciled, and not by the estate. The rate of tax and allowances vary according to the relationship between the beneficiary and the deceased. There are allowances for close relatives, after which inheritance tax is levied on a sliding scale at 5 to 40 per cent.

Value Added Tax (VAT): The standard rate of VAT in France is 19.6 per cent, which is included in the purchase price of properties less than five years old when sold for the first time. There are reduced rates of 2.1 per cent on medicines subject to reimbursement by social security and daily newspapers, 4 per cent on magazines, and 5.5 per cent on food, agricultural products, medicines, books, public transport, gas, electricity, canteen food, cinema, theatre and concert tickets, hotel accommodation and travel agency fees.

Property

Market: The property market has been generally good in France since 1997 when the French franc fell in value by around 20 per cent against sterling (and against other currencies). Rural property remains excellent value, particularly if you're after a large plot, and some excellent bargains are available. However, coastal and city properties are at a premium and cost up to double the price of similar rural properties. Property on the French Riviera remains among the most expensive in the world, and Paris is one of Europe's most expensive cities, although property in the capital remains a good long-term investment. New properties are widely available and include coastal and city apartments, ski and golf developments, and a wide range of individually designed houses and chalets. Many new properties are part of purpose-built developments, often located along the coast or in mountain areas, encompassing a golf course, swimming pool, tennis and squash courts, a gym or fitness club, and a restaurant.

Areas: The most popular areas for foreign buyers include Paris, the Loire Valley (famous for its *châteaux*), the South of France (particularly the French Riviera or Côte d'Azur and Provence), south-west France (e.g. Charente, Dordogne and Gascony), and Brittany and Normandy, which are particularly popular with the British. Winter holiday homes in French alpine ski resorts are also popular, especially in fashionable resorts such as Chamonix, Courchevel, Mégève, Méribel, Val d'Isère and Val Thorens. Properties in French ski resorts are usually an excellent investment and also make fine summer holiday homes, especially if you're a keen hiker.

Cost: Apart from obvious points such as size, quality and land area, the most important factor influencing the price of a house is its location. A restored or modernised two-bedroom house costs between €48,000 and €81,000 in the north-west (e.g. Normandy) but sells for double or treble that price in the south-east (e.g. Provence). Similarly, the closer you are to the coast or Paris the more expensive property is, with properties on the French Riviera the most expensive of all (and among the most expensive in Europe). A Charente farmhouse with a barn and a large plot costs around the same as a tiny studio apartment in Paris or on the Côte d'Azur.

In most rural areas it's still possible to buy an old property for as little as €20,000 to €35,000, although you usually need to carry out major renovation or restoration which can double or treble the price. Modern one-bedroom apartments in main cities or in resorts cost from around €100,000 and two-bedroom apartments from €150,000. A rural two-bedroom renovated cottage costs from around €31,000 and a modern two-bedroom bungalow from €80,000. Villas situated near the south coast with a swimming pool cost from €300,000. Property in ski resorts varies considerably in price according to the resort and the location of the property. A tiny studio in a purpose-built resort costs from around €37,500, while a one-bedroom apartment close to the ski lifts in a resort such as Courchevel, Méribel or Tignes costs from €55,000, rising to around €75,000 in Chamonix or Val d'Isère. Small chalets start at €100,000, although you need to spend around €125,000 or more to buy a family-size chalet in a top resort.

Local Mortgages: Mortgages are available from all major French banks (both for residents and non-residents) and many foreign banks. Crédit Agricole is the largest French lender with a 25 per cent share of the market. Mortgages can be obtained for any period from 2 to 20 years, although the usual term is 15 years. French mortgages are usually limited to 70 or 80 per cent of a property's value.

Property Taxes: There are two property-based taxes in France. Property tax (*taxe foncière*) is similar to the property tax (or rates) levied in most countries and is paid by property owners based on the average (notional) rental value of the property in the previous year, adjusted for inflation, as calculated by the land registry. Rates vary considerably according to the region and even within a region from as little as around €300 to €1,500 or more per year. Residential tax (*taxe d'habitation*) is payable by whoever is residing in a property on 1st January, whether as an owner, tenant or rent free and is calculated according to income, number of children, etc. It's normally around half as much as property tax.

Purchase Procedure: The purchase of property in France is strictly controlled and regulated. Property sales are conducted by a notary (*notaire*), who's a government official representing neither the vendor nor buyer (although you can engage another notary to act solely for you). However, it's wise to hire a local lawyer to protect your interests and carry out the usual checks concerning title, outstanding debts, etc. A good estate agent is invaluable when buying in France, but he shouldn't be relied upon with regard to legal matters. There are various types of purchase contract, the most common being a bilateral agreement (*compromis de vente*), which is binding on both parties. When the preliminary contract is signed a deposit is payable, which is usually 5 per cent for a new property and 10 per cent for a resale property. An agent must be bonded to hold money on behalf of clients and must display the sum of his financial guarantee (*pièce de garantie*). Note that the deposit isn't returnable unless you're unable to obtain a mortgage or there are serious legal problems involved in the purchase. The balance of the purchase price and all fees are due on completion of the sale, which is a fixed time after the signing of the purchase contract (normally six weeks), when the deed of sale (*acte de vente*) is signed.

Offshore Companies: Offshore companies can be used to purchase property in France, but for most people there's little or no advantage.

Fees: The total fees payable when buying a house in France are between 10 and 15 per cent of the price for a small to medium-size property over five years old. Fees for new properties less than five years old are 3 or 4 per cent, but VAT at 19.6 per cent is included in the purchase price. The fees comprise the notary's fee (2 to 5 per cent), stamp or transfer duty (0.6 per cent on new homes, 7.5 per cent on old homes), registration fees (6 to 7 per cent) and agent's fees. Note that prices may be quoted inclusive or exclusive of agent's fees, so you should check whether these are included in the price quoted and who's to pay them.

Precautions: The legal procedure in France regarding the purchase of real property is very safe. However, any special conditions regarding a purchase *must* be included as conditional clauses in the preliminary contract. It's wise to have a survey on an older habitable dwelling or at the very least have it checked by a building expert, as a property is purchased 'as seen' and the vendor isn't liable for any defects unless he knowingly withheld information at the time of sale. Buyers should be particularly cautious when buying old properties requiring extensive restoration, as the cost can escalate wildly. Before going ahead with a purchase you should obtain written detailed quotations (*devis*) from *at least* two local builders. You should *always* expect the final cost of restoration to be higher than the highest estimate you receive! If a property has already been renovated, you should check who did it, how it was done (i.e. professionally or by cutting corners) and whether there's a guarantee.

Holiday Letting: No restrictions, although tax is payable by non-residents on letting income.

Restrictions on Foreign Ownership: None.

Building Standards: Excellent. The standard of new buildings in France is strictly regulated and most homes are built to official quality standards that are higher than in many other countries. The quality of renovation and restoration varies considerably with the builder.

Personal Effects: Goods purchased within the European Union (EU) can be imported duty-free and don't need to be retained for a minimum period. An inventory must be provided. If you're a non-EU resident planning to take up permanent or temporary residence in France, you're permitted to import your furniture and personal effects free of duty. These include vehicles, mobile homes, pleasure boats and aircraft. However, to qualify for duty-free import, articles must have been owned and used for at least six months and cannot be sold for one year after import. All items should be imported within one year of the date of your change of residence, in one or a number of consignments, although it's best to have only one.

General Information

Crime: France has a similar crime rate to most other major European countries and, in common with them, crime has increased considerably in recent years as unemployment has soared. Inner-city violence is now a particular problem, and house-breaking and burglary are rampant in some areas, where holiday or second homes are a popular target. Car theft and theft from cars is also rife in Paris and other cities. The crime rate is low in rural areas, however, and it's common for people in many villages and small towns not to lock their homes and cars.

Medical Facilities: Excellent. French doctors are highly trained and general hospitals are superbly equipped, although they're few and far between in some rural areas. There are foreign-run hospitals in major cities, e.g. American and British hospitals in

Paris. France has an excellent national health scheme for those contributing to social security and retirees. If you aren't covered by the national health scheme, private health insurance is essential and often obligatory for residents.

Pets: You can take up to three animals into France at a time, one of which may be a puppy (three to six months old), although no dogs or cats under three months of age can be imported. There's generally no quarantine period. If you're importing a dog into France, it must be vaccinated against rabies or have a health certificate signed by an approved veterinary surgeon issued no more than five days before your arrival. For visitors with pets, a rabies vaccination is compulsory only for animals entering Corsica, being taken to campsites or holiday parks, or participating in shows in a rabies-affected area. Resident dogs must be vaccinated against distemper and hardpad and need an annual rabies booster. Cats aren't required to have rabies vaccinations, although if you let your cat roam free outside your home it's wise to have it vaccinated annually. Cats must, however, be vaccinated against feline gastro-enteritis and typhus.

Residence Permits: A formality for EU nationals, although non-working residents must have sufficient income or financial resources to live in France without working. Visitors can stay in France for a maximum of 90 days at a time, although many nationalities require a visa. Non-EU nationals require a long-stay visa (*visa de long séjour*) to live in France for longer than three months.

Work Permits: Work permits are unnecessary for EU nationals, but are difficult for non-EU nationals to obtain.

Reference

Further Reading

BUYING A HOME IN FRANCE, David Hampshire (Survival Books). *Everything you need to know about buying a home in France.*
LIVING & WORKING IN FRANCE, David Hampshire (Survival Books). *Everything you need to know about living and working in France.*
English-French Dictionary of Building and Property, J. Kater Pollock (Flowerpoll).
Focus on France, Outbound Publishing, 1 Commercial Road, Eastbourne, East Sussex BN21 3XQ, UK (☎ 01323-726040). Quarterly property magazine.
France Magazine, Dormer House, Stow-on-the-Wold, Glos. GL54 1BN, UK. Monthly lifestyle magazine.
French Property News, 6 Burgess Mews, Wimbledon, London SW19 1UF, UK (☎ 020-8543 3113, 🖳 www.french-property-news.com). Monthly property newspaper.
French Real Property and Succession Law, Henry Dyson (Robert Hale).
Living France, The Picture House, 79 High Street, Olney MK46 4EF, UK (☎ 01234-713203, 🖳 www.livingfrance.com). Monthly lifestyle magazine
The News, Brussac SARL, BP 23, Chancelade, France. Monthly English-language newspaper.
The Riviera Reporter, 56 Chemin de Provence, 06250 Mougina, France (☎ 0493-457719, ✉ info@riviera-reporter.com). Monthly magazine.
Traditional Houses of Rural France, Bill Laws (Collins & Brown).

Useful Addresses

French Embassy, 4101 Reservoir Rd., NW, Washington, DC 20007, USA
(☎ 202-944 6000, 💻 www.info-france-usa-org).
French Embassy, 58 Knightsbridge, London SW1X 7JT, UK (☎ 020-7201 1000).
French Government Tourist Office, 178 Piccadilly, London W1V 0AL, UK
(☎ 090-6824 4123, 💻 www.franceguide.com).
💻 **www.paris-anglo.com**. Expatriate website.

GERMANY

Background Information

Capital: Berlin.
Population: 82 million.
Foreign Community: Germany has a large foreign community of over 4 million immigrant workers, mostly Italians, Turks and Yugoslavs. A considerable number of Americans and Britons also work there.
Area: 356,844km² (137,777mi²).
Geography: Germany is situated in the heart of Europe and has borders with Austria, Belgium, the Czech Republic, Denmark, France, Luxembourg, the Netherlands, Poland and Switzerland. It extends from the North Sea and Baltic coasts in the north to the flanks of the central Alps in the south. Germany is characterised by three topographical features: lowlands (in the north and centre); medium-altitude mountains; and high mountains (in the south), including the Alps.
Climate: Germany forms the connecting link between maritime western Europe and continental eastern Europe, and between the cooler north and the warmer south. It has a predominantly mild, temperate climate, with occasional continental influences from the south creating periods of extreme heat or cold. Oceanic airstreams provide cooling in summer, although 'Indian' summers created by high pressure systems are common. Rainfall is evenly distributed throughout the year, with April and October the driest months. Summers are usually warm with average temperatures of 17°C/63°F, although temperatures of around 22 to 23°C/72 to 74°F are common in many regions and can rise to over 30°C/86°F in Berlin. Winters are cold throughout the country and can be severe in mountainous regions. The average winter temperature is 0°C/32°F, although it can drop to -10°C/14°F in the Bavarian Alps.
Language: German (with regional dialects). English is widely spoken, although less so in the former East German states.
Political Stability: Germany, particularly the former West Germany, has been one of the most politically stable countries in Europe since the Second World War. It's divided into 16 self-governing states, which have a large degree of autonomy. The reunification of Germany in 1990 created enormous economic and social problems, although these are gradually being overcome. Germany is a founder member of the European Union.

Finance

Currency: Euro (€).
Exchange Rate: £1 = €1.60.
Exchange Controls: None.
Interest Rate: 3.75 per cent.
Cost/Standard of Living: Germany enjoys a high standard of living with low inflation. The cost of living is relatively high, although only slightly higher than Britain and France.
Income Tax: Germany has a PAYE system with rates from 24 to 53 per cent (on incomes above €235,280). Taxes increased substantially in the '90s to finance the cost of reunification and the regeneration of eastern Germany. A 'solidarity' surcharge (*Solidaritätszuschlag*) of 5.5 per cent is levied on income tax to help pay for the cost of reunification.
Capital Gains Tax (CGT): Capital gains on property sold within two years of purchase are subject to income tax at normal rates.
Wealth Tax: None.
Inheritance & Gift Tax: Inheritance tax is paid by the beneficiary, and gift tax is paid by both the donor and the recipient. For non-residents, tax is limited to property located in Germany. Exemptions and tax rates vary according to the relationship of the donor and recipient and the value of the property inherited or received as a gift. Inheritance tax ranges from 7 to 30 per cent for relatives of the first degree and from 17 to 50 per cent for non-related people.
Value Added Tax (VAT): The standard rate of VAT is 16 per cent, which applies to most goods and services. There's a reduced rate of 7 per cent for certain items of food and 'necessary' social services.
Other Taxes: Members of the Roman Catholic and Lutheran (Protestant) churches pay around 9 per cent of their income tax liability as church tax (pensioners are exempt).

Property

Market: The majority of Germans rent their homes and home ownership at around 40 per cent is one of the lowest rates in western Europe. Most Germans live in apartments in the cities and their suburbs, where there's an acute shortage of housing (exacerbated by reunification). Some 75 per cent of German housing has been built since the Second World War, although there are still many beautiful villages and rural areas with period and traditional houses. Best buys are often older properties in need of restoration, particularly in eastern Germany, although the ownership of a large number of dwellings there is in dispute.
Areas: Among visitors and residents who don't need to live close to a major city the most popular areas are the Rhine and Mosel valleys, Franconia, the Swabian Jura, the Black Forest and Bavaria. There's excellent skiing in the German Alps in Upper Bavaria and Allgäu. Garmisch-Partenkirchen is the most famous German ski resort.
Cost: German property is among the most expensive in Europe, particularly in the cities where prices have soared in recent years, and the situation has been exacerbated by the large number of refugees. Nevertheless, property is an excellent long-term

investment. Prices vary considerably according to the city and region, the cost of a townhouse ranging from €127,500 to well over €300,000, and detached family houses costing from €180,000 to over €840,000. Affordable apartments in cities are at a premium, although there's a surplus of prestige properties in many cities. Prices are highest in Munich where prime apartments cost between €8,500 and €10,250 per m². Properties are slightly cheaper in rural areas and in the former East German states, although many are in poor repair and the infrastructure is also poor. Properties can often be purchased at auction at below market prices.

Local Mortgages: The maximum mortgage (*Hypothek*) available in Germany is 60 or 70 per cent, which means that buyers must make a 30 or 40 per cent deposit. Most German banks and building societies (*Bausparkasse*) expect borrowers to make regular savings for a number of years before they will make a home loan. Usually a loan can only be taken out four to six years after paying a fixed amount monthly to a building society (and virtually no interest is paid!). Bank mortgage terms are usually a maximum of 30 years on loans of up to €205,000 with a low fixed rate of interest for the whole period. Many buyers have a combination of a building society loan and a mortgage from a bank. Despite the high deposit and low rates of interest, Germany has the highest average mortgage repayments in the EU of over €870 per month, and mortgages are often assumed by the next generation.

Property Taxes: A land tax (*Grundsteuer*) is levied by local communities and is calculated on the rentable value (which is below the market value) of land and buildings. The amount payable is between 0.5 and 1.5 per cent of a property's rentable value.

Purchase Procedure: All contracts must be certified by a public notary (*Notar*) or a lawyer (*Rechtsanwalt*) specialising in property transactions, and property must be sold free of any liabilities. When a buyer and seller have agreed on a price, a notary is engaged to carry out the legal formalities. When the sale has been completed, the title deed (*Eigentumsrecht verbriefende Urkunde*) is registered at the local land registry (*Grundbuchamt/Katasteramt*), after which title passes to the buyer.

Fees: Transfer tax (*Grundwerbsteuer*) on land and buildings is 2 per cent of the purchase price, and the notary's fee is between 1 and 1.5 per cent. The estate agent's commission (*Provisionssatz*) of up to 6 per cent, usually split between the vendor and buyer, can add a considerable sum to the price (which is why many Germans sell their homes privately).

Holiday Letting: No restrictions.

Restrictions on Foreign Ownership: None.

Building Standards: Excellent and among the best in the world. However, in the former East German states housing stock is poor, particularly the ubiquitous high-rise apartment blocks. Most pre-war housing stock in eastern Germany is also dilapidated and most hasn't been modernised or renovated since before the Second World War.

Personal Effects: Goods purchased within the EU can be imported duty-free and don't need to be retained for a minimum period. However, goods (including cars) purchased outside the EU must have been owned for at least six months and cannot be sold for one year after import in order to be exempt from import duty.

General Information

Crime Rate: Relatively low, although it has increased significantly since unification and the consequent rise in unemployment. Burglaries and car crime are particularly high in the major cities. Violent crime is low, although muggings have increased in the last five years.

Medical Facilities: Excellent. German hospitals and clinics are among the best equipped and staffed in the world (Germany has the highest number of hospital beds per capita in the EU). Germany has a national health scheme whereby employees pay around 6.75 per cent of their gross income for membership of a health insurance fund (*Krankenkasse*). Membership is compulsory (some 90 per cent of the population are members) and almost all medical treatment and medicines are provided 'free'. Pensioners must continue to pay health contributions. If you aren't covered by social security, private health insurance is essential.

Pets: Pet owners require a veterinary certificate (with a German translation) attesting to the good health of a cat or dog and stating that it has been vaccinated against rabies at least 30 days and less than one year prior to its import. An import licence is required for certain animals or when more than three animals are imported.

Residence Permits: A formality for EU nationals, although non-working residents must have sufficient income to maintain themselves. Residents must register with the Residents' Registration Office and the Foreign Nationals Authority within three months of arrival. Nationals of most non-EU countries require a visa to work or reside permanently in Germany. Visitors can remain for three months.

Work Permits: Unnecessary for EU nationals, but difficult for others to obtain.

Reference

Further Reading

LIVING & WORKING IN GERMANY, Nick Daws (Survival Books). *Everything you need to know about living and working in Germany.*
Germany and the Germans, John Ardagh (Penguin).
The Germans: Who Are They Now?, Alan Watson (Thames-Methuen).
How to Live & Work in Germany, Christine Hall (How To Books).
Live & Work in Germany, Victoria Pybus (Vacation Work).

Useful Addresses

German Embassy, 4645 Reservoir Rd, NW, Washington, DC 20007, USA (☎ 0202-298 4000, 💻 www.germany-info.org).
German Embassy, 23 Belgrave Square, 1 Chesham Place, London SW1X 8PZ, UK (☎ 020-7824 1300, 💻 www.german-embassy.org.uk).
German National Tourist Office, Chanin Building, 122 East 42nd Street, 52nd Floor, New York, NY 1068-0072, USA (☎ 212-661 7200).
German National Tourist Office, PO Box 2695, London W1Y 8NE, UK (☎ 020-7317 0908, 💻 www.germany-tourism.de).
💻 **www.german/expat.html**. Comprehensive expatriate website.

GIBRALTAR

Background Information

Capital: Gibraltar.
Population: 30,000.
Foreign Community: Around 25,000 of the population are native Gibraltarians. The remainder are mostly Britons, although there are also some Moroccans and Indians.
Area: 6.5km² (2.5mi²).
Geography: Gibraltar lies at the tip of southern Spain where the Mediterranean sea and the Atlantic ocean meet, 20km (12mi) north of Africa (Morocco). It consists of an isthmus 6km (3.6mi) in length, dominated by the Rock of Gibraltar (427m/1,400ft), from which it gets its colloquial name 'The Rock' (one of Hercules' legendary pillars between Africa and Europe).
Climate: Gibraltar has a Mediterranean climate with hot, sunny summer days and mild winters, and benefits from the climate of the western Mediterranean. The average temperature is between 11 and 15°C/52 and 59°F in winter and 19 to 27°C/66 to 81°F in summer. Rain is infrequent, but can be heavy. Like southern Spain, Gibraltar is susceptible to periodic droughts but has its own desalination plant and therefore suffers no acute water shortages.
Language: English is the official language, but Spanish is also spoken by native Gibraltarians. Gibraltar also has a non-written dialect called Llanito, which is a bizarre mixture of English and Spanish.
Political Stability: Gibraltar is a British dependent territory and has been a crown colony since 1713 under the terms of the Treaty of Utrecht. It's a largely autonomous city-state with a parliamentary system and a House of Assembly consisting of 15 elected members. Although Gibraltar has been a self-governing dependency since 1969, executive authority remains in the hands of a British-appointed governor (who represents the British crown) and Britain is responsible for defence, foreign policy and internal security. Gibraltar joined the EU in 1973 (with Britain) under the provisions relating to European dependent territories, although it's excluded from VAT, the Customs Union and the Common Agricultural Policy (CAP). There's continuing friction with Spain over Gibraltar's ownership and the smuggling of tobacco and drugs into Spain from Gibraltar. Harassment by Spanish customs often results in interminable queues for those entering and leaving Gibraltar by road. However, in 2001 Spanish and British diplomats agreed to enter into greater co-operation over the Gibraltarian question.

Finance

Currency: The official currency is the £sterling,
although the Gibraltar pound circulates freely and has parity with sterling. Most businesses also accept euros, but you may be offered a poor exchange rate.
Exchange Controls: None.
Cost/Standard of Living: The cost of living is low and similar to Spain's. Gibraltar is a duty-free port and therefore luxury goods are relatively inexpensive, as are

tobacco, alcohol and petrol. Tax-free cars on Gibraltar plates can be purchased by non-residents.

Income Tax: Employees pay income tax via a PAYE system with progressive rates from 20 (first £1,500) to 50 per cent (above £19,500). 'High net worth individuals' (HNWI) qualify for a special tax allowance under which income tax is a minimum of £10,000 and a maximum of £19,750, irrespective of income (although this is to be phased out). To qualify you must have accommodation available in Gibraltar for your exclusive use for seven months of the year and you must be physically resident for a minimum of 30 days per year. The maximum income liable for tax is £45,000 a year and only income remitted to Gibraltar is taken into account. A non-refundable fee of £500 is payable with an application for HNWI status. Non-residents with Gibraltar source income are taxed at 30 per cent on the first £7,000. Gibraltar has no double taxation treaties.

Capital Gains Tax (CGT): None.

Wealth Tax: None.

Inheritance & Gift Tax: Inheritance tax (called estate duty) is levied progressively from 5 per cent on estates valued between £20,000 and £40,000 to a maximum of 25 per cent on the amount above £100,000. Estate duty for non-residents is payable only on Gibraltar-based property and a home valued at up to £100,000 is exempt if it passes to a surviving spouse or children. Gift tax is levied on gifts made within three years of death.

Value Added Tax (VAT): None. Duty on most imported goods is 12 per cent. Food, books and building materials are zero-rated, and there's a low rate of duty on alcohol, cigarettes and petrol.

Property

Market: Gibraltar has a small property market consisting mostly of new luxury apartments in high-rise blocks built on reclaimed land. Very few old properties are for sale.

Cost: Property in Gibraltar is expensive, reflecting the scarcity of land. Apartments in new luxury developments (e.g. Watergardens and Cormorant Wharf) cost from £90,000 to £300,000 for a two-bedroom apartment. Apartments are sold leasehold (150 years).

Local Mortgages: Most banks and building societies (mainly British) offer mortgages at competitive rates.

Property Taxes: Property tax at 62 per cent is based on the 'net annual value' (NAV) of a property (calculated according to its location and rental value) and is payable in quarterly instalments. Owners of new properties are often exempt from paying full property taxes for a period, e.g. 10 years.

Purchase Procedure: Similar to Britain (see page 148).

Offshore Companies: Property can be owned through an offshore company in order to avoid inheritance tax.

Fees: Stamp duty is 1.26 per cent of the purchase price. Legal fees are around £200 for the first £30,000 of the purchase price and 0.5 to 1 per cent on the balance. There are also small fees for land registry and land title registration.

Precautions: Buyers should employ a local lawyer.

Holiday Letting: There are generally no restrictions, although residents under the HNWI scheme (see **Income Tax** above) must have accommodation available in Gibraltar for their exclusive use for seven months of the year and must be physically resident for one month a year.

Restrictions on Foreign Ownership: None.

Building Standards: New properties are built to very high standards. The quality of old properties is variable.

Personal Effects: No duty is payable on previously owned personal effects. Duty of between 25 and 35 per cent is payable on permanently imported vehicles, although their age and condition is taken into consideration.

General Information

Crime Rate: Gibraltar's crime rate is low (although smuggling tobacco and drugs into Spain is a major industry).

Medical Facilities: Very good. Gibraltar has an international health centre and a general hospital with British-trained medical staff, plus a number of private clinics and many general practitioners. There's a free health service for those who contribute to social security, and EU visitors can take advantage of reciprocal health arrangements. Private health insurance is essential for residents who aren't covered by social security.

Pets: An export health certificate is required and cats and dogs must be vaccinated against rabies, although this isn't necessary if they're imported directly from Britain.

Residence Permits: EU citizens don't require permission to live in Gibraltar, but must have sufficient income to maintain themselves. Non-EU nationals may find obtaining a residence permit difficult unless they have a work permit.

Work Permits: EU nationals have the right to work in Gibraltar, although they must find work within six months of arrival. Work permits are very difficult for non-EU nationals to obtain.

Reference

Useful Addresses

Gibraltar Chronicle, 2 Library Gardens, Gibraltar (☎ 78589).

Gibraltar Information Bureau, 710 Madison Offices, 1155 Fifteenth Street NW, Washington DC 20905, USA (☎ 202-542 1108).

Gibraltar Information Bureau and National Tourist Board, 4 Arundel Great Court, 179 Strand, London WC2R 1EH, UK (☎ 020-7836 0777).

Gibraltar International Business Development Board (GIBDB), PO Box 561, PMB 6194, Suite 944, Europort, Gibraltar (☎ 73175). GIBDB Publishes a comprehensive free guide to Gibraltar.

GREECE

Background Information

Capital: Athens.
Population: 10.7 million.
Foreign Community: Although becoming more popular with foreigners from northern Europe, particularly retirees, Greece doesn't have a large foreign community. However, a significant number of Britons and other EU nationals are resident in Corfu, Crete and other islands.
Area: 131,990km² (50,965mi²).
Geography: Mainland Greece consists of a mountainous peninsula extending some 500km (310mi) into the Mediterranean from the southwest corner of the Balkans, with the Aegian Sea to the east, the Ionian Sea to the west and the Mediterranean Sea to the south. In addition to the mainland, Greece also has some 3,000 islands, around 150 of which are inhabited, comprising around 20 per cent of Greek territory. The mainland and islands have a combined coastline of some 13,350km (8,300mi). The principal structural feature of Greece is the Pindos Mountains extending south-eastwards from the Albanian border and covering most of the peninsula. Some 80 per cent of the mainland is mountainous with 20 mountains over 2,000m/6,560ft (the highest peak is Mount Olympus at 2,900m/9,500ft) and permanently covered in snow. Greece has little flat or cultivated land, and woodland covers around half the country (almost 90 million hectares). Greece has borders with Albania, Bulgaria, Turkey and the former Yugoslavian state of Macedonia (now independent).
Climate: Greece has a Mediterranean climate with long, hot, dry summers and mild sunny winters in the south, although winters can be cold in northern areas. It has some 3,000 hours of sunshine a year and average temperatures above 25°C/77°F in summer, when the oppressive heat is often tempered by a cooling breeze. Spring and autumn are the most pleasant seasons, sunny but not too hot. Annual rainfall varies from around 1.5m in (59in) the north to under 50cm (20in) in the south and is rare anywhere in summer. Athens has the highest high air pollution in western Europe and is often choked with smog, particularly in summer.
Language: Greek. English and other foreign languages such as German are widely spoken in tourist areas.
Political Stability: The least stable country in the EU (only Italy provides any competition), although it has been reasonably stable in recent years. Greek politics are traditionally volatile and are characterised by shaky coalition governments and political and financial scandals. The country was ruled by a military dictatorship from 1967 to 1974. Membership of the EU (since 1981) has brought much needed political and economic stability, although economic performance remains the lowest in the EU. Greece is an enthusiastic member of the EU, although it's unpopular and frequently out of step with its EU partners. It has historically poor relations with its neighbour Turkey, which are exacerbated by Turkey's continuing military occupation of northern Cyprus, although diplomats from both countries have recently been making efforts to resolve the situation, as Cyprus bids to join the EU.

Finance

Currency: Euro (€).
Exchange Rate: £1 = €1.60.
Exchange Controls: Funds imported to buy a property should be officially documented so that the proceeds can be re-exported when it's sold.
Interest Rate: 3.75 per cent.
Cost/Standard of Living: Greece has a lower living standard and cost of living than most other EU countries, although cars and luxury items are expensive, and it has a relatively high rate of inflation. Athens is much more expensive than the rest of the country and is expected to be even more so in the period before the 2004 Olympic Games.
Income Tax: Greece has a PAYE system of income tax with rates ranging from 5 to 45 per cent. Income tax evasion is rife and tax can be increased by the authorities if they decide that your lifestyle is incompatible with your declared income!
Capital Gains Tax (CGT): Gains made by individuals in Greece on the sale of personal assets and property generally aren't subject to CGT. Companies are, however, liable for CGT at 30 per cent on gains from the transfer of any right connected with a company (e.g. a sublease), and there's a 20 per cent tax on gains from the transfer of an entire company or of shares in a limited liability company.
Wealth Tax: Greece has an annual property tax of between 0.3 and 0.8 per cent on property valued at over €205,040, although there are generous personal allowances.
Inheritance & Gift Tax: Inheritance and gift tax are based on the value of the bequest and the relationship between the donor and recipient. Rates are between 25 per cent for relatives of the first degree (spouses and children) and 60 per cent for unrelated beneficiaries.
Value Added Tax (VAT): The standard rate of VAT is 18 per cent. There are reduced rates of 8 per cent (food, medicines, water, transport services) and 4 per cent (books, magazines, newspapers and theatre tickets). Note that on certain island groups such as the Dodecanese, North-Eastern Aegean and the Sporades, the standard and reduced rates are 12.6 and 5.6 per cent respectively.

Property

Market: Greece has a fairly lively property market, as the country has become more popular with foreign homebuyers in recent years. Greece is largely undeveloped, with most areas as unspoilt as Portugal and Spain were 20 or 30 years ago. It has a largely untapped holiday-home market and many areas have good investment potential. There are strict controls over development and renovation to ensure that local character is preserved, particularly in coastal and country areas. Old village houses are reasonably priced and in plentiful supply in most areas, although they usually require extensive renovation. Note that buying and renovating a property in a remote area is unlikely to be a good investment, however low the initial cost. Many foreigners buy a plot of land and build a new house. You can expect to pay a premium for a coastal or island property. Prices are stable in most areas and largely unaffected by world recessions.

Areas: A large number of areas and islands attract foreign property buyers in Greece. The most popular islands include Crete, the Cyclades (e.g. Ios, Mykonos, Naxos, Paros), the Dodecanese (e.g. Rhodes, Kos, Kalymnos), the Ionian Islands (e.g. Corfu, Paxos, Zakynthos), the Sporades (e.g. Skiathos, Skopelos, Alonissos and Skyros), the Saronic Gulf Islands and the Peloponnese Islands. Crete is the most favourable location if you're seeking winter sunshine. The most popular mainland area among foreigners is the Peloponnese.

Cost: Costs vary considerably according to the location and whether you buy a new or an old property. Athens is expensive (although not popular with foreign buyers). New apartments on the islands cost from around €60,000 for one bedroom, €75,000 for two bedrooms and €100,000 for three bedrooms. A new two-bedroom townhouse or villa costs from around €100,000, although prices rise to €150,000 or more in a good location on a small island. A three-bedroom, two-bathroom villa costs from €150,000 (plus €15,000 to €22,000 for a pool). Inland properties are much cheaper than coastal properties.

Old stone houses are common in many areas (e.g. Crete) and can be purchased from around €14,000. However, renovation costs are around two to three times the purchase price. Note that most old village houses tend to be small, e.g. 50 to 75m², with only a few rooms. Like houses, building plots vary considerably in price, although the average cost of a 4,000m² (around an acre) plot in the country is around €60,000. Houses can be built on small plots, e.g. 250m², which can cost as little as €15,000 in a coastal location. However, minimum plot sizes vary with the location (e.g. whether the plot is in a village or in the country), as does the size of building that can be built. A 200m² building usually requires a one-acre site. For smaller plots, the permitted floor area is usually a maximum of 60 to 70 per cent of the plot size.

Local Mortgages: Interest rates in Greece are in line with those set for the whole euro-zone, but local mortgages are only obtainable by Greek residents (Greek banks don't like lending on property). Most people find it's better to obtain a mortgage or loan abroad.

Property Taxes: In 1997 a property tax was introduced, which is levied at between 0.3 and 0.8 per cent on property valued at over €205,040, although there are generous personal allowances.

Purchase Procedure: All property in Greece is owned freehold. A deposit of 10 to 30 per cent (normally 10 per cent) is often paid after a preliminary agreement is signed, detailing the price and date of completion (usually within 30 days). The balance of the purchase price (less the deposit) is payable on signing the purchase deed before a public notary in Greece (or a Greek Consulate General abroad). A property must have full and unencumbered title, or the notary won't proceed with the sale. Your lawyer will pay the transfer and local community tax and register the property deeds with the Land Registry. Note that the origin of funds used to buy property in Greece must be declared to the Bank of Greece using an official import document.

Offshore Companies: Offshore companies can be used to purchase property in Greece and have various financial advantages (as well as making a property easier to sell). However, expert legal advice is essential.

Fees: The fees associated with buying a home in Greece are high and usually total around 15 per cent of the purchase price. Transfer (or purchase) tax is at 10 per cent and an extra 2 per cent is charged on properties in areas covered by the public fire protection service. The tax is assessed on a property's 'objective value' by the local tax office, based on tables issued by the Greek Ministry of Finance. The assessed value is usually around two-thirds of the purchase price. Land registry fees are 0.3 per cent of the assessed value plus a small sum for stamp duties and certificates. A community tax equal to 3 per cent of the property transfer tax is paid to the local municipality for general public services such as road maintenance. Lawyer's fees are normally 1 to 1.5 per cent and notary's fees around 1 to 2 per cent of a property's value. Estate agent's fees are usually paid by the vendor.

Precautions: It's essential that all contracts are checked by a Greek lawyer before you sign any papers or pay any money. You must ensure that the vendor has full title and that a property is free of debts. There are Greek lawyers based in many countries outside Greece (ask your local Greek embassy for a list).

Holiday Letting: No restrictions, although tax is payable on rental income.

Restrictions on Foreign Ownership: There are a few restrictions on foreign property ownership for security reasons, e.g. in some border areas and islands close to Turkey. EU citizens have the same rights as Greeks in most of Greece.

Building Standards: New homes are generally well built and designed. The quality of old properties and restored buildings is variable.

Personal Effects: No duty is payable on imported personal effects, although a five-year residence permit must have been issued by the authorities and an import certificate is required from a Greek embassy or consulate listing all belongings to be imported. A car can be imported duty-free, but must have been owned and used for at least six months abroad.

General Information

Crime Rate: Greece is generally safe and serious crime is rare, although 'petty' crime such as burglary is common.

Medical Facilities: Greece has a national health service for those paying social security, but there are long waiting lists for non-essential treatment. Private health insurance is recommended, even for those covered by social security. Greece has reciprocal health agreements with many countries, and retirees from EU countries enjoy free medical treatment. Note that local medical facilities vary considerably with the area, and you should check the location of the nearest general hospital with emergency facilities, which, if you live on an island, may be on the mainland or another island.

Pets: All animals must have a health certificate issued within 10 days of import stating that they're in good health and free from contagious diseases. Dogs (except those under three months old) must be vaccinated against rabies not less than 20 days or more than 11 months before import.

Residence Permits: A formality for EU nationals, although non-working residents must have sufficient income to maintain themselves in Greece. Visitors can stay for three months without formalities, but a residence permit is required for longer stays: a temporary residence permit for six months followed by a five-year permit.

Work Permits: Work permits are unnecessary for EU nationals but are difficult for others nationals to obtain.

Reference

Further Reading

BUYING A HOME IN GREECE AND CYPRUS, Joanna Styles (Survival Books). *Everything you need to know about buying a home in Greece and Cyprus.*

Useful Addresses

Greek Embassy, 2221 Massachusetts Ave., NW, Washington, DC 20008, USA (☎ 202-939 5800, 💻 www.greekembassy.org).
Greek Embassy, 1A Holland Park, London W11 3TP, UK (☎ 020-7229 3850, 💻 www.greekembassy.org.uk).
National Tourist Office of Greece, 4 Conduit Regent Street, London W1R 0DJ, UK (☎ 020-7734 5997).
National Tourist Office of Greece, 645 Fifth Avenue, Olympic Tower, New York, NY 10022, USA (☎ 212-421 5777).
💻 **www.geocities.com/Athens/7243**. Expatriate information.

IRELAND

Background Information

Capital: Dublin.
Population: 3.7 million.
Foreign Community: Britons make up the largest expatriate community in Ireland and there's also a large American community in Dublin.
Area: 70,280km² (27,137mi²).
Geography: Ireland is the large island situated to the west of Britain in the North Atlantic and is part of the British Isles. However, the Republic of Ireland, with which this section deals, comprises only some 80 per cent of the island of Ireland (or 26 of the 32 counties of Ireland) and excludes the six counties in Northern Ireland that remained part of the United Kingdom when the Republic of Ireland was formed in 1921. Ireland is separated from Britain by the Irish Sea. The Irish landscape consists of rich farmland interspersed with rolling hills, bleak moors and lakes, surrounded by a rocky coastline. The country is largely unspoilt and has little industry and no large cities apart from Dublin.
Climate: Ireland is wet at most times of the year, particularly in the west, hence its green countryside and popular name, the 'Emerald Isle'. It has cold winters and warm summers, when July and August are the hottest months. The climate is similar to that of Britain (see page 148), i.e. cool, damp and changeable for most of the year.
Language: Ireland has two official languages: Irish (or Gaelic) and English. It's mandatory for many government employees to speak Irish, although relatively few people speak it fluently. The everyday language is English, which is spoken by virtually everybody.
Political Stability: Ireland is very stable, and the 'troubles' in Northern Ireland have rarely caused much political unrest in the Republic. Ireland has a conservative

coalition government, which is no longer slow to effect change. Ireland is a member of the European Union (EU), which it joined with the UK and Denmark in 1973. EU subsidies created the highest growth rate in Europe between 1994 and 2000, but this has now slowed and zero growth is predicted for 2002. Relations with the UK government have improved in recent years and both countries have worked hard together towards the peace process in Northern Ireland.

Finance

Currency: Euro (€).
Exchange Rate: £1 = €1.60.
Exchange Controls: None.
Interest Rate: 3.75 per cent.
Cost/Standard of Living: The cost of living is high in Ireland, particularly in relation to salaries, which are relatively low in rural areas. Cars, petrol and luxuries are particularly expensive, although the country also has a rapidly rising standard of living. An increasing number of Britons retire to Ireland, often to take advantage of the high level of benefits paid to pensioners which include free public transport and TV licences, free phone rental plus a number of free calls, free healthcare, and allowances for clothing, electricity and gas.
Income Tax: Ireland has a PAYE system of income tax with rates from 20 to 44 per cent (above €215,190). The first €5,950 is exempt. There's a special dispensation for artists, writers and sports stars, who don't pay tax on their royalties. Non-residents are taxed only on their income from Irish sources. There are large tax allowances for those with a mortgage and dependants.
Capital Gains Tax (CGT): CGT is levied at 20 per cent (except on development land, which attracts CGT at 40 per cent). Gains made on the sale of your principal residence are exempt.
Wealth Tax: None.
Inheritance & Gift Tax: Inheritance tax is called Capital Acquisition Tax (CAT) and is levied at 20 per cent above certain thresholds. The wife and children of a donor are granted exemptions of up to €379,747 each. CAT is payable by the recipient and not the estate. The tax on lifetime gifts is 75 per cent of the inheritance tax rates, with the first €633 exempt.
Value Added Tax (VAT): The standard rate of VAT is 20 per cent. There are reduced rates of 12.5 and 10 per cent on certain goods and services including adults' clothing, footwear and theatre tickets. Most food, children's clothing, medicines and books are zero-rated and services such as insurance, health, education and finance are exempt.

Property

Market: Ireland has a flourishing property market, with home ownership around 80 per cent and the highest in Europe. Ireland has always been popular with the British for holiday homes and an increasing number of Britons retire there. It's particularly popular with outdoor sports enthusiasts (e.g. the hunting, fishing and shooting fraternity) and is becoming a popular destination for continental Europeans seeking holiday homes (e.g. Dutch and Germans). For those with deep pockets, there are period 'stately' homes and large estates in all areas. For those of more modest means, there's a multitude of picturesque cottages and farmhouses. Less attractive, modern bungalows are also popular in all parts of the country. Irish property has been a good investment, with annual price rises of up to 40 per cent, although prices have now stabilised in most areas. (Note that Northern Ireland also has a strong property market and is a popular location for holiday homes – see **Britain** on page 148).

Areas: Those who don't need to live close to Dublin or another town can choose from a wealth of unspoilt rural settings throughout Ireland. Among the most popular areas are almost anywhere on the southern and western coasts, most of which are only a short journey from a regional or international airport. The southern counties are especially popular with foreign buyers, particularly Cork, Kerry and Waterford.

Cost: Property is expensive in Dublin, where the average price is around €112,500 and suburban family homes sell for up to €450,000. As the cost of houses rises, apartments are becoming more popular, particularly in Dublin where a one-bedroom apartment costs from €160,000 and two bedrooms from €250,000. Property in rural areas, however, is good value and a modern semi-detached three-bedroom house costs from around €90,000, a detached three-bedroom house from €105,000 and a four-bedroom bungalow around €130,000. Smaller rural properties in need of modernisation can be purchased from around €50,000, and renovated cottages from around €80,000. Many old rural properties have a large plot of land. Note, however, that in fashionable regions, such as the south-west, prices have risen considerably in recent years as a result of high demand from foreign buyers and you may pay a premium of up to 100 per cent. There are also many fine country houses and estates at prices upwards of €1 million, some of which have been converted into expensive apartments with golf and country club facilities.

Local Mortgages: Mortgages are available from Irish banks. The maximum loan is usually 90 per cent, payable over a period of 15 years. There's a small stamp duty (0.1 per cent) on mortgages above €25,316.

Property Taxes: There's no property tax in Ireland. The only charge normally made to householders is for refuse collection, which ranges from nothing to €650 a year or more, depending on the location of a property.

Purchase Procedure: The purchase procedure is similar to Britain (see page 148), completion taking place six to eight weeks after signing a preliminary contract.

Fees: The fees associated with buying a property in Ireland amount to between 2 and 12 per cent of the price. Legal fees are 1 to 1.5 per cent of the purchase price plus VAT (20 per cent) and there are small fees for land registration (between €125 and €650) and a surveyor (if necessary). VAT is included in the price of new properties. The main fee is stamp duty, which ranges from zero per cent on properties costing up to €126,582 to 9 per cent on properties costing over €632,911 and all properties purchased for investment. Stamp duty is waived for first-time buyers and isn't payable on new properties.:

Holiday Letting: No restrictions.

Restrictions on Foreign Ownership: None.

Building Standards: Generally very good.

Personal Effects: Personal effects (including a motor vehicle) can be imported duty-free provided they've been owned and used for six months. Importation must take place within six months of your arrival or 12 months after the date of the transfer of your normal residence. VAT is payable on vehicles imported into Ireland from outside the EU.

General Information

Crime Rate: The crime rate is low in Ireland, particularly serious crime, although burglary and car theft are a problem in some areas, particularly parts of Dublin.

Medical Facilities: Medical facilities are generally excellent in Ireland, which has a national health scheme for residents paying social security and retirees. However, there's a limited number of public hospitals and practitioners, and it's wise to have private health insurance.

Pets: There are no restrictions on cats and dogs imported from Britain and the Channel Islands, and no documentation is required. Pets imported from most other countries must spend six months in quarantine, although regulations are in process of change, so pet owners should check with a local embassy or consulate before making arrangements.

Residence Permits: Residence permits are a formality for EU nationals, although non-working residents must have sufficient income to maintain themselves. Visitors can stay for three months without formalities, after which a residence permit must be obtained from the Department of Justice.

Work Permits: Unnecessary for EU nationals, but difficult for other foreigners to obtain.

Reference

Further Reading

BUYING A HOME IN IRELAND, Joe Laredo (Survival Books). *Everything you need to know about buying a home in Ireland.*

LIVING & WORKING IN IRELAND, Joe Laredo (Survival Books). *Everything you need to know about living and working in Ireland.*

Useful Addresses

Department of Justice, 72/76 St. Stephen's Green, Dublin 2, Ireland (☎ 01-602 8415).

The Incorporated Law Society of Ireland, Blackhall Place, Dublin 7, Ireland (☎ 01-672 4800, 🖳 www.lawsociety.ie).

The Irish Auctioneers' and Valuers' Institute, 129 Lower Baggot St, Dublin 2, Ireland (☎ 01-678 5685, 🖳 www.ipav.ie).

Irish Embassy, 2234 Massachusetts Ave, NW, Washington, DC 20008, USA (☎ 202-462 3939, 🖳 www.irelandemb.org).

Irish Embassy, 17 Grosvenor Place, London SW1X 7HR, UK (☎ 020-7235 2171, ✉ ir.embassy@lineone.net).

Irish Tourist Board, 150 New Bond Street, London W1Y 0AQ, UK (☎ 020-7493 3201).

ITALY

Background Information

Capital: Rome.
Population: 56.8 million.
Foreign Community: There are many foreigners in the major Italian cities and also foreign communities in many resorts and rural areas, particularly in central and northern Italy, including some 40,000 Britons.
Area: 301,302km² (116,342mi²).
Geography: Italy has a wide variety of landscape and vegetation, characterised by its two mountain ranges, the Alps and the Apennines (almost 80 per cent of the country is covered by hills and mountains). The Alps, where there are a number of peaks over 4,000m (13,000ft), extend across northern Italy and include the Dolomite range in the east. The Apennines, where the Corno Grande (2,912m/9,554ft) is the highest peak, form the backbone of the Italian peninsula. The Alpine foothills are characterised by the vast Po Valley and the lakes of Como, Garda and Maggiore. The Po is Italy's longest river, flowing from east to west across the plain of Lombardy in the north into the Adriatic. Northern Italy has large areas of wood and farmland, while the south is mostly scrubland. Italy's principal islands are Sicily (with the active volcano of Mount Etna at 3,342m/10,965ft) and Sardinia, plus Elba, Capri and Ischia. Italy, which is shaped like a boot, has a vast coastline of some 7,500km (4,660mi) and borders with Austria, France, Slovenia and Switzerland.
Climate: Italy has a temperate climate influenced by the Mediterranean and Adriatic Seas. Summers are generally very hot everywhere, with average summer temperatures in July and August around 24°C/75°F. Winters are cold and dry in the Alps, damp in the Po Valley and mild on the Italian Riviera and in Sicily. Rainfall is moderate to low in most regions and is rare anywhere in summer; fog is common in the north in autumn.
Language: Italian. Minorities speak German (Alto Adige), French (Valle d'Aosta), Slovene and Ladino, and there are also numerous regional dialects. French is widely understood and English is spoken in the major cities and tourist centres.
Political Stability: Italy is one of the most politically unstable countries in the European Union (EU), although this appears to have little outward effect on the country's economy. There have been numerous changes of government since the Second World War, largely because Italy's system of proportional representation almost guarantees fragmented and shaky coalition governments (an attempt at electoral reform in recent years appears to have had little effect). In April 2001, the country held its 59th general election since 1945, which was won by a right-wing coalition led by Silvio Berlusconi, who has several trials pending for corruption and misuse of public funds! Italy is a founder member of the EU.

Finance

Currency: Euro (€).
Exchange Rate: £1 = €1.60.

Exchange Controls: None. Sums above €10,000 must be declared and their source registered.

Interest Rate: 3.75 per cent.

Cost/Standard of Living: There's a huge disparity between the cost and standard of living in the prosperous north and central regions of Italy, and the relatively poor south. The cost of living in the major cities is much the same as in cities in Britain, France and Germany, although overall Italy has a slightly lower cost of living than northern European countries. Luxury and quality products are expensive, as are cars, but wine and spirits are inexpensive.

Income Tax: Income tax (IRPEF) is high in Italy and ranges from 19 (up to €7,745) to 46 per cent (over €82,350). Tax evasion is widespread. Residents require a fiscal number (*codice fiscale*) which must be used in all communications with the tax authorities. Non-residents must file a tax return stating the details of their Italian property, as property is considered to provide an income whether it's let or used as a private residence. The 'assumed' income is based on the cadastral value (*rendita catastale*).

Capital Gains Tax (CGT): CGT isn't levied on property but gains made on stocks and shares are levied at two rates: 12.5 and 27 per cent depending on the gain.

Wealth Tax: None.

Inheritance & Gift Tax: Inheritance tax varies between 3 and 33 per cent according to the relationship of beneficiaries to the deceased. Estates valued below €152,500 left to a spouse, children or parents and estates valued below €61,000 left to direct relatives are exempt.

Value Added Tax (VAT): The standard rate of VAT is 20 per cent and there are reduced rates of 10 and 4 per cent. VAT is payable on new properties at 4 per cent for non-luxury property and 20 per cent for luxury property.

Property

Market: There's a lively property market in Italy where there's a high and steady demand for second homes from both Italians and foreigners, although few developments are built solely for foreigners, particularly holiday-home developments such as are common in some other European countries. In many areas the countryside and coastline have been damaged by uncontrolled development (only around 10 per cent of Italy's 7,500km coastline remains undeveloped, while others (such as Tuscany) have hardly changed in centuries. New development in Tuscany and some other areas is prohibited and renovation is strictly regulated, e.g. existing buildings must be replaced with properties built in the same style and or the same size.

Many inland towns and villages are almost totally unspoilt. In cities, people generally live in apartments, houses being rare and prohibitively expensive. The best buys are old rural or village period houses requiring renovation. Properties are advertised in local property newspapers such as **Panorama Casa** in Tuscany and national property magazines such as the weekly **Casa per Casa** or the monthly *Ville & Casali* (mainly for up-market properties). Despite high prices in many areas, Italian property is generally an excellent investment, particularly in cities and popular resort areas.

Areas: There are numerous alluring areas for foreign property buyers in Italy. The most popular areas are those north of Rome including Tuscany, Liguria, Umbria, Lombardy, Le Marche, Veneto and Piedmont. So many Britons have purchased homes in Tuscany that the Chianti region has been dubbed 'Chiantishire'. However, much of Tuscany is and poor value, although it can still be a good investment. Reasonably priced homes can be found in northern Tuscany (e.g. in Lunigiana north of Lucca), which offers much better value than most of southern Tuscany. Rising prices in Tuscany have led British and other foreign buyers to cast their nets wider and many have turned to Umbria, le Marche and Liguria.

The northern Adriatic coast, the Italian Lakes, the Italian Riviera (e.g. Portofino, San Remo), and the Amalfi coast (e.g. Positano, Sorrento) are also popular for holiday homes, as are Sardinia and Sicily. Property on the Italian Riviera is expensive, but is better value than the French Riviera. Italy also has a wide choice of resorts for those seeking a winter holiday home, including Bormio, Cervinia, Cortina, Courmayeur and Sestriere.

Cost: Property prices in Italy vary considerably and are generally high in cities and towns and relatively low in rural areas (except where high demand from foreign buyers has driven them up). Prices were flat or slumped in Italy's major cities during the recession, in stark contrast to the most popular areas for second homes where they remained stable or even rose. Although you can spend €hundreds of thousands on a luxurious *palazzo* or a large country estate, it's also possible to buy a small one or two-bedroom renovated apartment or village house from around €55,000. In many areas, old village houses in need of complete restoration can be purchased from as little as €30,000. However, you should expect to pay two or three times the purchase price in restoration costs (which are around €720 to €800 per m² plus architect's and surveyor's fees). In many rural areas, around €95,000 will buy a restored two-bedroom farmhouse and a bit of land. However, you can pay over €400,000 for a small farmhouse in a fashionable area of Tuscany.

Prices have remained stable in recent years on the Italian Riviera and are between €6,000 and €7,000 per m² for a quality apartment with a view in a top resort such as Portofino. In the Cinque Terre villages of Liguria, apartments can be purchased for around €2,500 per m². In some Riviera towns, small one-bedroom apartments cost from around €120,000 and two-bedroom apartments from €135,000. The Italian lakes are another popular area, which is reflected in the above average prices, e.g. €95,000 for a new or restored one-bedroom apartment on Lake Como or Maggiore and €145,000 for a two-bedroom apartment. If you dream of living in Venice, a studio on the Grand Canal will set you back around €550,000! On the other hand, holiday apartments in Sicily start at around €65,000. Winter holiday homes are a good investment and have good letting potential, although they're relatively expensive. In a top resort such as Cortina, you will pay around €95,000 to €130,000 for a studio, €130,000 to €160,000 for a one-bedroom apartment, and up to €240,000 for a two-bedroom apartment. **Always barter over the price of property in Italy, as owners invariably ask for more than they expect to receive (but don't show too much enthusiasm or the price is likely to increase suddenly!).**

Local Mortgages: Mortgages are available from Italian banks, although they usually take a long time to be approved and you can generally obtain better terms and a larger loan from a foreign lender. Maximum loans from Italian banks are generally 50 or 60 per cent for second homes and 75 per cent for principal homes. The usual term is 5 to 15 years. If you import funds to buy a property in Italy, it should be officially registered by your Italian bank.

Property Taxes: A local community tax (*imposta comunale sugli immobili*//ICI) is paid by all owners of property or land in Italy, whether they're resident or non-resident. It's levied at between 0.4 to 0.7 per cent of a property's cadastral value (*valore catastale*), the actual rate being decided by the local municipality depending on a property's size, location, class and category. ICI is paid in two instalments in June and December.

Purchase Procedure: When buying a property in Italy, you must sign a preliminary contract (*contratto preliminare di vendita, promessa di vendita* or *compromesso di vendita*), which may be drawn up by the vendor, the estate agent or a lawyer. The preliminary contract, which can be hand-written or a standard printed document, may be preceded by a binding 'buying proposal', where the buyer is legally bound to buy, but the vendor and agent are free to consider other offers. On signing the preliminary contract, both parties are bound to the transaction. A deposit (*capara penitenziale*) of around 10 per cent (but possibly up to 30 per cent) is paid to a notary (*notaio*), which is forfeit if the buyer doesn't go through with the purchase (if the vendor reneges, he must pay the buyer double the deposit). Note that the deposit should be described as *caparra penitenziale* and not as *caparra confirmatoria*, as the latter allows the vendor to take legal action to force a buyer to go through with a purchase.

The preliminary contract contains the essential terms of the sale, including the purchase price, the financing plan, the closing date, and any other conditions that must be fulfilled prior to completion. A sale must be completed within the period stipulated in the *compromesso*, usually six to eight weeks (although it can be from two weeks to three or four months). The sale is completed before a notary when the final deed or 'conveyance of transfer' (*atto di compravendita* or *scrittura privata*) is signed. The notary issues a certified copy of the deed of sale and registers the original document with the land registry (*Registro Immobiliare*). Registration is of paramount importance, as until a property is registered you aren't the legal owner. Note that there are two kinds of deed in Italy: a private deed and a public instrument, which provides more protection but is more expensive. When a property is purchased by private deed and is subsequently found to have a charge against it, such as a mortgage, the notary isn't responsible. When buying by public instrument, you can happily sue the notary for professional misconduct. All properties in Italy are owned freehold.

Offshore Companies: It's possible to buy a property in Italy through an offshore or overseas company.

Fees: Total fees when buying a property in Italy are usually between 8 and 15 per cent of the purchase price. Registration tax or stamp duty ranges from 4 to 19 per cent of the declared price plus a fixed fee. Notary fees depend on the price of a property and are higher (as a percentage of the price) on cheaper properties. They're generally between 2 and 4 per cent of the declared price and legal fees around 2 per cent. A surveyor's fee is usually from around €300, but can be up to €825 for a large property with an extensive plot. The estate agent's fee (and who pays it) varies considerably, although it's usually shared between the vendor and buyer, e.g. around 3 per cent each. VAT is payable on new homes at 4 per cent (on non-luxury buildings) or 20 per cent (for luxury homes with a rating of A1 in the property register) and is included in the price. Registration tax on new homes is levied at a flat rate of €77.

Precautions: It's important to deal only with a qualified and licensed agent, and to engage a local lawyer (*avvocato*), before signing anything or paying a deposit. A local surveyor (*geometra*) may also be necessary, particularly if you're buying an old property or a property with a large plot. Your lawyer or surveyor will carry out the necessary searches regarding such matters as rights of way. Enquiries must be made to ensure that the vendor has a registered title and that there are no debts against a property (e.g. mortgages or taxes). It's also important to ensure that a property has the relevant building licences, conforms to local planning conditions and that any changes have been notified to the local town hall. If a property is owned by several members of a family, which is common in rural areas, *all* owners must give their consent before it can be sold. With regard to a rural property, it's important to ensure that there's a reliable water supply.

Holiday Letting: No restrictions.

Restrictions on Foreign Ownership: None.

Building Standards: Vary from excellent to poor. New buildings are generally very well constructed. The quality of renovations varies, but is usually very good.

Personal Effects: Personal effects (including a motor vehicle) can be imported duty-free provided they've been owned and used for at least six months. A certificate of residence or proof of having purchased a home is required, and belongings must be imported within six months of taking up residence. It's necessary to make an inventory of all items being imported and to have it stamped by an Italian consulate.

General Information

Crime Rate: The crime rate in Italy varies considerably from region to region. Violent crime is rare, although muggings do occur in resort areas and there are armed (and dangerous) bandits in some parts of southern Italy. Burglary is a problem in most areas and car crime is widespread. Vespa (motor scooter) thieves are common in some cities. Although organised crime and gang warfare is rife in some areas, it has no discernible impact on the lives of most foreigners in Italy (particularly in rural areas).

Medical Facilities: Medical facilities in Italy vary from poor to excellent. Italy has a public health service, although it's over-stretched and under-funded and the quality of service varies considerably with the region. Private health insurance is highly recommended.

Pets: There's no quarantine period for pets in Italy, but they need a certificate of health from an approved veterinary surgeon. Cats and dogs over 12 weeks old need a rabies vaccination not less than 20 days and not more than 11 months prior to the date of issue of the health certificate. Animals may be examined at the Italian port of entry by a veterinary officer.

Residence Permits: Prospective residents must obtain a residence permit within eight days of arrival, which is valid for one year and renewable annually. Visitors may remain for three months and extensions can be obtained.

Work Permits: Unnecessary for EU nationals, but difficult for others to obtain.

Reference

Further Reading

BUYING A HOME IN ITALY, David Hampshire (Survival Books). *Everything you need to know about buying a home in Italy.*
LIVING & WORKING IN ITALY, Nick Daws (Survival Books). *Everything you need to know about living and working in Italy.*
Belle Cose, c/o Brian French & Associates, The Nook, Sowerby St, Sowerby Bridge, West Yorkshire HX6 3AJ, UK (☎ 0870-730 1910, 💻 www.brianfrench.com). Quarterly property magazine.
Casa e Country, Via Burigozzo 5, 20122 Milan, Italy (☎ 02-58219). Glossy home decoration and country homes magazine with some property listings.
Casa per Casa, Via Valtellina 21, 20092 Cinisello Balsamo (MI), Italy (☎ 02-660 6161, 💻 www.casapercasa.it). Weekly free property magazine published in regional editions.
The Informer, BuroService Snc, Via dei Tigli 2, 20020 Arese (MI), Italy (☎ 02-935 81477, 💻 www.theinformer.it). Monthly magazine for people living in Italy.
La Mia Italia (Italian State Tourist Board). Free booklet.
A Small Place in Italy, Eric Newby (Picador).
Urban Land and Property Markets in Italy, Gastone Ave (UCLP).
Ville e Casali, Via Anton Giulio Bragaglia, 33, 00123 Rome, Italy (☎ 06-3088 4122, ✉ direzione@eli.it). Glossy monthly property and home decoration magazine.

Useful Addresses

Italian Embassy, 1601 Fuller St, NW, Washington, DC 20009, USA (☎ 202-328 5500).
Italian Embassy, 14 Three Kings Yard, Davies St, London W1Y 2EH, UK (☎ 020-7312 2200, 💻 www.embitaly.org.uk).
Italian Government Travel Office, 630 Fifth Avenue, Suite 1565, New York, NY 10111, USA (☎ 212-245 4822).
Italian State Tourist Board, 1 Princes St, London W1R 8AY, UK (☎ 020-7408 1254, 💻 www.enit.it/uk).

MALTA

Background Information

Capital: Valletta.
Population: 375,000.
Foreign Community: There are around 5,000 British residents in Malta and many more holiday homeowners, but relatively few residents from other countries.
Area: 316km² (122mi²).
Geography: Malta is situated in the middle of the Mediterranean 93km (58mi) south of Sicily and 290km (180mi) from North Africa (Libya), and consists of three main

islands, Malta, Gozo, Comino, and the small uninhabited islands of Cominotto and Filfla. The island of Malta, by far the largest, is 27km long and 14.5km wide at its maximum and has a coastline of 137km/85mi, indented with natural harbours, sandy beaches and rocky coves. Most of Malta consists of an undulating limestone plateaux with no mountains, woodland, rivers or lakes. All available land is under cultivation.

Climate: Malta has hot, dry summers and mild, damp winters. The temperature ranges from 10 to 21°C/50 to 70°F in January and 25 to 33°C/77 to 91°C in July. Malta enjoys an average of eight hours' sunshine a day. Most rain falls in winter and spring, with around 7.5cm (3in) between October and March and just 1cm in the remaining six months.

Language: Maltese. Most Maltese speak English, which is also an official language. Italian is widely understood.

Political Stability: The political stability of Malta has been excellent in recent years and the government encourages (through tax breaks) foreign retirees to live in Malta. Malta is a member of the British Commonwealth and has applied for membership of the European Union. It has had a high growth rate and low inflation in recent years and is an offshore financial centre.

Finance

Currency: Maltese lira (Lm).

Exchange Rate: £1 = Lm0.60.

Exchange Controls: Yes. Funds imported to buy a property should be officially documented so that on its sale the proceeds can be re-exported.

Interest Rate: 4.5 per cent.

Cost/Standard of Living: Malta's cost of living is around 10 to 15 per cent lower than northern European countries. However, although food and essential services are reasonably priced, imported 'luxury' goods are expensive.

Income Tax: Malta has a PAYE income tax system for employees at rates of from 15 to 35 per cent. There are a number of tax concessions for retirees and temporary residents. Foreign residents must have an income of at least Lm10,000 a year or assets of Lm150,000 and must remit to Malta at least Lm6,000 (for a single person) a year plus Lm1,000 a year for each dependant. Tax is assessed on these remittances at 15 per cent, less personal allowances, with a minimum income tax bill of Lm1,000 per year. Income that isn't remitted to Malta isn't taxed there. Visitors can spend six months per year in Malta without paying income tax; those whose stay exceeds six months per year are taxed at between 10 and 35 per cent on remittances to Malta.

Capital Gains Tax (CGT): CGT at 7 per cent is levied on gains made since January 1993 on income and property, although property is exempt from CGT after three years' ownership.

Wealth Tax: None.

Inheritance & Gift Tax: Malta levies a transmission (transfer) tax of 5 per cent on property inherited in Malta. If the recipient is the spouse, transfer tax is levied on half the property's value.

Value Added Tax (VAT): The standard rate of VAT is 15 per cent, with a reduced rate of 10 per cent for hotel and holiday accommodation and restaurant food.

Property

Market: A wide range of properties are available, both old and new. Old character village homes and farmhouses that have been restored and modernised are popular with foreigners. Old properties are usually full of charm, although garages are rare and much sought-after. Modern properties are generally larger than the average in many other countries, although modern apartment buildings are often uniform in style and externally unattractive. A number of new developments are targeted at the foreign retirement market. All property is sold freehold.

Areas: There are numerous attractive areas to live in Malta, including both inland villages and coastal areas. Among the most popular towns are Bugibba, Mellieha, Marsaxlokk, Qawra, St Pauls Bay and Xemxija. Other popular areas include Mdina, Mosta, Rabat and Sliema (particularly St Julians). The island of Malta has a high population density, particularly in the area surrounding Valletta, where two-thirds of the population lives. Gozo is quieter than Malta with a slower pace of life, although its population has increased considerably in recent years.

Cost: Property prices are lower than in northern Europe, although strong local demand has pushed them up in recent years. The minimum price of a property purchased by a non-resident foreigner is Lm15,000 and to qualify as a permanent resident the minimum cost is Lm30,000 in the case of an apartment and Lm50,000 for a house. Typical prices are two or three-bedroom apartments from Lm30,000, converted two-bedroom village houses from Lm70,000, two or three-bedroom townhouses from Lm80,000, and three-bedroom detached houses from Lm180,000 (although a detached house in a fashionable area can cost around Lm350,000). Prices on Gozo are lower and include two-bedroom apartments from Lm20,000, three-bedroom bungalows from Lm75,000 and three-bedroom detached villas from Lm120,000.

Local Mortgages: Mortgages are available from Maltese banks, although facilities are limited and you can usually obtain better terms from a foreign lender. Local mortgages are usually for a maximum of 25 per cent of a property's value and terms are limited to 10 years.

Property Taxes: None.

Purchase Procedure: Permission is required from the Ministry of Finance to buy a property, although this is only a formality. Documentary evidence is required that the funds used to purchase a property originated abroad. A preliminary or 'promise of sale' agreement is signed, binding both vendor and purchaser to the sale, subject to good title and the issue of any appropriate permits. A deposit of 10 per cent is paid and deposited in a trustee (escrow) account. The preliminary agreement is usually valid for three months (or longer if both parties agree), during which time a public notary undertakes searches to prove good title and submits applications for government permits. The final purchase contract is signed once the permits are issued, when the balance is paid plus all fees. Contracts may be written in English.

Fees: Total fees are around 6.5 per cent of the purchase price. They include 5 per cent stamp duty, 1 per cent notary's fee, a Ministry of Finance fee of Lm100, and search and registration fees. Estate agents' fees are usually paid by the vendor.

Precautions: No particular precautions are necessary when buying property in Malta, although you should deal with a reputable local agent and engage a local lawyer to carry out the necessary checks.

Holiday Letting: Non-Maltese can only let a property if it's a villa, bungalow or farmhouse with a private swimming pool, although apartments in some new developments in designated areas may also be let. Permission must be obtained through estate agents and costs around Lm350 per year.

Restrictions on Foreign Ownership: Foreigners are permitted to buy only one property per family. Permits to build new properties are almost impossible to obtain.

Building Standards: Good, although the design of new buildings, particularly apartment blocks, often leaves much to be desired.

Personal Effects: There's no import duty on personal effects (including one car) for anyone who spends at least 200 days a year in Malta. Goods must have been owned and used for at least six months and must be imported within six months of your arrival. A motor vehicle imported duty-free must not be sold in Malta for three years. Holiday homeowners must obtain an import licence and pay customs duty on imported goods.

General Information

Crime Rate: The crime rate in Malta is exceptionally low, although precautions must be taken against burglary.

Medical Facilities: Medical facilities are generally very good and there's a major general hospital on the island of Malta (with mostly British-trained medical staff) and a number of 24-hour health centres. Free health care is provided for permanent residents and reduced hospital charges for holders of temporary residence permits. Residents and visitors who aren't covered by reciprocal agreements need private health insurance.

Pets: There's a quarantine period of three weeks for dogs and cats imported from Australia, Britain and New Zealand; for pets imported from other rabies-free countries the quarantine period is six months. Pets cannot be imported from countries which aren't free of rabies.

Residence Permits: Permanent residents need to purchase a property of a minimum value and have a minimum income level (see above under **Income Tax** and **Cost**). Visitors may remain for three months and can obtain a three-month extension. A special category of 'temporary residence' allows foreigners to remain in Malta 'permanently' without becoming residents. However, they must provide evidence that they have sufficient income to support themselves.

Work Permits: Very difficult to obtain.

Reference

Further Reading

Malta Property News, Frank Salt, 2 Paceville Avenue, Paceville, Malta (🖳 www. franksalt.com.mt). Free bi-monthly property magazine.

Guide to Buying Property in Malta, Frank Salt (see above).

Useful Addresses

Acquisition of Immovable Property Section, Ministry of Finance, St Calcedonius Square, Floriana CMR 02, Malta (☎ 236306).
Association of Estate Agents in Malta, PO Box 18, Sliema, Malta (☎ 343370, 🖳 www.maltaestateagents.com).
Department for Citizenship and Expatriate Affairs, 3 Castille Place, Valletta CMR 02, Malta (☎ 250569).
Maltese Consulate, 2017 Connecticut Ave, NW, Washington, DC 20008, USA (☎ 202-462 3611).
Maltese High Commission, Malta House, 36–38 Piccadilly, London W1V 0PP, UK (☎ 020-7292 4800).
Malta National Tourist Office, Suite 300, Mappin House, 4 Winsley Street, London W1N 7AR, UK (☎ 020-7292 4900).

NEW ZEALAND

Background Information

Capital: Wellington.
Population: 3.7 million.
Foreign Community: New Zealand is largely a nation of migrants (around three-quarters of the population is of European descent) and a cosmopolitan country, although less so than Australia. The bulk of migrants still come from Britain (and a few other European countries), although in recent years there has been an increasing number of Asian and South African immigrants. The indigenous Maori race makes up around 10 per cent of the population (some 350,000) and Polynesians (mostly from Fiji, Samoa and Tonga) 4 per cent. Auckland has the largest concentration of Polynesians in the world. Chinese and Indians each comprise around 1 per cent of the population.
Area: 268,680km^2 (103,737mi^2).
Geography: New Zealand is situated in the South Pacific, some 2,200km (1,370mi) east of Australia. It comprises two main islands, called simply North Island and South Island, which differ considerably in geography, vegetation and character. The country is almost 1,600km (994mi) long and 420km (260mi) wide at its widest point. New Zealand also comprises a number of outlying islands, including Stewart and Chatham Islands and territories in the Pacific such as the Kermadec Islands and Kiribati. It's a mountainous country with some three-quarters of the land above 200m (650ft) and over half forested. The highest peak is Mount Cook in the Southern Alps (3,764m/ 12,349ft) on the South Island, which divides the wet rain forests on the west coast from the dry pasture lands on the east coast. New Zealand is one of the world's most beautiful and unspoilt countries, with some 30 per cent consisting of protected conservation sites. The country is noted for its wealth of volcanoes, geysers, glaciers, fjords (lakes), rivers and lush vegetation. The South Island in particular has an abundance of unspoilt mountain scenery and a thriving skiing industry in winter.
Climate: Most of New Zealand has a temperate oceanic climate (the exception being the far north, which is sub-tropical) and four distinct seasons that are opposite to those

in the northern hemisphere. Summers are hot throughout the country and there are sometimes heat waves in December or January. Winters are cold and temperatures sometimes fall below freezing during the day on the east coast and snow isn't uncommon in Christchurch (South Island). The northern part of the South Island usually has the mildest weather and the most sunshine (an average of around 6.5 hours a day). Average rainfall in the North Island is 135cm (53in) per year, while in the South Island it varies considerably between the east and west coasts. Rainfall is very high (usually torrential) on the west coast, where many areas receive over 5m (195in) of rain per year. The eastern coasts of both islands are much drier, e.g. in Auckland it rains on around 12 days a month in winter and six days a month in summer, while Christchurch has rain on around six days a month all year round. New Zealand's major cities also suffer from strong winds, Wellington being the windiest capital city in the world, deserving its nickname of 'The Windy City'. Temperatures are moderate outside the mountainous areas, averaging 23°C (73°F) in summer and 14°C (57°F) in winter in Auckland, 22°C (72°F) and 11°C (52°F) in Christchurch, 19°C (66°F) and 11°C (52°F) in Dunedin, and 20°C (68°F), and 14°C (57°F) in Wellington.

Language: English and Maori are both official languages, and most official signs and forms are bi-lingual.

Political Stability: Excellent. New Zealand is a parliamentary democracy modelled on the British system. Politics have traditionally been dominated by the Labour (left) and National (conservative) parties, although a system of proportional representation introduced in recent years has made it more difficult for one party to obtain an overall majority. New Zealand is a member of the British Commonwealth and Queen Elizabeth II is head of state.

Finance

Currency: New Zealand dollar (NZ$).

Exchange Rate: £1 = NZ$3.45.

Exchange Controls: None.

Interest Rate: 5.57 per cent.

Cost/Standard of Living: New Zealand enjoys a high standard of living, ranked as the tenth highest in the world according to a recent survey and exceeding that of Australia. The cost of living is reasonable, with food and essential goods and services relatively inexpensive. Imported goods such as motor vehicles and electrical goods are expensive, although prices have fallen in real terms in recent years. Many New Zealanders own second homes (known as a *bach* or a *crib*) in the country or on the coast.

Income Tax: New Zealand has a PAYE system where income tax is deducted from gross salaries at source. Income tax rates are 15 per cent (on income up to NZ$9,500), 19.5 per cent (NZ$9,500 to NZ$38,000), and 33 per cent (over NZ$38,000).

Capital Gains Tax (CGT): None.

Wealth Tax: None.

Inheritance & Gift Tax: There's no inheritance tax in New Zealand. Gifts above NZ$27,000 in any year are taxed on a graduated scale up to 25 per cent (on gifts exceeding NZ$72,000).

Value Added Tax (VAT): New Zealand has a goods and services tax (equivalent to VAT) of 12.5 per cent. It's usually included in the advertised price rather than added when you pay (as in the USA). There are various exemptions including residential property, financial services and rented accommodation.

Property

Market: New Zealand has a thriving property market with some 75 per cent of families owning their own homes. The most common home is a single-storey detached house built on a plot known as a section, traditionally a quarter of an acre and dubbed 'the quarter acre paradise' (although plots are now often smaller, as many sections have been subdivided by developers). Apartments (usually called units) and townhouses are common in cities, but are rare elsewhere. Most homes are constructed of wood and brick, and the variety of architecture is limited. Wooden Victorian villas are popular. (Most older houses are made of Kauri wood.)

Areas: The most popular areas are the major cities, i.e. Auckland, Christchurch and Wellington. Popular regions for second homes are the Coromandel Peninsula and the Bay of Islands in the extreme north of the North Island, and the Southern Alps, the Glaciers, Mount Cook and Milford Sound on the South Island. The most popular areas for retirement homes on the North Island include the Coromandel Peninsula, the Bay of Islands, the Bay of Plenty and the Kapati Coast (north of Wellington). In the South Island, the northern Marlborough region (e.g. Blenheim, Nelson and Picton) is popular, as is Banks Peninsula south of Christchurch.

Cost: The average price of a three-bedroom detached house ranges from around NZ$80,000 in Otago to NZ$200,000 in Auckland, the average being around NZ$160,000. Apartments are often more expensive than houses and townhouses, as they're invariably located in inner cities (inner city living has become fashionable in recent years), whereas most houses are located in suburbs or in the country. Advertised prices are usually up to 10 per cent above a property's actual market value.

Local Mortgages: Mortgages of up to 80 per cent are available from all major banks and building societies. The maximum repayment term is 25 years, although the current trend is for 20 or even 15 years.

Property Taxes: Property taxes (residential rates), which usually include water charges, are levied by local authorities according to the size of a property. The annual bill for an average family house is between NZ$1,000 and NZ$2,000 (the average in Auckland is NZ$1,142). In some areas there are additional fees for certain services, e.g. refuse collection and water.

Purchase Procedure: A deposit of 10 per cent is payable when a contract is signed. This is usually non-refundable, but most contracts include a clause requiring its return if the title to the property isn't clear or land is subject to government requisition (compulsory purchase).

Fees: Lawyer's fees are usually between NZ$1,000 and NZ$2,000, and there's a land transfer registration fee of NZ$150. Banks levy a mortgage processing fee of 1 per cent of the mortgage amount and require a deposit (usually a minimum of NZ$500) on application.

Precautions: It isn't wise to sign a contract before taking legal advice and confirming that the title is clear, as this commits you to the purchase. Many estate agents try to get purchasers to sign as soon as a sale is agreed. If you feel obliged to sign a contract before the conveyance checks are complete, you should ask your lawyer to insert a clause in the contract to the effect that it's is null and void if any problems arise.

Holiday Letting: No restrictions.

Restrictions on Foreign Ownership: Foreigners can buy property of less than one acre without any restrictions. For property exceeding one acre, permission is required from the District Land Registrar or the Land Value Tribunal. Permission isn't required if permanent residence has been granted.

Building Standards: Generally excellent, although corrugated iron roofs and weatherboard (wooden) exterior walls are used on cheaper houses, which don't always stand up well to the inclement weather.

Personal Effects: Permanent residents can import goods owned for 12 months (including a car) without payment of duty, subject to certain restrictions.

General Information

Crime Rate: Low. New Zealand is a safe country with a low rate of violent and serious crime. However, in common with most other western countries, crime has risen in the last decade. Auckland has a substantially higher crime rate than rural areas.

Medical Facilities: Very Good. New Zealand has a national health system for residents, although there are long waiting lists for non-urgent hospital treatment. The state scheme does not pay for visits to a doctor, prescriptions (although they're subsidised), optometrists (opticians) or dental treatment. Over 30 per cent of New Zealanders have supplementary private health insurance, which is highly recommended as it pays the cost of treatment that isn't covered by the state system and includes private hospital care. Reciprocal agreements cover visitors from many countries, including Britain, and medical treatment for injuries sustained in an accident is provided free for all visitors.

Pets: The regulations for importing animals into New Zealand are rigorous and include vaccinations and veterinary checks. An import permit is required and most pets are subject to a quarantine period. The exceptions are animals from Australia, Norway, Sweden, the UK and Hawaii, which aren't subject to quarantine but must undergo veterinary checks.

Residence Permits: New Zealand has a permanent programme of immigration with an annual quota, e.g. 45,000 in 2001. As with Australia, immigration is decided on a selective policy based on a points system, with priority given to those with special skills that are in demand and those wishing to start a business.

Work Permits: Authorisation is required from a New Zealand Consulate under the points system mentioned above.

Reference

Further Reading

LIVING & WORKING IN NEW ZEALAND, Mark Hempshell (Survival Books). *Everything you need to know about living and working in New Zealand.*

Destination New Zealand, 1 Commercial Road, Eastbourne, East Sussex BN21 3XQ, UK (☎ 01323-726040, 💻 www.outbound-newspapers.com).
New Zealand Outlook, 3 Buckhurst Road, Bexhill-on-Sea, East Sussex TN40 1QF, UK (☎ 01424-223111, 💻 www.consylpublishing.co.uk).
New Zealand News UK, PO Box 10, Berwick-upon-Tweed, Northumberland TD15 1BW, UK (☎ 01289-306677).

Useful Addresses

Department of Land Information, 160 Lambton Quay, PO Box 5501, Wellington, New Zealand (☎ 04-473 5022, 💻 www.linz.govt.nz).
Harcourts Group, 28 Grey Street, PO Box 151, Wellington, New Zealand (☎ 0800-804805, 💻 www.harcourts.co.nz). New Zealand's largest estate agency group. Publishes 'Blue Book' guides to the property market in the major areas.
The New Zealand High Commission, New Zealand House, Haymarket, London SW1Y 4TQ, UK (☎ 020-7930 8422, 💻 www.nzembassy.com).
New Zealand Embassy, 37 Observatory Circle, NW, Washington, DC 20008, USA (☎ 202-328-4800, 💻 www.nzemb.org).
New Zealand Tourism Board, New Zealand House, Haymarket, London SW1Y 4TQ, UK (☎ 020-7973 0360).
Real Estate Agents Licensing Board, PO Box 1247, Wellington, New Zealand (☎ 04-520 6949).

PORTUGAL

Background Information

Capital: Lisbon.
Population: 10.3 million.
Foreign Community: Portugal has large expatriate communities from Britain, Germany and various Scandinavian countries, mostly on the Algarve and in Lisbon, and a considerable number of Brazilians.
Area: 92,000km² (32,225mi²).
Geography: Portugal is situated in the extreme south-west corner of Europe, occupying around one sixth of the Iberian peninsula, with an Atlantic coastline of over 800km (500mi). It has a huge variety of landscapes including sandy beaches, rugged mountains, rolling hills, vast forests (over a quarter of the country is forested) and flat grasslands. Portugal also owns Madeira (and its neighbouring island of Porto Santo) and the Azores in the Atlantic. Madeira, which is situated off the West African coast north of the Canary Islands and around 1,000km (620mi) south-west of Lisbon, is 56km (34mi) in length and 21km (13mi) wide and has a population of 300,000. Like the Azores it has volcanic origins and is green and mountainous with few beaches. The Azores, north-west of Madeira and approximately 1,500km (960mi) west of Lisbon, comprise nine islands covering an area of 2,350km² (907mi²), with a population of around 250,000.
Climate: Mainland Portugal is noted for its generally moderate climate with mild winters and warm summers, with the notable exception of the north-east, which has

long, cold winters and hot summers. The Algarve has one of the best year-round climates in Europe, with hot summers tempered by cooling breezes from the Atlantic and warm winters. Most rain falls in winter, with the heaviest rain in the north-west. Average temperatures in the Algarve are 12°C/54°F in January and 24°C/75°F in July/August, although temperatures may fall to 5°C/41°F in winter and can be over 30°C/86°F in summer. Lisbon and Oporto are only a few degrees cooler than the Algarve for most of the year. Madeira is sub-tropical with wet winters and hot summers. The average temperature is around 16°C/61°F in winter (January) and 22°C/72°F in summer (July/August).

Language: Portuguese. English is widely spoken in resort areas.

Political Stability: Since the bloodless revolution in 1974 which ended 50 years of dictatorship, Portugal has had a stable democracy. Its stability was enhanced in 1986 when it joined the European Union, a move which has brought huge economic benefits, although Portugal remains one of the EU's poorest members.

Finance

Currency: Euro (€).

Exchange Rate: £1 = €1.60.

Exchange Controls: None. Note, however, that if you import funds to pay for the purchase of a property you must obtain a licence from the Bank of Portugal (*Boletim de Autorizacao de Capitals Privados*).

Interest Rate: 3.75 per cent.

Cost/Standard of Living: Portugal has a relatively low cost of living, although it has increased considerably since the country joined the EU so that it's no longer a cheap country to live in. Food and wine are inexpensive, but imported goods are expensive

Income Tax: Foreign property owners need a tax card and a fiscal number (*número de contribuinte*). Portugal has a PAYE system of income tax with rates from 12 to 40 per cent. There are numerous tax credits. Non-residents must pay tax on income received in Portugal, e.g. letting income, at a flat rate of 15 per cent. When a property is owned by an offshore company, tax on letting income is paid at a flat rate of 25 per cent, although the offshore company must fulfil certain requirements.

Capital Gains Tax (CGT): In general CGT is levied at the same rates as personal income tax rates up to a maximum of 40 per cent, although gains from property are taxed only to the extent of 50 per cent of the gain. Property acquired before 1st January 1989 is exempt as are gains from a personal residence if the proceeds are reinvested in another personal residence in Portugal within two years of the sale. Gains from property are indexed to allow for inflation according to an official government coefficient.

Wealth Tax: None.

Inheritance & Gift Tax: Inheritance tax is levied at between 3 and 50 per cent, depending on the relationship between the donor and the beneficiary. Inheritance tax is payable by the beneficiary and not the estate.

Value Added Tax (VAT): The standard rate of VAT is 17 per cent, which is levied on most products including new homes. There's a reduced rate of 12 per cent for some foodstuffs, restaurants, farming equipment and miscellaneous items, and a rate of 5 per cent on books. In Madeira and the Azores there are VAT rates of 12, 8 and 4 per cent.

Property

Market: The Portuguese property market is fairly lively in most areas and there's a strong market in properties on luxury developments (offering a wide range of leisure and sports facilities) and sheltered housing for retirees. In the past, overdevelopment has spoilt some areas of the Algarve and there are now much stricter planning controls. A planning law (*Plano Regional de Ordenamento do Território Algarve*/PROTAL) was introduced in 1993 to curb development, which has stabilised and increased prices. Most new developments are tasteful and in harmony with their surroundings. Older properties requiring renovation are available in rural areas.

Areas: The most popular area for foreign buyers is the Algarve in the south, which extends from the Spanish coast to Cape St Vincent in the west, although the main tourist area is between Faro and Lagos. Apart from a few towns (e.g. Albufeira, Quarteira and Vilamoura) few Algarve towns have been spoilt by over-development and there are still many unspoilt fishing villages, particularly east of Faro, an area largely ignored by tourists. Other coastal areas popular with foreign buyers include Cascais and Estoril west of Lisbon, the Obidos lagoon area (silver coast) north of Lisbon, and the Costa Verde north of Oporto. Those seeking a peaceful life in completely unspoilt surroundings may wish to investigate developments in central Portugal (e.g. Beita Litoral), which has been discovered by developers from Belgium and the Netherlands. There's a relatively small property market in Madeira and few foreign agents.

Cost: Property prices in Portugal vary considerably and are generally higher than Spain because of the higher cost of land and the often superior quality of developments. Resale apartments on the Algarve cost from around €65,000 for one bedroom, from €124,700 for two bedrooms and from €140,000 for three bedrooms. Two-bedroom detached villas cost from around €140,000 and three-bedroom villas from €175,000. Note that it can be cheaper to build a new villa than to buy a resale property, with building costs from around €400 per m². In inland areas, old cottages and houses on large plots in need of total restoration can be purchased from around €40,000. However, you should expect to spend two or three times the purchase price in renovation costs.

In the last decade the Algarve has seen a flood of luxury developments (mostly built by foreign, often British, developers) with a wide range of leisure and sports facilities, including golf courses. Prices can be high, e.g. €150,000 for a tiny studio or one-bedroom apartment, €200,000 for a two-bedroom apartment and from €250,000 for a three-bedroom apartment or townhouse. The price usually includes free golf membership plus the use of all country club facilities. Luxury developments generally have high annual maintenance fees, e.g. from around €1,000 for a studio apartment to over €3,000 for a three-bedroom villa. Prices in other areas (apart from major cities and a few fashionable areas such as Cascais and Estoril) are generally lower than on the Algarve, although prices vary considerably depending on a property's age, location, size and quality.

Local Mortgages: Local mortgages on second homes are difficult for foreigners to obtain, as Portuguese banks are reluctant to lend to non-Portuguese nationals. In any case, you can usually get better terms and a larger loan from a foreign lender.

Property Taxes: Property or municipal tax (*contribuiçao predial*) is based on a property's value, location and the standard of local services. It ranges from 0.7 to 2 per cent of a property's fiscal value (*valor matrical*) per year and is paid in two instalments in April and November. Principal homes in urban areas costing less than €50,000 are exempt for ten years. It's likely that municipal taxes will be raised in the near future to 20 per cent for property owned by offshore companies.

Purchase Procedure: Foreign property buyers must obtain a fiscal number (*número de contribuinte*). It's no longer necessary to declare the funds imported to buy a property in Portugal, but it's still recommended. When buying a property in Portugal, the buyer signs a preliminary or promissory contract (*contrato de promessa de compra e venda*) containing the property details, price, completion date and date of possession. When buying off plan, a small holding deposit, e.g. €750, is necessary to reserve a property until a promissory contract is signed (usually around four weeks later). The deposit is agreed between the parties and is usually between 10 and 30 per cent of the purchase price, depending on the price and the date of completion. It's forfeited if the buyer fails to go through with the purchase; if the vendor withdraws, he must pay the buyer double the deposit. A buyer must engage a lawyer (*advogado*) to check for outstanding debts such as a mortgage, charges or restrictive covenants.

Completion is performed by a notary when the deeds (*escritura de compra e venda*) are signed by both parties and the balance of the purchase price is paid. The original deeds are stored in the notary's office and a stamped certified copy is given to the buyer. Ownership is registered at the local land registry office (*Conservatória de Registo Predial*) by the buyer or his legal representative. Note that it can take several months to complete the registration. Most properties in Portugal are owned freehold.

Offshore Companies: There are considerable advantages to buying a home in Portugal through an offshore company. These include no conveyance costs (as the shares of the company are simply transferred to the new owner), no property transfer tax (SISA), no capital gains tax and no inheritance tax. The cost of buying a property through an offshore company is around €750 plus annual fees of around the same amount. Owning a property through an offshore company is a big advantage when you're selling and may increase its value.

Fees: The fees when buying a property in Portugal are usually between 10 and 15 per cent of the purchase price. Notary and registration fees are between 3 and 3.5 per cent and legal fees usually between 1 and 2 per cent of the price. VAT (at 17 per cent) is included in the price of new properties. The main fee is stamp duty or transfer tax (SISA), which ranges from 8 to 10 per cent of the purchase price.

Precautions: When buying property in Portugal you should deal only with a government-registered estate agent (*mediador autorizado*) and employ an English-speaking lawyer to protect your interests and carry out the necessary searches. It's necessary to ensure that a property is free of debts and liens via a certificate (*certidao de registro*) from the local land registry. The deeds (*escritura*) must be registered as soon as possible after completion.

Holiday Letting: No restrictions.

Restrictions on Foreign Ownership: None.

Building Standards: Generally excellent, particularly for luxury developments. The quality of renovations is variable.

Personal Effects: Household goods and cars can be imported duty-free provided they've been owned for at least six months, although you must produce a property deed (*escritura*) or a residence permit (*residência*). VAT and duty is payable on vehicles imported from outside the EU.

General Information

Crime Rate: Portugal has a relatively low crime rate, particularly regarding serious and violent crime, although as in most European countries crime has risen dramatically in the last decade. It's important to protect your property against burglary, particularly if it's a holiday home.

Medical Facilities: Health care in Portugal has greatly improved in the last decade or so and is generally of a high standard. There are many English-speaking and foreign doctors in resort areas and major cities, although hospital facilities are limited in some rural areas. Residents who aren't covered by social security need private health insurance.

Pets: Pets must be vaccinated and have an import permit and a health certificate issued by an authorised veterinary surgeon not less than 14 days prior to import. Dogs over the age of four months must be vaccinated against rabies and must be kept isolated in your home for a period after importation (as indicated on the import permit or determined by the Portuguese Animal Health Services).

Residence: Residence permits are a formality for EU nationals, although non-working residents must have sufficient income to maintain themselves. Residents require a residence card (valid for five years) and a fiscal number. Visitors can remain for three months, after which a residence permit is necessary.

Work Permits: Unnecessary for EU nationals, but difficult for others to obtain.

Reference

Further Reading

BUYING A HOME IN PORTUGAL, David Hampshire (Survival Books). *Everything you need to know about buying a home in Portugal.*
Algarve Resident Magazine (weekly), Rua 16 de Janeiro, N° 6, 8400 Lagos, Portugal (☎ 282-342936).
Anglo-Portuguese News (APN), Avda Sao Pedro 14-D, 2765 Monte Estoril, Portugal.
Essential Algarve Magazine (bi-monthly), HDP, Apt 59, 8400 Lagoa, Portugal.
Madeira Island Bulletin, Apt 621, 9008 Funchal, Madeira, Portugal (🖳 www. madeiraonline.com).

Useful Addresses

The Anglo-Portuguese Society, Canning House, 2 Belgrave Square, London SW1X 8PJ, UK (☎ 020-7245 9738).
The Association for Residents and Home Owners in Portugal, Apartado 23, Alvor, 8500 Portimao (Algarve), Portugal.

Portuguese Embassy, 2125 Kalorama Rd., NW, Washington, DC 20008, USA (☎ 202-462-3726, 🖳 www.portugal.org).
Portuguese Embassy, 11 Belgrave Square, London SW1X 8PP, UK (☎ 020-7235 5331, 🖳 www.portembassy.gla.ac.uk).
Portuguese National Tourist Office, 2nd Floor, 22–25a Sackville Street, London W1X 1DE, UK (☎ 020-7494 1441).

SOUTH AFRICA

Background Information

Capital: Pretoria.
Population: 41.5 million.
Foreign Community: South Africa has some 6 million residents of European origin, including over 500,000 Britons. After the Second World War South Africa was one of the most popular countries for migrants from Europe, particularly from Britain, France, Germany and Holland. It's an extremely cosmopolitan country, and although the bulk of post-war immigrants came from Europe, many African-Americans have migrated to South Africa since the end of Apartheid. However, in recent years there has been a net outflow of qualified workers, those leaving (including a high number of professionals) outnumbering new arrivals by around two to one.
Area: 1,221,040km^2 (471,444mi^2).
Geography: South Africa is the second-largest country in southern Africa (five times the size of Britain), occupying the southernmost region of the African continent. It's an ancient land comprising two natural zones: the interior and the coastal fringe, which is separated from the interior by the Fringing Escarpment, a major communications barrier. The coastline covers almost 2,900km (1,800mi) and borders the Atlantic Ocean in the south-west and the Indian Ocean (which is much warmer than the Atlantic) in the south and east. South Africa is one of the world's most beautiful countries and contains a wealth of breathtaking natural beauty. It contains a wide variety of landscapes including majestic mountains extending to over 2,500m (8,000ft), numerous placid lakes and raging rivers, vast plains, huge tracts of dense forest and jungle, and many magnificent game parks and reservations.
Climate: South Africa has a temperate and sub-tropical (on the Kwazulu-Natal coast) climate, with the southern coast around Cape Town enjoying an almost Mediterranean climate, recognised as one of the best in the world. Being in the southern hemisphere, the seasons in South Africa are opposite to those in the northern hemisphere, which makes the country a popular choice for a winter holiday home for Europeans and North Americans. Coastal regions enjoy a hotter climate than inland regions, although the extreme summer heat is tempered by balmy sea breezes. The coolest months are June to September (winter), which is also the rainy season.
Language: The main languages are English and Afrikaans, although South Africa has 11 official languages. The major African languages are Xhosa and Zulu. Over 60 per cent of the population speaks English.
Political Stability: Good but with an uncertain future. Apartheid officially ended in 1991 and a government of National Unity was established after the 1994 general election, with Nelson Mandela (African National Congress) as president. Mandela

retired in 1999 leaving his successor, Thabo Mbeki, with many social and economic problems, including high unemployment and widespread AIDS. While South Africa's democracy seems stable, there are sporadic outbreaks of civil unrest in the country. However, the South African government encourages foreign investment.

Finance

Currency: Rand (R).
Exchange Rate: £ = R12.40.
Exchange Controls: None for import, although there are controls on the export of foreign currency.
Interest Rate: 11 per cent.
Cost/Standard of Living: The cost of living in South Africa is lower than most western European countries, but higher than in North America. Food and alcohol is inexpensive, but imported goods are expensive, including motor vehicles (although there are concessions for migrants). Homes are a bargain by international standards.
Income Tax: South Africa has a PAYE system of income tax, with rates from 19 per cent (on annual income up to R34,200) to 45 per cent (on income above R120,000). There are rebates for all individuals. Income tax is payable on all income earned in South Africa, even by non-residents.
Capital Gains Tax (CGT): CGT is levied on gains made from the sale of non-primary residences.
Wealth Tax: None.
Inheritance & Gift Tax: A donations (gift) tax of 25 per cent is levied on gifts, and an estate (inheritance) tax, also of 25 per cent, on estates valued at over R1 million.
Value Added Tax (VAT): VAT at 14 per cent is levied on goods and services, with the exception of basic foodstuffs. Duty at 57.5 per cent is payable on motor vehicles, although this is waived for tourists, business people and first time immigrants (provided the vehicle has been owned for one year). VAT is, however, still payable after an addition of 10 per cent to the vehicle's value. Visitors may apply for a refund of VAT on goods taken out of the country when their value exceeds R250.

Property

Market: In the last few years there has been a booming market for second and permanent homes in South Africa, prompted by the relatively stable political climate and low prices, although property prices have risen somewhat as a result. The market has been fuelled by a strong demand from overseas buyers, particularly Britons and Germans. There are many superb examples of colonial architecture, including beautiful Dutch gable houses, thatched cottages and 19th century homesteads. New marina and golf apartment and townhouse developments are also attracting foreign buyers. Larger homes contain a wealth of luxury features such as swimming pools, jacuzzis, saunas, tennis courts, large landscaped gardens, barbecue patios and extensive security features. Many older homes (including most detached properties) contain self-contained apartments, which were originally designed as servants' quarters. Most property is sold freehold, although it can also be leasehold, sectional title (condominiums) or share block.

Areas: The most popular provinces with foreign buyers are the Western and Eastern Capes, followed by Kwazulu-Natal. The coastal areas around Cape Town on the Western Cape, Port Elizabeth, Port Alfred and East London on the Eastern Cape, and Durban in Kwazulu-Natal are the most popular areas among foreign buyers. Cape Town is one of the world's most attractive cities and is noted for its beautiful countryside and magnificent coastline. There are numerous prestigious residential areas including the suburbs of Claremont, Constantia and Kenilworth, and the nearby towns of Somerset West and Stellenbosch. Hout Bay on the Atlantic coast is also popular, as are Fish Hoek and Simon's Town on the Indian Ocean, which, although not as attractive, are cheaper than the Central and Western Cape areas. Knysna on the Western Cape (between Cape Town and Port Elizabeth) has become a prime retirement area and Port Alfred is also becoming increasingly popular. The Northern Cape, which runs north of Cape Town to the Botswana and Namibia borders, mainly appeals to those looking for tranquillity.

Cost: Property in South Africa is excellent value (because of the low value of the rand and the emigration of many white residents in recent years), and is among the cheapest in the world. However, prices have been increasing in recent years and have risen by 25 per cent or more in many areas, particularly in Cape Town where the property market is booming. In many coastal areas you can buy new apartments and townhouses from R135,000 and resale three-bedroom detached houses with servants' quarters from around R300,000. New marina apartments are available in Cape Town for around R250,000 and a four-bedroom detached house on a large plot in a good area costs as little as R375,000. Large colonial-style homes are in high demand and a five or six-bedroom property with a swimming pool and a few acres of land can be purchased from around R800,000 rising to over R1,200,000 in exclusive areas such as Constantia Valley. Retirement villages are springing up around Cape Town and prices start at R170,000 for a one-bedroom unit with alarm and on-site medical attention.

Local Mortgages: Mortgages (called bonds in South Africa) of up to 90 or even 100 per cent over 10 to 20 years are available to residents from local banks and building societies, although interest rates are high. Mortgages up to 50 per cent of the purchase price are available to non-residents. Stamp duty of 0.2 per cent is payable on a mortgage. Most buyers find it's cheaper to obtain a mortgage abroad.

Property Taxes: Property taxes are levied by local communities and vary according to the size of a property and other factors. There are plans to unify the criteria in the near future.

Purchase Procedure: Buying property in South Africa is usually trouble-free and the country has a highly efficient system of land registration. Agents must be qualified and register with the Estate Agents Board. Offers must be made in writing and when an offer is accepted, a deposit of 10 per cent is paid to the seller's estate agent, which is held in the agent's trust (escrow) account. Contracts contain the obligations of both vendor and buyer, and the buyer has the right to nominate a lawyer to carry out the necessary checks and register the new ownership at the Registrar of Deeds office. Deeds are held by the buyer's bank when there's a mortgage. Completion usually takes two to three months.

Offshore Companies: It's possible to buy property in South Africa through an offshore company, which provides certain advantages concerning inheritance.

Fees: The tariffs for legal fees, conveyance costs and transfer duty are set by the government. Transfer duty is levied at 1 per cent on the first R60,000, 5 per cent on the amount between R60,001 and R250,000, and 8 per cent on the balance. Where the purchaser is a legal entity, transfer duty is a flat 10 per cent. Transfer duty isn't payable on new properties when VAT (at 14 per cent) is included in the purchase price. Conveyance costs (payable to the seller's lawyer) are variable and are usually between 1 and 2 per cent of the purchase price. Legal and other fees total around 1 per cent.

Precautions: It's usual to have a survey (inspection), which should include checks for damp and termites. It's also necessary to engage a lawyer to oversee a sale and carry out the necessary checks.

Holiday Letting: No restrictions.

Restrictions on Foreign Ownership: None.

Building Standards: Variable but generally excellent.

Personal Effects: Can be freely imported without any restrictions but you must pay a deposit equivalent to the duty payable on the goods. This deposit is refunded when you leave the country permanently or become a resident. Migrants may import a motor vehicle (that has been owned for at least a year) up to an insured value of R100,000 free of duty.

General Information

Crime Rate: The crime rate is very high in some cities and urban areas, particularly crimes against property and robberies (including muggings). South Africa's murder rate is the highest in the world, but is distorted by the high level of inter-tribal fighting (over 5,000 have died in the last decade), and most 'white' areas where foreigners buy property, for example in the Eastern and Western Capes, are relatively crime-free. However, it's necessary to take precautions to protect your property and avoid high crime areas. In many areas, private properties and estates have extensive security systems (including barbed wire and high walls) and many employ private security guards. The hijacking of cars is rife in some cities (such as Johannesburg), where it can be dangerous to stop a car at night, even at a red light. Police corruption is widespread and up to 25 per cent of police officers have a criminal record (many officers are linked to robbery, rape and murder).

Medical Facilities: Good to excellent, depending on the town or city. South Africa has no national health scheme, although one is planned, and private health insurance is essential.

Pets: There's no system of quarantine in South Africa.

Residence Permits: Note that *all* applications for immigration to South Africa have a *non-refundable* fee of £1,112 (late 2001). Amongst those who qualify for immigration are close relatives (under the family reunion scheme), retirees (who must provide evidence that they have sufficient income to support themselves and that they can transfer funds to South Africa immediately), financially independent people (who must transfer around R1.5 million, of which R700,000 must be invested in South Africa for a period of three years), and business investors, who require a minimum investment of around R250,000 to obtain a residence permit (there's no fixed minimum and the investment required is decided by the Immigrants Selection Board). If you plan to employ South Africans, your application will be looked upon more favourably.

Work Permits: South Africa doesn't have a points system and those wishing to work (aged 18 to 51) require an offer of employment; employers must produce evidence as to why a position cannot be filled by a South African. Migrants must pay a deposit (£400 in early 2001), which is refunded when they leave South Africa.

Reference

Further Reading

Live and Work in South Africa, Avril Harper (Grant Dawson).
South Africa News, Outbound Newspapers, 1 Commercial Road, Eastbourne, East Sussex BN21 3XQ, UK (☎ 01323-726040, 🖥 www.outbound-newspapers.com). Monthly newspaper for those planning to live or work in South Africa.

Useful Addresses

Institute of Realtors of South Africa, Suite 15, Howard Centre, Forest Drive, Pinelands, 7405, South Africa (☎ 021-531 3180).
South African Embassy: 3051 Massachusetts Ave., NW, Washington, DC 20008, USA (☎ 202-232 4400, 🖥 www.southafrica.net).
South African High Commission, South Africa House, Trafalgar Square, London WC2N 5DP, UK (☎ 020-7451 7299, 🖥 www.southafricahouse.com).

SPAIN

Background Information

Capital: Madrid.
Population: 40 million.
Foreign Community: Spain has a large expatriate community in its major cities and resort areas including many Americans, British, Germans, Scandinavians and other Europeans.
Area: 510,000km^2 (197,000mi^2).
Geography: The Spanish mainland measures 805km (500mi) from north to south and 885km (550mi) from east to west, making Spain the second largest country in western Europe after France. The Balearic Islands off the eastern coast comprise the islands of Mallorca (Majorca), Ibiza, Menorca (Minorca) and Formentera, and cover an area of 5,014km^2 (1,936mi^2), while the Canary Islands, situated 97km (60mi) off the west coast of Africa, cover 7,272km^2 (2,808mi^2). Spain also has two North African enclaves, Ceuta and Melilla, administered by the provinces of Cadiz and Malaga respectively. The Pyrenees in the north form a natural barrier between Spain and France, while to the west is Portugal. To the north-west is the Bay of Biscay and the province of Galicia with an Atlantic coast. In the east and south is the Mediterranean. The southern tip of Spain is just 16km (10mi) from Africa across the Strait of Gibraltar, a British territory claimed by Spain and a constant source of friction between Britain and Spain. Spain's mainland coastline totals 2,119km (1,317mi).

The country consists of a vast plain (the *meseta*) surrounded by mountains and is the highest country in Europe after Switzerland, with an average altitude of 650m (2,132ft) above sea level. The *meseta* covers an area of over 200,000km² (77,000mi²) at altitudes of between 600 and 1,000m (2,000 and 3,300ft). Mountains fringe the coast on three sides with the Cantabrian chain in the north (including the Picos de Europa), the Pénibetic chain in the south (including the Sierra Nevada, which has the highest peaks in Spain) and a string of lower mountains throughout the regions of Catalonia and Valencia in the east. The highest peak on the mainland is the Pico de Mulhacén in the Sierra Nevada range (3,482m/11,423ft), which is topped by Mount Teide (3,718m/12,198ft) on the Canary island of Tenerife.

Climate: Spain is the sunniest country in Europe and the climate (on the Costa Blanca) has been described by the World Health Organisation as among the healthiest in the world. Spain's Mediterranean coast, from the Costa Blanca to the Costa del Sol, enjoys an average of 320 days' sunshine per year. Continental Spain experiences three climatic zones: Atlantic, Continental and Mediterranean, in addition to which some areas, particularly the Balearic and Canary Islands, have distinct micro-climates. In coastal areas there can be huge differences in the weather between the seafront and mountains a few kilometres inland. In Mallorca rainfall varies from 30 to 40cm (12 to 16in) in the south to over 1.2m (47in) in the north, and Menorca experiences strong winds in winter.

Language: Spanish, or more correctly Castilian (*castellano*), is the main language, although Basque, Catalan and Galician are also official languages in the respective regions. There are also a number of dialects including *Mallorquin* (Mallorca), *Menorquin* (Menorca) and *Ibiçenco* (Ibiza). English is widely spoken in resort areas and the major cities.

Political Stability: Very good. Since the death of General Franco on 20th November 1975, which heralded the end of 36 years of dictatorship, Spain has become a parliamentary democracy, with arguably the most liberal constitution in western Europe (since 1978). Spain has been a member of the European Union since 1986.

Finance

Currency: Euro (€).
Exchange Rate: £1 = €1.60.
Exchange Controls: None. Funds imported to buy a property should be officially documented so that on its sale the proceeds can be re-exported.
Interest Rate: 3.75 per cent.
Cost/Standard of Living: In the last decade or so, inflation has brought the price of many goods and services in Spain in line with most other European countries, although many things remain cheaper, including property and rents, food, alcohol, dining out and general entertainment. With the exception of the major cities, where the higher cost of living is generally offset by higher salaries, the overall cost of living in Spain is lower than in many other European countries, particularly in rural and coastal areas.
Income Tax: Income tax is levied on a sliding scale from 18 (on annual income up to €3,606) to 48 per cent (on annual income over €66,111). Non-resident property owners in Spain are liable for income tax at a flat rate of 25 per cent on income arising

in Spain, including that from letting a property. All property owners in Spain (both residents and non-residents) must have a fiscal number (*número de identificación de entranjero*/NIE).

Capital Gains Tax (CGT): Capital gains tax (*impuesto sobre incremento de patrimonio*) is payable on the profit from sales of certain assets in Spain, including property. After the first two years there's an annual deduction (for inflation) of 11.11 per cent for property, which means that after 10 years' ownership there's no capital gains tax liability. CGT isn't payable when you're a resident of Spain and sell your principal home, provided the proceeds are used to buy a new home in Spain within two years. The CGT rate is a flat 35 per cent for non-residents and a maximum of 18 per cent for residents. Individuals over 65 are exempt from CGT on property provided they've owned the property for more than three years.

Wealth Tax: Spain has a wealth tax (*impuesto extraordinario sobre el patrimonio*), known simply as *patrimonio*. A resident is exempt from paying tax on assets worth up to €108,182 and pays no tax on a primary residences. If a property is registered in the names of both spouses (or a number of unrelated people), each is entitled to claim the €108,182 exemption. Non-residents must pay tax on the total value of their assets in Spain. The rate ranges from 0.2 per cent on assets of up to €167,130, up to a maximum of 2.5 per cent on assets above €10,696,000.

Inheritance & Gift Tax: Inheritance tax (*impuesto sobre sucesiones y donaciones*) in Spain is paid by the beneficiaries and not by the deceased's estate. The amount payable depends upon the relationship between the donor and the recipient, the amount inherited, and the wealth of the recipient, and varies from 0.2 to 34 per cent. There are allowances for close relatives, e.g. direct descendants, direct ascendants and relatives to a third degree.

Value Added Tax (VAT): The standard rate of VAT (called IVA in Spain) is 16 per cent. There are reduced rates of 7 per cent (e.g. drinks other than alcohol and fizzy drinks, fuel, water, communications, drugs and medicines, transport, hotel accommodation restaurant meals; and theatre and cinema tickets) and 4 per cent (e.g. food and books). Certain goods and services are exempt, including health care (e.g. doctors' and dentists' services), educational services, insurance and banking.

Property

Market: The Spanish property market is lively and the last few years have seen an unprecedented boom in construction. Prices have risen sharply in mainland coastal and resort areas, although in late 2001 it was expected that prices would begin to stabilise. Prices in the major cities have remained fairly stable, being less dependent on foreign buyers and the vagaries of the world economic climate, although Madrid and Barcelona have some of Europe's most expensive property. Resort property remains good value, particularly for those paying in currencies that made large gains against the peseta in recent years (e.g. sterling). Spain suffered in the 1980s from a reputation for 'crooked' agents and developers and, although it's now a safer place to buy, it's still plagued by red tape and a plethora of property-related taxes.

Areas: The most popular locations are the Costa Blanca, Costa Del Sol, the Balearics (Ibiza, Mallorca and Menorca) and the Canaries (Gran Canaria, Tenerife and Lanzarote), followed at some distance by the other *costas* (Costa Brava, Costa

Dorada, Costa Almería, Costa Cálida and the Costa de la Luz). The major cities, particularly Barcelona and Madrid, are also popular with foreigners, who are also to be found in many inland villages along the *costas*. There is, however, much more to Spain than the Mediterranean coastal resorts and the islands, and less popular regions such as the northern Cantabrian coast and inland cities such as Seville and Granada also have their enthusiasts. The Costa del Sol is Europe's sunniest region during the winter, although if you want really hot weather and wish to swim in the sea during winter without freezing, the only choice is the Canaries.

Cost: Prices in Spain vary considerably with the region and town, and with the size and quality of a property. On the Costa del Sol, resale studios and one-bedroom apartments start at around €60,000, two-bedroom apartments at around €90,00 and three-bedroom apartments at €120,000. Two-bedroom townhouses cost from around €120,000 and three-bedroom townhouses from €180,000. Small two-bedroom detached villas can be purchased from around €180,000 and three-bedroom villas from around €270,000. For those with deep pockets the sky's the limit and there's a huge choice of luxury villas and estates costing from around €475,000 upwards. Prices are generally lower on the eastern Costa del Sol than at the western end (i.e. west of Malaga). Prices on the Costa del Sol are generally around 10 to 20 per cent higher than on the Costa Blanca and property in the Balearics and the Canaries is usually around 20 per cent more expensive than on the *costas*.

There's little difference between the price of new and resale properties, although new properties may be slightly cheaper. Second-hand or resale properties are often good value in Spain, particularly in resort areas, where the majority of low to medium-priced apartments and townhouses are sold fully furnished. You usually pay a premium for a beachside property or a property with a sea view. Property is less expensive in rural areas, where a farmhouse (*finca*) with outbuildings and a fair amount of land can cost the same as a studio apartment in a fashionable resort. In inland areas, old cottages and houses in need of total restoration can be purchased for around €48,000, although you will need to spend two or three times the purchase price in modernisation and renovation costs. When buying a community property always check the community fees, which can run into €thousands per year.

Local Mortgages: Mortgages are freely available from Spanish banks for both principal and second homes, up to a maximum of 80 per cent of purchase price (50 per cent for non-residents). Spanish mortgages are usually payable over 10 to 15 years, although loans can be repaid over 5 or 25 years. You should shop around, as you may be able to obtain better terms from a foreign or offshore bank.

Property Taxes: Property tax (*impuesto sobre bienes inmuebles*/IBI) in Spain is based on the fiscal value (*valor catastral*) of a property, which is assessed by the local authority and may be different from a property's actual or market value. It's important to check the fiscal value of a property, as a number of taxes are linked to it, including income, wealth and inheritance tax. In general, property tax rates in Spain are 0.5 per cent of the fiscal value for urban (*urbana*) properties and 0.3 per cent for those on agricultural land (*rústicas*), although in some municipalities they're as high as 1.7 per cent. However, there's another value ascribed to property, which is assessed by the tax authorities and published in a set of tables. This 'tax value' is often higher than a property's fiscal value, as the tax authorities revise their tables more frequently than local authorities. In addition to property tax, you must pay an imputed 'letting' tax (*rendimientos del capital inmobiliario*) at 0.5 per cent of a property's fiscal value, 'tax value' or purchase price, whichever is the highest. Many municipalities also charge an annual fee for refuse collection.

Purchase Procedure: When buying an unfinished property off plan, take care when signing a reservation or option contract that it isn't a binding purchase contract. A reservation deposit, e.g. €3,000, usually secures a property for up to 30 days. If you pay a reservation fee, this is usually lost if you back out of the purchase, although some developers return it. If a property is still to be built or completed, payment is made in stages. **When buying an unfinished property it's important to ensure that the developer is financially secure and that any money paid are protected if he goes bust.**

When you sign the contract (*contrato privado de compraventa*) for a new or resale property (or a plot), you must pay a deposit. If you're buying a property privately, you must usually pay a deposit of 10 per cent when signing the initial contract, although the actual deposit is negotiable, particularly on expensive properties. Once you've paid the deposit there's a legally binding agreement between you and the vendor. If there's any doubt about whether you can complete a sale in the time specified in the contract, you should sign a contract with an option to purchase (*contrato de opción de compra*). In this case the deposit is paid in the form of an *arras* or *señal* and the contract can be cancelled by either party: if the buyer cancels, he forfeits his deposit; if the vendor cancels, he must pay the buyer double the deposit. A deposit should always be held in a separate bonded (escrow) account. **Always ensure that you know precisely the terms under which a deposit will be repaid or forfeited** *before paying it!*

The final act of the sale is the signing of the deed of sale (*escritura de compraventa*) and the payment of the balance due, usually paid by banker's draft unless otherwise arranged. Non-resident purchasers must obtain a certificate from a Spanish bank stating that the amount to be paid has been exchanged or converted from a foreign currency, a copy of which is attached to the title deed. It's normal for both parties to be present when the deed of sale is read, signed by both buyer and vendor, and witnessed by the *notario*. In practice, a copy of the *escritura* will usually be available for scrutiny before the official signing and, if you don't understand it, you should obtain an official translation. You can give a representative in Spain general power of attorney (*poder general*) so that he can sign a contract on your behalf.

Since 1993, a notary has been required to check the property register (not more than 48 hours before making the title deed) for any debts against a property or other restrictions which would 'inhibit' a sale. When the contract is signed, the notary will give you a certified copy (*primera copia*) of the deeds. A notarised copy is lodged at the property registry office (*registro de la propiedad*) and the new owner's name is entered on the registry deed. You should ensure that the *escritura* is registered *immediately* after signing it, if necessary by registering it yourself. Registering your ownership is the most important act of buying property in Spain, as until it's registered – even after you've signed the contract before a notary – charges can be levied against it. Only when the *escritura* is registered in your name do you become the legal owner of a property. Following registration, the original deeds are returned to you, usually after a few months.

Offshore Companies: It's possible to buy a property through an offshore company, but the advantages have been largely negated by a law requiring the name of the owner to be declared to the Spanish tax authorities; otherwise a punitive annual tax (*impuesto especial*) equal to 5 per cent of the property's value is imposed. When selling a property owned by an offshore company, you can save fees such as transfer tax, notary and land registry fees, but it's no longer possible to avoid capital gains and inheritance tax. You should therefore buy a property through an offshore company in certain special cases only, e.g. when there's a complicated family or inheritance situation.

Fees: The fees payable when buying a property in Spain amount to around 10 per cent of the purchase price and may include the notary's fees, VAT (IVA), transfer tax, legal fees and a property registration fee. A land tax (*plus valía*) is also payable when a property is sold and should be paid by the vendor (but you should confirm this). Most fees are based on the 'declared' value of a property, which must be no less than the 'tax value' assessed by the tax authorities (see **Property Taxes** above).

Property buyers purchasing resale property must pay a transfer tax (*impuesto de transmisiones patrimoniales*/ITP) of 6 per cent (4.5 per cent in the Canaries). There's no transfer tax on new properties, but VAT at 7 per cent is payable. Legal fees are usually around 1 to 2 per cent of the purchase price for an average property. The notary who officiates at a sale is paid a fixed fee based on a sliding scale depending on the amount of land, the size of the building(s) and the price. The fee for an average property is around €600. The registration fee is usually between €240 and €300, according to the declared value.

Precautions: Buying property in Spain is continually the subject of much adverse publicity, with some commentators even going so far as to advise people *not* to buy at all! It should be noted that most purchasers who have had problems didn't suffer so much from fraud, but from the insolvency of developers. Developers are now required to have financial guarantees and the legal situation has been tightened to prevent fraud, although the possibility must never be ignored. Nevertheless, **it cannot be emphasised too strongly that anyone planning to buy (or sell) property in Spain *must* take expert, independent legal advice.** Never sign anything or pay any money until you've sought legal advice in a language in which you're fluent from an experienced, Spanish-registered lawyer. If you aren't prepared to do this, you shouldn't even think about buying property in Spain!

Among the myriad problems experienced by buyers in Spain have been properties purchased without legal title, properties built without planning permission, properties sold that were subject to mortgages or embargoes, properties with missing infrastructure, properties sold to more than one buyer, and even properties sold that didn't exist! Checks must be carried out *both* before signing a 'preliminary' contract *and* before signing the deed of sale (*escritura*). Note that, if you get into a dispute over a property deal, it can take many years for it to be resolved in the Spanish courts, and even then there's no guarantee that you will receive satisfaction.

One of the Spanish laws that property buyers should be aware of is the law of subrogation, whereby property debts, including mortgages, local taxes and community charges, remain with a property and are inherited by the buyer. This is an open invitation for dishonest sellers to 'cut and run'. It's possible, of course, to check whether there are any outstanding debts on a property and this should be done by your legal advisor. However, it's virtually impossible to prevent a seller fraudulently taking out a loan on a property after you've made a check. The procedure has been tightened in recent years, but still isn't foolproof. This also applies in other countries.

Many problems can arise when buying an unfinished property (i.e. buying off plan) or a property on an unfinished development (*urbanisation*). Because of the problems associated with buying off plan, such as the difficulty in ensuring that you actually receive what is stated in the contract and that the developer doesn't go broke, many experts advise buyers against buying an unfinished property. A 'finished' property is a property where the building is complete in every detail (as confirmed by your own architect or legal advisor), all communal services have been completed, and all infrastructure is in place, such as roads, parking areas, lighting, landscaping, water, sewerage, swimming pools, tennis courts, electricity and telephone services.

Holiday Letting: No restrictions. An imputed letting tax is payable by all property owners in Spain, both residents and non-residents, irrespective of whether you let a property. Tax is also payable on letting income at a flat rate of 25 per cent.

Restrictions on Foreign Ownership: None.

Building Standards: Building standards vary enormously from excellent to poor. Care must be taken when buying a property, whether new or old, and unless you're absolutely confident that a property is sound you should have a survey carried out. The quality of properties in Spain varies considerably with regard to materials, fixtures and fittings, and workmanship, probably as much or more so than in any other European country.

Personal Effects: European Union (EU) nationals planning to take up permanent or temporary residence in Spain are permitted to import their furniture and personal effects free of duty or taxes, provided they were purchased tax-paid within the EU or have been owned for at least six months. Non-EU nationals must have owned and used all goods for at least six months to qualify for duty-free import. A vehicle owned and used for six months in another EU country can be imported into Spain tax and duty-free. VAT (16 per cent) and duty (10 per cent) are payable on vehicles imported from outside the EU, the rates being based on a vehicle's value. A registration tax (*impuesto municipal sobre circulación de vehículos*) of 13 per cent is payable on all vehicles imported into Spain, including those from EU countries, and is calculated on the vehicle's current market value.

General Information

Crime Rate: Spain's crime rate is among the lowest in Europe, although in common with most other European countries it has increased dramatically in the last decade. Violent crime is rare, although muggings have increased in resort areas. However, petty crime such as handbag snatching, pick-pocketing and theft from vehicles are widespread throughout Spain. You should *never* leave anything on display in your car, including your stereo system, which should be removed when parking in cities and resorts. Burglary is also a big problem throughout Spain, particularly for holiday homeowners. It's necessary to take comprehensive measures to protect your property in Spain to ensure that it's as thief-proof as possible and not to leave valuables or money lying around (a home safe is recommended).

Medical Facilities: Medical facilities in Spain vary and are generally very good in resort areas and major cities but limited in some rural areas. There are English-speaking Spanish and foreign doctors and dentists in resort areas and major cities. If you aren't covered by the public health service, private health insurance is essential; it's recommended in any case if you want the widest possible choice of practitioners and the best treatment without waiting.

Pets: A maximum of two pets may accompany travellers to Spain. A rabies vaccination is usually compulsory, although this *doesn't* apply to accompanied pets (including cats and dogs) entering Spain directly from Britain or for animals under three months old. A rabies vaccination is necessary if pets are transported by road from Britain to Spain via France. If a rabies vaccination is given, it must be administered not less than one month or more than 12 months prior to export. Pets over three months old from countries other than Britain must have been vaccinated against rabies. If a pet has no rabies certificate, it can be quarantined.

Residence: A residence permit is a formality for EU nationals, although non-working residents must have sufficient income to maintain themselves in Spain. There's no fixed income required to obtain a visa to retire to Spain, but proof of income or receipt of a pension is required. An investment of around €90,000 is usually necessary for a non-EU national to start a business in Spain and 30 per cent of this amount must be readily available. Visitors may remain in Spain for up to six months in a calendar year without a residence permit.

Work Permits: Unnecessary for EU nationals, but difficult for other foreigners to obtain.

Reference

Further Reading

BUYING A HOME IN SPAIN, David Hampshire (Survival Books). *Everything you need to know about buying a home in Spain.*
LIVING & WORKING IN SPAIN, David Hampshire (Survival Books). *Everything you need to know about living and working in Spain.*
Costa Blanca News (✉ cbnews@ctv.es). Weekly English-language newspaper.
Island Connections (✉ info@ic-web.com). Fortnightly English-language newspaper issued in the Canary Islands.
Lookout, Lookout Publications SA, Urb. Molino de Viento, C./Rio Darro, Portal 1, 29650 Mijas Costa (Málaga), Spain (✉ lookout@jet.es). Quarterly lifestyle magazine.
Property World, Edif. Buendía, 1°A, C/ España 1, 29640 Fuengirola, Spain (☎ 0952-888 234, 🖳 www.propertyworldmagazine.com).
The Reporter, C./Los Naranjos, 5, Pueblo Lopez, 29640 Fuengirola (Málaga), Spain (✉ thereporter@alsur.es). Free monthly news magazine.
Spanish Homes Magazine, 2 Paragon Place, Blackheath, London SE3 0SP, UK (🖳 www.spanishhomesmagazine.com). Monthly property magazine.
Spanish Property Owners' Handbook, David Searle (Santana).
Sur in English, Diario Sur, Avda. Doctor Marañón, 48, 29009 Málaga, Spain (🖳 www.surinenglish.com). Weekly free newspaper.

Villas & ..., SKR Española SL, Apdo de Correos 453, 29670 San Pedro de Alcántara, Spain (☎ 0952-884 994, ✉ skrespanola@jet.es). Monthly property magazine with articles in English, French, German and Spanish.
You and the Law in Spain, David Searle (Santana).

Useful Addresses

Institute of Foreign Property Owners, Apartado de Correos 418, 03590 Altea (Alicante), Spain (☎ 096-584 2312, 🖳 www.fipe.org).
Spanish Embassy, 2375 Pennsylvania Ave, NW, Washington, DC 20037, USA (☎ 202-452 0100, 🖳 www.spainemb.org).
Spanish Embassy, 39 Chesham Place, London SW1X 8SB, UK (☎ 020-7235 5555, 🖳 www.cec-spain.org.uk).
Spanish National Tourist Office, Metro House, 57-58 St. James's Street, London SW1A 1LD, UK (☎ 020-7499 0901).

SWITZERLAND

Background Information

Capital: Berne.
Population: 7.3 million.
Foreign Community: Switzerland has a large foreign resident population, around 20 per cent of the total and higher in cities such as Geneva. They include a large number of expatriates of France, Germany, Italy, Portugal, Spain and the former Yugoslavia, and a significant number from the USA and Britain.
Area: 41,288km^2 (16,100mi^2).
Geography: Switzerland is situated in the central Alpine region of Europe and has borders with five countries: Italy to the south, Austria and Liechtenstein to the east, Germany to the north and France to the west. Switzerland is the highest country in Europe. The Alps, mainly in the central part of the country, reach altitudes of over 4,000m (around 13,000ft), the highest point being the Dufour Peak of the Monte Rosa (4,634m/15,203ft) and the lowest Lake Maggiore (193m/633ft above sea level). The Swiss Alps the sources of both the Rhine and Rhône rivers and are crossed the St Gotthard, Grimsel, Furka and Oberalp passes.
Climate: It's almost impossible to give a general description of the Swiss climate, as it varies considerably from region to region (probably no country in Europe has such diverse weather conditions in such a small area). The Alps, extending from east to west, form a major weather division between the north and south of Switzerland, and separate weather forecasts are usually given for each area. The climate north of the Alps is continental with hot summers and cold winters, although prolonged periods when the temperature is below freezing are rare during daytime (unless you live on top of a mountain). South of the Alps in Ticino, a mild Mediterranean climate prevails and even in winter it's significantly warmer here than elsewhere in Switzerland. Spring and autumn are usually mild and fine in most areas, although it can be dull and wet in some regions.

Language: Switzerland has three official languages: German, French and Italian. Rhaeto-Romanic (Romansch), spoken by around 60,000 people (1 per cent) in the canton of Graubünden, is a national but not an official language. English is widely spoken.

Political Stability: Switzerland is the most politically stable country in the world. The Swiss constitution provides both the confederation and cantons with the system of a democratic republic, in the form of either direct or representative democracy, with all important decisions made by the people and cantons through referendums. The Swiss voted against joining the European Economic Area (EEA), which was seen by many as a first step to joining the European Union (EU). However, there's a wide division between the German and Italian speakers, who mostly oppose membership of the EU, and the French speakers, who are largely in favour.

Finance

Currency: Swiss franc (Sfr).
Exchange Rate: £1 = Sfr2.35.
Exchange Controls: None.
Interest Rate: 1.75 per cent.
Cost/Standard of Living: Switzerland has one of the highest costs of living in the world, but also has one of the highest standards of living and the highest GDP per head (and the highest per capita spending power in the world). Geneva and Zurich are among the most expensive cities in the world.
Income Tax: Each of the 26 Swiss cantons is autonomous as far as taxes are concerned and therefore tax rates vary from canton to canton, and even from community to community. Income tax is levied by the federal government (direct federal tax) and by cantons and communities. In 2001, the maximum federal income tax rate was 11.5 per cent. Maximum canton tax rates range from approximately 14 to 35 per cent. Non-working residents, e.g. retirees, can arrange to pay a lump sum tax in some cantons, which is often negotiated individually. Non-residents are liable to pay Swiss income tax only on income from property and business activities in Switzerland.
Capital Gains Tax (CGT): With the exception of property, there's no capital gains tax in most cantons. Capital gains tax on property depends on the profit level and the length of ownership. Capital gains are usually taxed separately and not with general income.
Wealth Tax: Wealth tax is levied on individuals by all cantons (there's no federal wealth tax) on all assets except property. The rate is progressive and depends on the canton and community where you live.
Inheritance & Gift Tax: Inheritance and gift taxes aren't levied by the federal government in Switzerland, but by all cantons except Schwyz (which levies neither tax) and Lucerne (which doesn't have a gift tax). Inheritance tax, which may be as low as 4 or 5 per cent, varies with the canton and usually the relationship of the beneficiary to the deceased. The closer the relationship, the lower the rate. The tax levied on the estate of a foreigner who's domiciled but has never been employed in Switzerland is reduced in some cantons, e.g. by 50 per cent in Vaud.

Value Added Tax (VAT): The standard rate of VAT is 7.5 per cent and there are reduced rates of 3.5 per cent on hotel accommodation and 2.3 per cent on food and drink, medicines, books, newspapers and water.

Other Taxes: If you're a member of the Reformed, Catholic or Old Catholic (Protestant) churches, you must pay a church tax (*Kirchensteuer/impôt du culte*) based on your salary, your community and your religion, which can amount to Sfrthousands per year if you earn a high salary. You can, however, have your religion officially changed (on paper) in order to reclaim church tax!

Property

Market: Because of the high cost and the restrictions on foreign property ownership (see below), there isn't a booming property business in Switzerland, particularly for second homes. In many towns and regions there are few properties for sale, even to Swiss nationals and qualifying foreign residents, as many properties are built for rental. Home ownership in Switzerland is among the lowest in western Europe at around 30 per cent.

Areas: Unless you're a resident, the areas and towns where you can buy a home in Switzerland are limited to those where sales to non-residents are permitted (see below). Among the most popular are Crans-Montana, Gstaad, Montreux and Villars. Ticino is also popular.

Cost: Swiss property is among the most expensive in the world, particularly when you're paying in a currency which has lost value against the Swiss franc in recent years. The restricted property market is reflected in high prices, which usually start at over Sfr130,000 for a studio apartment and increase to Sfr900,000 or more for a chalet. Prices vary considerably with the area and with the location and age of a property. One-bedroom apartments generally start at around Sfr200,000, two-bedroom chalet apartments cost from Sfr350,000, and three-bedroom chalet apartments start at over Sfr450,000. Three-bedroom apartments in exclusive developments can cost anywhere between Sfr600,000 and Sfr750,000. The average price per m^2 of new buildings in Switzerland is around Sfr6,500 (the highest in the world). A parking space or garage isn't usually included in the price of an apartment or townhouse and costs from around Sfr37,000.

Local Mortgages: Swiss mortgages of 50 to 75 per cent of the purchase price are available to non-residents, payable over 15 to 50 years. If you have additional security, other than the property that you're buying, you may qualify for a larger mortgage. Mortgage rates for non-residents are usually around 1 per cent higher than for residents. A mortgage in Switzerland is usually split between a first mortgage (60 to 65 per cent) and a second mortgage (15 to 20 per cent), repayable at different interest rates. The first mortgage is never normally repaid, as you pay only the interest, while the second mortgage is repaid over 10 to 20 years. Mortgage interest rates are usually variable, but fixed rate mortgages are also available (although they must be re-negotiated every three to five years). Swiss franc mortgages have the lowest interest rates in Europe, although you should be wary of taking out a mortgage in Swiss francs if your income is earned in a different currency. Not surprisingly, Switzerland has the world's highest per capita indebtedness in the mortgage sector.

Property Taxes: Property taxes in Switzerland are included in community income tax and aren't taxed separately.

Purchase Procedure: The process of buying a property in Switzerland is among the most efficient and secure in the world. Property sales in Switzerland are handled by a public notary (*Notar/notariat*), who acts for both the vendor and buyer. Contracts are written in the local language (French, German or Italian) and a certified translation is provided if necessary. A 10 per cent deposit is paid when the preliminary contract is signed. The purchase contract is always contingent on the buyer obtaining a mortgage (if necessary). On completion of the purchase and registration of ownership, legal fees and a transfer tax (*Übertragungssteuer/impôt sur les transferts*) amounting to around 5 per cent of the purchase price are payable to the notary. The title deed must be registered at the local land registry (which takes just a few days) and the Central Land Registry in Berne.

Fees: Fees total between 2.5 and 5 per cent of the purchase price and include transfer tax, notary's fees and land registry fees. VAT at 7.5 per cent is included in the price of new properties.

Precautions: Switzerland is one of the safest countries in the world in which to buy property. However, if you take out a mortgage in Swiss francs and your income is earned in another currency, you should beware of currency swings. Buying in Switzerland should be seen as a long-term commitment, as restrictions on sales and high prices often make it difficult to sell a property quickly without making a loss.

Holiday Letting: A foreign owner must occupy a Swiss property for a minimum of three weeks a year and rentals can be for a maximum of 11 months a year.

Restrictions on Foreign Ownership: Non-resident foreigners are restricted to buying property in certain cantons only, where there are also quotas. The annual quota for second homes sold to non-resident foreigners is around 1,400 for the whole of Switzerland, the majority in the cantons of Valais, Grisons, Ticino and Vaud. No quotas are set for Basle city, Geneva or Zurich and it's generally impossible for non-residents to buy property in the major cities. Nevertheless, in recent years quotas haven't been filled because of the recession, high property prices and resale restrictions. There are fewer opportunities to buy in German-speaking cantons than in French-speaking cantons. Swiss property law demands that where foreigners are permitted to purchase homes, a percentage of every development (e.g. a group of chalets or an apartment chalet) must be acquired by Swiss citizens. In some towns, local laws prevent sales to non-residents.

Restrictions on residents buying property depend on the type of residence permit held. Those with a C permit (permanent residence) can buy property without restriction, while those with a B permit (temporary annual residence) must obtain permission from their local canton authorities. Foreigners and each of their children over 20, who must also be financially independent, may buy one property only, which is restricted to 100m² of living area (non-living areas may be any size) or 1,000m² of land. You aren't permitted to buy a property in the name of a foreign company, although joint-ownership is allowed. Property owned by foreigners cannot be left empty for a calendar year and the owner or a family member must occupy it for at least three weeks a year.

All house purchasers in Switzerland, including Swiss, are forbidden to sell property within two years of the purchase date to prevent property speculation. The only exceptions are *force majeure* sales, e.g. as a result of financial hardship, family illness or death, when an owner is obliged to sell without making a profit. Non-residents who purchase a property in Switzerland generally aren't permitted to sell for a profit within the first five years, except in exceptional circumstances. In the first five years a sale is permitted to a Swiss citizen or a resident foreigner only. After five to ten years' ownership, an application can be made to sell to a non-resident (although in some cantons, e.g. Fribourg, resales to foreigners aren't restricted). A proposal to increase quotas to non-residents and ease restrictions was heavily defeated in a referendum in June 1995.

Building Standards: Swiss building standards and the quality of materials and fixtures and fittings used are among the highest in the world.

Personal Effects: No duty is payable on personal effects (including a car) that have been used and owned for at least six months, although they should be imported within three months of taking up residence or buying a holiday home. However, VAT (at 7.5 per cent) is payable on belongings imported to furnish a secondary residence, although this may be waived if the country of origin grants reciprocal rights to Swiss citizens.

General Information

Crime Rate: The crime rate in Switzerland is among the lowest in the world. Crimes against property (e.g. homes and cars) are particularly low in relation to other western countries and violent crime is rare. Nevertheless, as in most European countries, the crime rate has increased in the last decade and you should take the usual precautions.

Medical Facilities: Medical facilities in Switzerland are among the best in the world. However, health care is also very expensive and only North Americans and Swedes spend more on it. Private health insurance is recommended, and compulsory for many residents.

Pets: There's generally no quarantine period for animals in Switzerland. All dogs and cats over five months old must have an international health certificate stating that they've been vaccinated against rabies. You must have an official letter stating that your pet was in good health before the vaccination, which must have been given at least 30 days and not more than one year before entering Switzerland. Certificates are accepted in English, French, German and Italian. Dogs and cats under five months of age may be imported from many countries without a vaccination, but require a veterinary attestation of their age and good health.

Residence Permits: Residence permits are difficult to obtain by the non-employed (euphemistically called 'leisured foreigners' by the Swiss authorities) and permits are normally issued only to those over 60 (i.e. pensioners) or people of independent means, particularly the *very* rich (and famous). You're required to furnish proof that you have sufficient assets or income to live in Switzerland, usually via a statement from your bank. Non-residents are permitted to spend up to six months a year in Switzerland, although each visit mustn't exceed three months.

Work Permits: Work permits are available and each canton has an annual quota. Short-term seasonal work of up to nine months a year is relatively easy to find in some areas, but permits for 'permanent' jobs are difficult to obtain. Note that under bilateral treaties between Switzerland and the EU, which came into effect in 2001, EU nationals will have the same rights to jobs as Swiss nationals from 2003.

Reference

Further Reading

LIVING & WORKING IN SWITZERLAND, David Hampshire (Survival Books). *Everything you need to know about living and working in Switzerland.*
George Mikes Introduces Switzerland (Andre Deutsch).
The Perpetual Tourist, Paul N. Bilton (Bergli Books).
Revue Switzerland, Vogt-Schild AG, Zuchwilerstr. 21, 4501 Solothurn, Switzerland (☎ 065-247304). Monthly tourist magazine.
Swiss World, c/o HandelsZeitung Publications, Seestr 37, Postfach, CH-8027 Zurich, Switzerland (☎ 01-288 3546). Monthly business and lifestyle magazine.
Swiss News, Köschenrütistr 109, Postfach 4341, 8052 Zurich, Switzerland (☎ 01-302 7606). Monthly lifestyle magazine.
Switzerland for Beginners, George Mikes (Andre Deutsch).
Switzerland: Land, People, Economy, Aubrey Diem (Media International).
Ticking Along With The Swiss, Dianne Dicks (Bergli Books, Aeuss Baselstr 204, 4125 Riehen, Switzerland, ☎ 061-601 3101).

Useful Addresses

American Citizens Abroad (ACA), 5 Rue Liotard, 1202, Geneva, Switzerland (☎ 022-340 0233, 💻 www.aca.ch).
The British Resident's Association of Switzerland (BRA), Chemin de Chenalettaz 105, 1807 Bloney, Switzerland (☎ 021-943 1788).
The Federation of Anglo-Swiss Clubs (FASC), Basle, Switzerland (☎ 061-461 4536, 💻 www.angloswissclubs.ch, ✉ info@fasc.ch).
Head Customs Office, Monbijoustr 40, 3003 Berne BE, Switzerland (☎ 031-322 6511, 💻 www.zoll.admin.ch).
Schweizerischer Verband der Immobilien-Treuhänder/Union suisse des Fiduciaires immobilières, EugenHuber Strasse 19a, 8048 Zurich, Switzerland (☎ 01-434 7888, 💻 www.sivt.ch). Swiss Professional Estate Agents' Association.
Swiss Embassy, 2900 Cathedral Ave, NW, Washington, DC 20008, USA (☎ 202-745 7900, 💻 www.swissemb.org).
Swiss Embassy, 16–18 Montagu Place, London W1H 2BQ, UK (☎ 020-7723 0701, 💻 www.swissembassy.org.uk).
Switzerland Tourism, Bellariastr 38, 8027 Zurich, Switzerland (☎ 01-288 1111).

TURKEY

Background Information

Capital: Ankara.
Population: 64.6 million.
Foreign Community: There isn't a large expatriate group in Turkey, although in recent years the country has become popular with western Europeans for the purchase of holiday homes, and the foreign community is growing.

Area: 774,815km² (299,179mi²).

Geography: Turkey is situated in the south-eastern extremity of Europe with some 95 per cent of the country considered to be part of Asia. The European part is located west of the Bosporus, linking the Sea of Marmara to the Black Sea. Istanbul, on the west bank of the Bosporus, is Turkey's largest city with a population of around 5.5 million. The capital, Ankara, is situated in the middle of the Anatolian peninsula in Asia, a large part of which is mountainous. Turkey has borders (which were established only in 1923) with Armenia, Bulgaria, Georgia, Greece, Iran, Iraq and Syria, and some 8,000km (around 5,000mi) of coastline – around half on the Mediterranean and Aegean Seas and half on the Black Sea.

Climate: Turkey is a huge country with a variety of climates ranging from temperate in the Black Sea region to continental in the centre and Mediterranean on the southern coast. The Aegean, Marmara and Mediterranean coasts have a typical Mediterranean climate with hot summers (over 300 days of sunshine a year), mild winters and low rainfall. The Black Sea coast has a temperate climate with warm summers, mild winters and relatively high rainfall. In Anatolia the climate is generally cold in winter (with snow in the east) and hot in summer (mild in the east), with most rain falling in winter in the south-east (which also has relatively mild winters). The average maximum temperature in the most popular holiday area of Antalya on the Mediterranean coast ranges from 10°C/50°F in January to around 28°C/82°F in July and August. Average maximum January and July temperatures in the major cities are Ankara 0/23°C (32/73°F), Istanbul 5/23°C (41/73°F) and Izmir 9/28°C (48/82°F).

Language: The main language is Turkish, spoken by some 86 per cent of the population, the remainder speaking Kurdish (11 per cent) and Arabic (2 per cent). Some English (and other major international languages) is spoken in tourist areas and main cities. Many Turks speak German as a result of working in Germany.

Political Stability: Turkey has a poor record of democracy and has a highly volatile political arena. Following a succession of military coups in the '60s and '70s, Turkey has had civilian rule since 1983, since when it has been relatively stable. However, Turkey is plagued by internal unrest (e.g. from the Kurds, who are seeking their own state, and Islamic militants) and has poor relations with some of its neighbours. It has a poor human rights record, particularly regarding its brutal treatment of the Kurds. Turkey has historically had poor relations with Greece, which were exacerbated by Turkey's military occupation of northern Cyprus in 1974. It has a long-standing application (1987) for European Union (EU) membership, although it's likely to be vetoed by Greece and others, at least until the Cyprus question is resolved.

Finance

Currency: Turkish lira (TL).

Exchange Rate: £1 = approximately TL2 million. Note that the Turkish lira is very unstable and the exchange rate varies tremendously.

Exchange Controls: Property buyers must provide proof that funds were imported from abroad.

Interest Rate: Interest rates are very high and, although constantly changing, are usually over 20 per cent.

Cost/Standard of Living: Turkey has a low standard of living, and basic foodstuffs and other necessities are relatively inexpensive. However, luxuries and imported items (including cars) are expensive. High inflation, around 90 per cent in 1997, is a problem.

Income Tax: Turkey has a PAYE system of income tax with rates between 25 and 55 per cent.

Capital Gains Tax (CGT): None, provided a property has been owned for three years.

Wealth Tax: None.

Inheritance & Gift Tax: Inheritance and gift tax is levied at between 1 and 30 per cent, depending on the relationship between the beneficiary and the donor or deceased.

Value Added Tax (VAT): The standard rate of VAT (KDV) is 17 per cent, with a reduced rate on foodstuffs of 1 per cent and a luxury rate of 25 per cent.

Property

Market: Turkey has a small but rapidly growing market for holiday homes, mostly on the Aegean and Mediterranean coasts. A number of developments targeted at foreign buyers have been built in recent years in 'holiday village' settings with a variety of sports and leisure facilities, including swimming pools, tennis and volleyball courts, football pitches, children's play areas and shops. As Turkey grows in popularity as a holiday destination, an increasing number of foreigners are buying homes there and property could have good investment potential. Turkey particularly appeals to those looking for something different, a largely unspoilt environment and a country with a colourful and fascinating history.

Areas: The most popular locations for foreign buyers are on the Aegean and Mediterranean coasts, particularly the areas around the resort of Belek and the towns of Antalya, Bodrum (opposite the Greek island of Kos), Izmir, Kalkan and Kas. Turkey also has a number of winter sports resorts, although available property is limited and of little interest to most foreign buyers.

Cost: Funds to buy a property in Turkey must be imported from abroad, for which official proof is required. Property prices are relatively low, particularly as the Turkish lira is a 'soft' currency and its value has decreased considerably in recent years against stronger currencies (including the US$ and sterling). Note that because of the fluctuation of the lira, the following prices, which were correct in mid-2001, should be taken only as a guide. Two-bedroom apartments on the Mediterranean coast cost from around TL90 billion and three-bedroom villas from TL150 billion. Old village houses can be bought from TL120 billion to TL240 billion, although some restoration may be required. Large new villas on seafront plots of around 1,300m^2 cost from TL300 billion. Note, however, that the quality of construction varies and it's important to compare finished properties in different price ranges.

Local Mortgages: Mortgages are available through some developers with local Turkish banks, although you can usually obtain better terms and a larger loan from a foreign lender. The maximum Turkish loan is usually around 75 per cent of a property's value and is repayable over a period of 15 years. Lenders take a first charge on the property as security.

Property Taxes: Property tax is levied on the estimated market value of land (0.6 per cent) and buildings (0.4 per cent) and is payable in two instalments in May and November. The tax on agricultural land is 0.5 per cent. Properties are re-valued every four years for tax purposes, and there's a 25 per cent reduction in property tax on new properties for the first four years.

Purchase Procedure: Note that the assistance of a lawyer in the purchase of property in Turkey is essential. Foreigners require permission from the Turkish authorities to buy a property and must pay in a convertible currency. When the vendor and buyer agree on a price, a preliminary contract is signed and a deposit paid, after which a lawyer is engaged to carry out the normal checks and draw up a notarised contract. Note that the checks can take from four to six months. At completion, the deeds (*tapu*) are signed in the presence of the Land Registrar and outstanding taxes, duties and the registration fee are paid. The buyer receives a copy of the deeds on the same day and the original is sent to Ankara to be registered.

Fees: Fees usually total between 7 and 9 per cent of the purchase price and include stamp duty at 4.8 per cent (the vendor also pays 4.8 per cent) of the declared value, notary fees of between 0.8 and 1.5 per cent, a registration fee for the sales contract and legal fees. If you're buying through an agent, you must usually pay his fee of around 3 per cent.

Precautions: It's essential to employ an English-speaking lawyer before signing anything (Turkish lawyers also practise in many foreign countries). If you use a proxy in Turkey to act on your behalf, you must take care whom you choose.

Holiday Letting: No restrictions.

Restrictions on Foreign Ownership: Usually none, although foreigners aren't permitted to buy property in certain villages or military areas.

Building Standards: Building standards in Turkey are variable and they aren't usually up to western European or North American standards (but are improving). Although some property is outstanding, there's generally a poor standard of construction and finishing of properties.

Personal Effects: Personal effects and household goods (including a car) may be imported duty-free by permanent residents. Non-residents may have to pay import duty on certain items.

General Information

Crime Rate: Serious crime is relatively rare in Turkey, particularly outside the main cities and in rural areas. You should take the usual precautions against burglary, however.

Medical Facilities: Medical services are adequate in major cities and towns, where there are many foreign-trained doctors who speak English and other foreign languages. There are foreign hospitals and clinics in Istanbul. Private health insurance is essential for foreigners.

Pets: An application for an import licence for a pet must be made at your nearest Turkish embassy. You require a 'certificate of origin' and a health record. There's no quarantine in Turkey, but a pet requires a certificate of health (issued not more than 15 days before the date of import) stating that it's in good health and has been vaccinated against rabies.

Residence Permits: Applications for residence permits must be made to the nearest Turkish embassy. Prospective residents require a visa and retirees must have sufficient income to maintain themselves in Turkey without working. Visitors can stay for three months at a time.

Work Permits: Work permits are difficult to obtain and applications must be for a position that cannot be filled by a Turkish national. Employers require permission from the Foreign Investment Directorate to employ foreigners.

Reference

Useful Addresses

Turkish Embassy, 1714 Massachusetts Ave, NW, Washington, DC 20036, USA (☎ 202-659 8200, 🖳 www.turkey.org/turkey).
Turkish Embassy, 43 Belgrave Square, London SW1X 8PA, UK (☎ 020-7393 0202, 🖳 www.turkishembassy-london.com).
Turkish Information Office, 821 United Nations Plaza, New York, NY 10017, USA (☎ 212-687 2194).
Turkish Office of Information, 1st Floor, 170–173 Piccadilly, London W1V 9DD, UK (☎ 020-7629 7711).

USA

Background Information

Capital: Washington DC.
Population: 281.4 million.
Foreign Community: The USA is extremely cosmopolitan, particularly in the major cities, and a nation of immigrants (although today only some 7.5 per cent of the population is foreign-born). There are large immigrant communities from all major countries.
Area: 9,399,300km² (3,615,125mi²).
Geography: The USA consists of 48 contiguous states on the mainland of North America, plus Alaska and Hawaii, and it's the third largest country in the world after Canada and China. It measures around 2,500mi (4,023km) from east to west (from the Atlantic to the Pacific coasts) and stretches some 1,200mi (1,931km) north to south, from the Canadian border (mostly along the 49th parallel) to the Gulf of Mexico. Alaska, which joined the Union as the 49th (and largest) state in 1959, is situated north-west of Canada and is separated from Russia by the Bering Strait. Hawaii joined the Union in 1960 as the 50th state and comprises a group of islands in the mid-Pacific Ocean, some 2,500mi (4,023km) to the south-west of continental America. The USA also administers over 2,000 islands, islets, cays and atolls in the Pacific and Caribbean, including American Samoa, Guam, Puerto Rico and the US Virgin Islands. The contiguous states consist generally of the highland region of Appalachia in the East, the Rocky Mountains in the West and the Great Plains in the centre. The highest point is Mount McKinley (6,193m/20,320ft) in Alaska and the lowest Death Valley in California (86m/282ft below sea level).

Climate: Because of its vast size and varied topography, ranging from sub-tropical forests to permanent glaciers, from deserts to swamplands, America's climate varies enormously. The range of weather in the contiguous states is similar to what is experienced in Europe (from northern Finland to the south of Spain). In winter it's cold or freezing everywhere except in the southern states. The coldest areas include the Plains, the Midwest and the Northeast, where temperatures can remain well below freezing for weeks on end. A long hot summer is normal throughout America, with the exception of northern New England, Oregon and Washington state.

Language: English (or American English) is the official language, although it isn't the primary language for some 15 per cent of Americans. Spanish is the main foreign language and is spoken by some 17 million people.

Political Stability: The USA is one of the world's most politically stable countries. The Constitution lays down the division of power, which is split between the executive (the President), the legislature (Congress) and the judiciary. Power is also split between federal, state and local governments. Each state has its own semi-autonomous government headed by a governor who's elected for four years. There's no system of proportional representation in America and elections are based on a 'winner takes all' system. This usually results in a very stable government, as coalition governments are unknown and independent politicians rarely get elected. American politics is dominated by just two parties, the Democrats and the Republicans, who fill every seat in Congress and provide most state governors and other posts at state and local government level.

Finance

Currency: US Dollar (US$).

Exchange Rate: £1 = US$1.45.

Exchange Controls: None.

Interest Rate: 2.5 per cent.

Cost/Standard of Living: The USA enjoys one of the highest standards and lowest costs of living in the world, although it varies considerably between different states and regions, and between cities and rural areas. The cost of 'luxury' imported goods is lower than in almost any other country. Cars are inexpensive and cost up to 50 per cent less than in some European countries.

Income Tax: Federal income tax rates are from 15 to 39.6 per cent, although state and local income taxes are also payable in some counties and states. Non-residents are generally taxed only on income from sources in America. State income tax rates vary considerably from state to state, although guidelines are set by the federal government, and some states have no state income tax, including Alaska, Florida, Nevada, New Hampshire, South Dakota, Tennessee, Texas, Washington and Wyoming. Non-resident homeowners must file an annual tax return. Tax on rental income earned by non-residents is at 30 per cent, although mortgage interest and other expenses can be offset against income. **Note that US citizens and residents are subject to tax on world-wide income, regardless of source**, although there are annual exclusions.

Capital Gains Tax (CGT): Capital gains are included in gross income and must be reported on a non-resident's tax return (form 1040NR). Net gains are taxed at ordinary rates, although the maximum rate for long-term gains is 20 per cent (10 per cent for individuals in the 15 per cent income tax bracket). Once every two years, US taxpayers may exclude up to $250,000 ($500,000 for married taxpayers filing jointly) of gains derived from the sale of a principal residence. The residence must have been owned and used for at least two of the five years preceding the sale. Non-residents generally pay CGT at 15 per cent up to US$23,350 and at 28 per cent above this amount. When a non-resident sells a property, the buyer in some states (e.g. Florida) is required to withhold 10 per cent of the purchase price as security against unpaid taxes.

Wealth Tax: None.

Inheritance & Gift Tax: An Estate Tax Return (form 706) must be filed when the gross estate of a US citizen or resident exceeds US$675,000 or the gross US estate of a non-resident exceeds US$600,000 at the time of death. Residents receive a credit against federal estate and gift taxes equivalent to the tax on an estate worth US$600,000. This credit will be indexed annually for inflation, up to a maximum estate value of $1 million in 2006. Non-residents are granted a credit of US$13,000, which effectively exempts the first US$60,000 of an estate from tax. A federal gift tax is imposed on the gratuitous transfer of property and is usually payable by the donor. You can give US$10,000 to any individual during any calendar year without incurring gift tax; a couple can agree to treat gifts to individuals as joint gifts and exclude up to US$20,000 a year. Gift and estate tax rates are from 18 to 55 per cent. In addition to federal estate tax, some 20 states also impose estate tax on estates left to a spouse or child.

Value Added Tax (VAT): There's no system of VAT in the USA, but sales tax is levied in 45 states at between 3 and 7 per cent. Sales tax must usually be added to advertised or displayed prices.

Other Taxes: Some states impose a sales tax on letting income, and certain counties in some states (e.g. Florida) levy other taxes on letting income, such as a tourist development tax, resort tax, tourist impact tax or a convention development tax.

Property

Market: The USA has a vast and flourishing property market, both domestically and internationally, and there's a vast range and quantity of homes to choose from. Millions of properties change hands each year and some 1.5 million new homes and apartments are built annually. Although the recession in the early '90s dealt the American property market a severe blow, it has now recovered. The demand for vacation homes by non-residents has increased dramatically in the last decade, particularly in America's 'sunbelt', stretching from California in the west to Florida in the east.

The choice and variety of property is huge and includes golf and country club developments, marina and waterfront homes with private moorings, and a vast range of inland sites with unique attractions. Developments usually consist of individual plots (e.g. for ranch or villa-style, one-family homes) and/or town-house/condo complexes with communal swimming pools, jacuzzis, saunas, heated spas, racquetball and tennis courts, golf courses, health clubs or fitness centres, and picnic and barbecue areas. Homes in ski resorts are also popular, as are residential communities with comprehensive fitness, recreational and social facilities (many free to residents). American homes are generally bigger, more luxurious and better equipped than homes in other western countries, particularly in rural areas. A large number of (usually free) property catalogues, magazines and newspapers are published in all states.

Areas: Every American state has a particular appeal, both for holiday homeowners and permanent residents, and many are ideal locations for both summer and winter holiday homes. Traditionally, the most popular US destinations for foreigners have been California, Florida and New York, although buyers are now spreading their wings, and homes in Georgia, North and South Carolina, Louisiana, Tennessee, Texas, Washington (e.g. Seattle), and Virginia and West Virginia are also in demand. The mountain states of Montana, Idaho, Wyoming, Utah, Colorado, Arizona and New Mexico are becoming increasingly popular with vacation home buyers, particularly with winter sports enthusiasts.

Although expensive, property in popular cities such as New York and San Francisco is a good investment and there's a constant demand for quality properties. Retirement communities, incorporating a wide variety of sports and leisure facilities, are common in many states. Although many Europeans, particularly the British, still think of Florida as the only American state in which to buy a vacation home, many other states offer excellent year-round weather and aren't as congested as Florida. The most popular areas in Florida include Clearwater, Orlando, Sarasota, St Petersburg and Tampa Bay.

Cost: Property prices in America have remained relatively stable and generally offer better value than equivalent homes in Europe (always depending, of course, on prevailing exchange rates), with prices in the sunbelt states (particularly Florida) kept down by intense competition. Prices vary considerably from region to region and area to area. A typical house of 167m² (1,800ft²)costs around $400,000 in Washington DC, $550,000 in Boston and San Francisco, and up to twice as much in New York city. However, in rural areas and small towns (including many areas popular for holiday and retirement homes such as Florida) the same size home can be purchased for as little as $75,000 to $100,000.

New homes in Florida cost from around $70,000 for a two-bedroom, two-bathroom detached home with a one-car garage or a two-bedroom, two-bathroom condominium (apartment) with a community pool. A 185m² (2,000ft²) property with jacuzzi and pool can be purchased for as little as $120,000. A wide range of quality fixtures and fittings is installed as standard equipment and homes in popular resort areas can be bought 'turn-key furnished' and ready to occupy. Although most foreigners buy new homes, resale homes are often better value. Southern and central Florida have become more expensive in recent years, particularly around Disney World and on the southern Gulf coast, and you generally need to look north of Tampa to find the best value. Rural building plots are available from as little as $6,000 to $12,000 in many states.

Local Mortgages: Mortgages in America are available from a number of sources, including savings and loan associations (who provide over half of all mortgages), commercial banks, mortgage bankers, insurance companies, builders and developers, and government agencies. Most American lenders won't lend more than 70 or 80 per cent of the value of a property over a period of 10 to 30 years (typically 30 years).

Credit and income checks are rigorous, although mortgages of up to 70 per cent are obtainable without proof of income or tax returns. Note that it's difficult and usually more expensive to raise finance for an American property abroad.

Property Taxes: Property tax is levied annually on property owners in all states to help pay for local services such as primary and secondary education, police and fire services, libraries, public transport, waste disposal, highways and road safety, maintaining trading standards, and personal social services. Property taxes on a house of average value vary considerably from zero (in some areas houses valued below a certain amount, e.g. US$75,000, are exempt) or around US$500 (e.g. in West Virginia) to around $6,000 a year in wealthy states (e.g. New Hampshire). Tax rates are fixed by communities and are expressed as an amount per US$100 or US$1,000 (the 'millage' rate) of the assessed market value of a property (e.g. US$15 per US$1,000).

Purchase Procedure: Usually you pay an initial 'good faith' deposit (also known as 'earnest money'), e.g. US$1,000 to US$5,000, to show that you're a serious buyer, and sign a contract that's binding on both parties. The deposit is usually 1 per cent of the purchase price, although it can be as high as 5 per cent. In California and some other states your deposit and all other funds must be placed with a neutral third party, the 'escrow agent', who's usually selected by the buyer's estate agent (but is subject to approval by all parties). He's responsible for compiling and checking documents and ensuring that the transaction can 'close' within the period specified in the purchase contract. Once the deal closes, the escrow agent records the deed and pays the funds to the appropriate parties.

If you withdraw from a purchase, you lose your deposit or can be forced to go through with it, so don't sign a contract without taking legal advice. A contract usually contains a number of conditions (riders or contingencies) that must be met before it becomes valid and binding, e.g. house and termite inspections and your ability to obtain a mortgage (if necessary) by a certain date. Conditions may vary from region to region and state to state. Some, such as a termite inspection, may be required by law, while others (e.g. a house inspection or survey) may be insisted upon by your estate agent or lender. The contract must list anything included in the price, such as furniture, fittings and extras, and should specify who pays the fees associated with the purchase. Standard contracts can usually be tailored to individual requirements.

Fees: You should allow around 5 per cent of the purchase price for closing or settlement costs. These may include a lender's appraisal (valuation) fee, legal fees, title search, title insurance, recording fees, survey/home inspection, homeowner's insurance and mortgage tax. Many people use a buyer's broker or agency, which doesn't usually cost any more than buying direct from a developer. Before you engage an agent, make sure you know exactly who will pay his fees. Usually agents' commissions are split between the buyer and seller, but this isn't always the case.

Precautions: From a legal viewpoint, America is one of the safest countries in the world in which to buy a home. However, you should take the usual precautions regarding deposits and obtaining proper title. Owner's title insurance is mandatory in some states and is usually required by lenders. In many states, hiring a lawyer for a property transaction is standard practice, although it isn't always necessary when a state (such as California) has mandatory escrow and title insurance (to protect against a future claim on the title by a third party). Before hiring a lawyer, compare the fees charged by a number of practices and make sure that they're experienced in property transactions. As when buying property in any country, you should never pay any money or sign anything without first taking legal advice.

Most experts believe that you should always have a house inspection (survey) on a resale house, and a termite inspection is almost mandatory on an older home, as America has numerous varieties of wood-boring insects. Make sure that all local taxes and water/sewerage bills have been paid by the previous owner, as these charges usually come with the property (and if unpaid are passed on to subsequent owners). You're afforded extra protection if you buy from a licensed and registered realtor, rather than an estate agent, as realtors are bound by a strict code of ethics. You must *never* sign anything pertaining to the purchase of property in the USA without going there and checking that the developer and land actually exist (they've been known not to!). As in most countries, there are crooks who prey on 'greenhorn' foreigners.

Holiday Letting: There are restrictions in some communities regarding short-term lets. In some developments, short-term rentals (generally less than 28 or 30 days, but in some cases less than six months) are prohibited, although if this is so you should be notified before buying. For example, Orange and Seminole counties in Florida don't permit lets of less than six months (usually because permanent residents don't wish to live in a community or development where people are coming and going every few months). Because most foreign property owners are limited to spending a maximum of six months in the USA, most developers (e.g. in Florida) provide management and letting services. Note that agents in America aren't permitted to offer guaranteed rental income, although some do. Rental income earned by non-resident aliens is taxable in America (e.g. 30 per cent in Florida) and you must also charge a sales tax on short-term rentals, payable to the state, plus local county taxes in some states (e.g. Florida).

Restrictions on Foreign Ownership: None.

Building Standards: Excellent. Building standards are strictly controlled and high quality fixtures and fittings are usually standard. American property generally provides excellent value with regard to size and quality of construction and of fixtures and fittings.

Personal Effects: When you enter America to take up permanent or temporary residence, you can usually import your belongings duty and tax-free. Any duty or tax payable depends on your country of origin, where you purchased the goods, how long you've owned them, and whether duty or tax has been paid in another country. Personal effects owned and used for at least one year prior to importation are usually exempt from import duty.

General Information

Crime Rate: One of the major drawbacks of living in the USA is the high crime rate, particularly of violent crime. The crime rate varies considerably with the state, county and city or town, and it's important to check crime statistics and avoid high crime areas. If you come from a country with a relatively low crime rate, e.g. anywhere in western Europe, it's important to bear in mind that **the ground rules aren't the same in America.** Avoid the ghetto areas of inner cities day and night, some of which are even no-go areas for armed policemen. Be extremely wary of where you go at night and always use a taxi rather than walk.

Medical Facilities: Health care in the USA is among the best in the world, provided you can afford it! There's no free treatment for visitors who fall ill in America and health insurance is essential for both visitors and residents alike. The health insurance cover required when visiting most other countries is totally inadequate in America, where the recommended minimum annual cover is around US$500,000. Health insurance in America is *very* expensive, with a typical policy for a family of four costing US$thousands a year (between US$1,000 and US$2,000 a month is typical). The average American family spends around 15 per cent of its income on health care!

Pets: All animals and birds imported into America must meet health and customs requirements (as are pets taken out of America and returned). Pets, particularly cats and dogs, must be examined at the port of entry for signs of disease that can be transmitted to humans. Dogs must be vaccinated against rabies at least 30 days prior to entry. Exceptions include puppies less than three months old and dogs originating from or having been located for at least six months in areas designated by the Public Health Service as being rabies-free. Vaccination against rabies isn't required for cats. Birds must be quarantined upon arrival for at least 30 days in a facility operated by the US Department of Agriculture (at the owner's expense).

Residence Permits: Residence permits are difficult to obtain unless you qualify for a green (residence) card, although with official immigration running at around 1 million a year, there are many opportunities. The easiest and quickest way for most people to obtain a green card is to buy a business, which qualifies you for an E-2 investor visa. Residence permits aren't issued to retirees (unless they're very rich!). Visitors can stay for 90 days at a time (six months a year), and nationals of most western countries (including Britain) don't need a visa for visits of up to three months.

Work Permits: A work permit (green card) is required to live or work in the USA and is difficult to obtain unless you qualify, for example through birthright, relationship, employment or investment.

Reference

Further Reading

BUYING A HOME IN FLORIDA, David Hampshire (Survival Books).
Everything you need to know about buying a home in Florida.
LIVING & WORKING IN AMERICA, David Hampshire (Survival Books).
Everything you need to know about living and working in America.
American Country Homes, 83 Clockhouse Road, Beckenham, Kent BR3 4JU, UK (☎ 020-8658 2094).
American Holiday & Life, PO Box 604, Hemel Hempstead, Herts HP1 3SR, UK. Tourist magazine.
Applying for a United States Visa, Richard Fleischer (How To Books).
The Complete Guide to Life in Florida, Barbara Brumm LaFreniere & Edward N. LaFreniere (Pineapple Press).
Essentially America, Warners Distribution, The Maltings, Manor Lane, Bourne, Lincs PE10 9PH, UK (☎ 01778-393652). Lifestyle and tourist magazine.

Florida Homes and Travel Newsletter, 9438 US Hwy 19, #318, Port Richey, Florida 34668-4623, USA (💻 www.floridahomesandtravel.com). Newsletter for Florida homeowners and frequent visitors published ten times a year.
Florida Trend, 490 First Ave South, St Petersburg, Florida 33701, USA (☎ 727-821 5800, 💻 www.floridatrend.com). Business magazine.
Going USA, Outbound Newspapers, 1 Commercial Road, Eastbourne, East Sussex BN21 3XQ, UK (☎ 01323-726040, 💻 www.outbound-newspapers.com). Monthly newspaper for those planning to live, work or holiday in the USA.
Life in America's Small Cities, G. Scott Thomas (Prometheus Books).
Welcome to New York, Roberta Seret (American Welcome Services Press).

Useful Addresses

American Association of Retired Persons (AARP), 601 East Street, NW, Washington, DC 20049 (☎1800-424 3410, 💻 www.aarp.org).
American Embassy, 24 Grosvenor Square, London W1A 1AE, UK (☎ 020-7499 9000, 💻 www.usembassy.org.uk).
Department of Housing and Urban Development, 451 7th Street, SW, Washington, DC 20410, USA (☎ 202-708 1112, 💻 www.hud.gov).
Florida Association of Realtors, 7025 Augusta National Drive, PO Box 725025, Orlando, FL 32872-5025, USA (☎ 407-438 1400, 💻 http://fl.living.net).
Florida Brits Club, Stanhope House, 18 Grange Close, Skelton, York YO3 6YR, UK (☎ 01904-471800, ✉ flabritscl@aol.com).
United National Real Estate, 4700 Belleview, PO Box 11400, Kansas City, Missouri 64112, USA (☎ toll-free 800-999 1020, 💻 www.unitedcountry.com).
USA Information Resource Centre in London, UK (☎ 020-7894 0925).
💻 **www.britishinamerica.com**. Expatriate website.

APPENDICES

APPENDIX A: USEFUL ADDRESSES

The addresses below are designed to help you obtain further information about buying property in the countries featured in this book. See also the listings under individual countries ('Useful Addresses') in **Chapter 6**.

Embassies in Britain (London)

American Embassy, Grosvenor Square, London W1A 1AE, UK (☎ 020-7499 9000, 🖳 www.usembassy.org.uk).

Australian High Commission, Australia House, Strand, London WC2B 4LA, UK (☎ 020 7438 4334, 🖳 www.australia.org.uk).

Austrian Embassy, 18 Belgrave Mews West, London SW1X 8HU, UK (☎ 020-7235 3731).

Canadian High Commission, Macdonald House, 1 Grosvenor Square, London W1X 0AB, UK (☎ 020-7258 6600, 🖳 www.canada.org.uk).

Cyprus High Commission, 93 Park Street, London W1Y 4ET, UK (☎ 020-7499 8272).

French Embassy, 58 Knightsbridge, London SW1X 7JT, UK (☎ 020-7201 1000, 🖳 www.ambafrance.org.uk).

German Embassy, 23 Belgrave Square, 1 Chesham Place, London SW1X 8PZ, UK (☎ 020-7824 1300, 🖳 www.german-embassy.org.uk).

Greek Embassy, 1A Holland Park, London W11 3TP, UK (☎ 020-7229 3850, 🖳 www.greekembassy.org.uk).

Irish Embassy, 17 Grosvenor Place, London SW1X 7HR, UK (☎ 020-7235 2171).

Italian Embassy, 14 Three Kings Yard, Davies Street, London W1Y 2EH, UK (☎ 020-7312 2200, 🖳 www.embitaly.org.uk).

Maltese High Commission, Malta House, 36–38 Piccadilly, London W1V 0PP, UK (☎ 020-7292 4800).

New Zealand High Commission, New Zealand House, Haymarket, London SW1Y 4TQ, UK (☎ 020-7930 8422, 🖳 www.nzembassy.com).

Portuguese Embassy, 11 Belgrave Square, London SW1X 8PP, UK (☎ 020-7235 5331, 🖳 www.portembassy.gla.ac.uk).

South African Embassy, South Africa House, Trafalgar Square, London WC2N 5DP, UK (☎ 020-7451 7299, 🖳 www.southafricahouse.com).

Spanish Embassy, 39 Chesham Place, London SW1X 8SB, UK (☎ 020-7235 5555, 🖳 www.cec-spain.org.uk).

Swiss Embassy, 16–18 Montagu Place, London W1H 2BQ, UK (☎ 020-7723 0701, 🖳 www.swissembassy.org.uk).

Turkish Embassy, 43 Belgrave Square, London SW1X 8PA, UK (☎ 020-7393 0202, 🖳 www.turkishembassy-london.com).

Embassies in the USA (Washington DC)

Australian Embassy, 1601 Massachusetts Ave, NW, Washington, DC 20036, USA (☎ 202-797 3000, 💻 www.ausemb.org).

Austrian Embassy, 3524 International Court, NW, Washington, DC 20008, USA (☎ 202-895 6700, 💻 www.austria-emb.org).

British Embassy, 3100 Massachusetts Ave, NW, Washington, DC 20008, USA (☎ 202-462 1340, 💻 www.britainusa.com).

Canadian Embassy, 501 Pennsylvania Ave, NW, Washington, DC 20001, USA (☎ 202-682 1740, 💻 www.cdnemb-washdc.org).

Cyprus Embassy, 2210 R St, NW, Washington, DC 20008, USA (☎ 202-462 5772).

French Embassy, 4101 Reservoir Rd, NW, Washington, DC 20007, USA (☎ 202-944 6000, 💻 www.info-france-usa.org).

German Embassy, 4645 Reservoir Rd, NW, Washington, DC 20007, USA (☎ 202-298 4000, 💻 www.germnay-info.org).

Greek Embassy, 2221 Massachusetts Ave, NW, Washington, DC 20008, USA (☎ 202-939 5800, 💻 www.greekembassy.org).

Irish Embassy, 2234 Massachusetts Ave, NW, Washington, DC 20008, USA (☎ 202-462 3939, 💻 www.irelandemb.org).

Italian Embassy, 1601 Fuller St, NW, Washington, DC 20009, USA (☎ 202-328 5500).

Maltese Consulate, 2017 Connecticut Ave, NW, Washington, DC 20008, USA (☎ 202-462 3611).

New Zealand Embassy, 37 Observatory Circle, NW, Washington, DC 20008, USA (☎ 202-328 4800, 💻 www.nzemb.org).

Portuguese Embassy, 2125 Kalorama Rd, NW, Washington, DC 20008, USA (☎ 202-328 8610, 💻 www.portugal.org).

South African Embassy, 3051 Massachusetts Ave, NW, Washington, DC 20008, USA (☎ 202-232 4400, 💻 www.southafrica.net).

Spanish Embassy, 2375 Pennsylvania Ave, NW, Washington, DC 20037, USA (☎ 202-452 0100, 💻 www.spainemb.org).

Swiss Embassy, 2900 Cathedral Ave, NW, Washington, DC 20008, USA (☎ 202-745 7900, 💻 www.swissemb.org).

Turkish Embassy, 1714 Massachusetts Ave, NW, Washington, DC 20036, USA (☎ 202-659 8200, 💻 www.turkey.org/turkey).

Publications

Holiday Villas Magazine, Merricks Publishing, Wessex Buildings, Somerton Business Park, Somerton, Somerset TA11 6SB, UK (☎ 01458-274447, 💻 www. holidayvillasmagazine.co.uk).

Homes Overseas, Blendon Communications, 207 Providence Square, Mill Street, London SE1 2EW, UK (☎ 020-7939 9888, 🖵 www.homesoverseas.co.uk). Bimonthly international property magazine.

International Homes Magazine, 3 St John's Court, Moulsham Street, Chelmsford, Essex CM2 0JD, UK (☎ 01245-358877, 🖵 www.international-homes.com). A bimonthly subscription magazine about property round the world.

Private Villas (Rentals), 52 High Street, Henley-in-Arden, Solihull, West Midlands B95 5BR, UK (☎ 01564-794011).

Resident Abroad, Maple House, 149 Tottenham Court Road, London W1P 9LL, UK (☎ 020-7896 2525, 🖵 www.ra.st.com). Monthly magazine for British expatriates.

Unique Homes, 327 Wall St, Princeton, NJ 08540, USA (🖵 www.uniquehomes. com). A magazine specialising in luxury properties around the world.

World of Property, Outbound Publishing, 1 Commercial Road, Eastbourne, East Sussex BN21 3XQ, UK (☎ 01323 726040).

Miscellaneous

American Citizens Abroad (ACA), 5 Rue Liotard, 1202, Geneva, Switzerland (☎ 022-340 0233, 🖵 www.aca.ch).

The British Association of Removers (BAR) Overseas, 3 Churchill Court, 58 Station Road, North Harrow HA2 7SA, UK (☎ 020-8861 3331, 🖵 www.bar movers.com).

The Centre for International Briefing, Farnham Castle, Farnham, Surrey GU9 0AG, UK (☎ 01252-720416, 🖵 www.cibfarnham.com). Organises briefing courses for people moving overseas.

Corona Worldwide, South Bank House, Blackprince Road, London SE1 7SJ, UK (☎ 020-7793 4020, ✉ hq@coronaww.prestel.co.uk). Organises expatriate briefing courses.

Employment Conditions Abroad, Anchor House, 15 Britten Street, London SW3 3TY, UK (☎ 020-7351 7151, 🖵 www.eca-international.com). Publishes *Outlines for Expatriates* for over 70 countries.

European Council of International Schools (ECIS), 21 Lavant Street, Petersfield, Hants GU32 3EL, UK (☎ 01730-268244, 🖵 www.ecis.org).

Federation of Overseas Property Developers, Agents and Consultants (FOPDAC), 3rd Floor, 95 Aldwych, London WC2B 4JF, UK (☎ 020-8941 5588, 🖵 www.fopdac.com).

First National Trustee Company, International House, Castle Hill, Victoria Road, Douglas, Isle of Man IM2 4RB, UK (☎ 01624 630630, ✉ iom@fntc.com). Timeshare trustees.

Going Places, 84 Coombe Road, New Malden, Surrey KT3 4QS, UK (☎ 020-8949 8811). Organises tailor-made expatriate briefing courses.

Homebuyer Events, Mantle House, Broomhill Road, London SW18 4JQ, UK (☎ 020-8877 3636, 🖵 www.homebuyer.co.uk). Organises property shows.

The Law Society, 50 Chancery Lane, London WC2A 1SX, UK (☎ 020-7242 1222, 💻 www.lawsociety.org.uk). Provides names of lawyers specialising in property sales in certain countries.

Medical Advisory Service for Travellers Abroad (MASTA), London School of Hygiene and Tropical Medicine, Keppel Street, London WC1E 7HT, UK (☎ 01276-685040, 24-hour travellers' 'healthline' ☎ 0906-822 4100, 💻 www.masta.org).

National Association of Estate Agents (NAEA), Arbon House, 21 Jury Street, Warwick CV34 4EH, UK (☎ 01926-496800, 💻 www.naea.co.uk).

The Retirement Letter, 28 Eccleston Square, London SW1V 1PA, UK (💻 www.retirementletter.com).

The Timeshare Council, 23 Buckingham Gate, London SW1E 6LB, UK (☎ 020-7821 8845).

APPENDIX B: FURTHER READING

The books listed below are just a small selection of the many books written for those planning to buy a home or live abroad. Some titles may be out of print, but may still be obtainable from book shops and libraries. Books prefixed with an asterisk (*) are recommended by the author. See also the listings under individual countries ('Further Reading') in **Chapter 6**.

Living and Working Abroad

*LIVING & WORKING ABROAD, David Hampshire (Survival Books).

*Guide to Living Abroad, Michael Furnell & Philip Jones (Kogan Page).

*Guide to Working Abroad, Godfrey Golzen (Kogan Page).

Getting a Job Abroad Roger Jones (How To Books).

*Money Mail: Moves Abroad, Margaret Stone (Kogan Page).

Working Abroad, Jonathan Golding (How To Books).

Your Own Business in Europe, Mark Hempshell (How To Books).

Moving and Living Abroad, Sandra Albright, Alice Chu & Lori Austin (Hippocrene Books).

*US Expat Handbook Guide to Living & Working Abroad, John W. Adams.

Retirement

*The Good Retirement Guide, Rosemary Brown (Enterprise Dynamics).

How to Retire Abroad (How To Books).

Life in the Sun, Nancy Tuft (Age Concern England).

Retirement Abroad, Robert Cooke (Robert Hale).

Your Retirement, Rosemary Brown (Kogan Page).

Health

*The ABC of Healthy Travel (British Medical Journal).

Health Advice for Travellers (Department of Health, UK).

*How to Stay Healthy Abroad, Dr. R. Dawood (Oxford University Press).

Travellers' Health, Richard Dawood (Oxford Paperbacks).

*A Travellers' Medical Guide, Paul Zakowich (Kuperard).

APPENDIX C: USEFUL WEBSITES

There are dozens of expatriate websites and as the Internet increases in popularity the number grows by the day. Most information is useful and websites generally offer free access, although some require a subscription or payment for services. Relocation and other companies specialising in expatriate services often have websites, although these may only provide information that a company is prepared to offer free of charge, which although it can be useful may be rather biased. However, there are plenty of volunteer sites run by expatriates providing practical information and tips. A particularly useful section found on most expatriate websites is the 'message board' or 'forum', where expatriates answer questions based on their experience and knowledge, and offer an insight into what a country or city is really like.

Below is a list of some of the best expatriate websites. Note that websites are listed under headings in alphabetical order and the list is by no means definitive. Websites relating to specific countries are listed under individual countries ('Country Profiles') in **Chapter 6**.

General Websites

Direct Moving: (💻 www.directmoving.com). The first world-wide relocation portal with a plethora of expatriate information, tips and advice, and good links.

ExpatAccess: (💻 www.expataccess.com). ExpatAccess is specifically for those planning to move abroad, with free online moving guides to help you through the relocation process.

ExpatBoards: (💻 www.expatboards.com). A comprehensive site for expatriates, with popular discussion boards and special areas for Britons, Americans, expatriate taxes, and other important issues.

Escape Artist: (💻 www.escapeartist.com). An excellent website and probably the most comprehensive, packed with resources, links and directories covering most expatriate destinations. You can also subscribe to the free monthly online expatriate magazine, *Escape from America*.

Expat Exchange: (💻 www.expatexchange.com). Reportedly the largest online community for English-speaking expatriates, provides a series of articles on relocation and also a question and answer facility through its expatriate network.

Expat Forum: (💻 www.expatforum.com). Provides interesting cost of living comparisons as well as over 20 country-specific forums and chats.

Expat Network: (💻 www.expatnetwork.com). The leading expatriate website in the UK, which is essentially an employment network for expatriates, although there are also numerous support services plus a monthly online magazine, *Nexus*.

Expat World: (💻 www.expatworld.net). Contains a wealth of information for American and British expatriates, including a subscription newsletter.

Expatriate Experts: (💻 www.expatexpert.com). A website run by expatriate expert Robin Pascoe, providing invaluable advice and support.

Global People: (⌨ www.peoplegoingglobal.com). Provides interesting country-specific information with particular emphasis on social and political aspects.

Living Abroad: (⌨ www.livingabroad.com). Provides an extensive and comprehensive list of country profiles, although they're available only on payment.

Outpost Information Centre: (⌨ www.outpostexpat.nl). A website containing extensive country-specific information and links operated by the Shell Petroleum Company for its expatriate workers, but available to everyone.

Real Post Reports: (⌨ www.realpostreports.com). Provides relocation services, recommended reading lists and plenty of interesting 'real-life' stories containing anecdotes and impressions written by expatriates in just about every city in the world.

World Travel Guide: (⌨ www.wtgonline.com). A general website for world travellers and expatriates.

American Websites

Americans Abroad: (⌨ www.aca.ch). Offers advice, information and services to Americans abroad.

Americans in Britain: (⌨ www.britain-info.org). Provides a comprehensive list of fact sheets regarding living and working in the UK.

American Teachers Abroad: (⌨ www.overseasdigest.com). A comprehensive website with numerous relocation services and advice plus teaching opportunities.

US Government Trade: (⌨ www.usatrade.gov). A vast website providing a wealth of information principally for Americans planning to trade and invest abroad, but useful for anyone planning a move abroad.

British Websites

British in America: (⌨ www.britishinamerica.com and www.british-expats.com). Two websites designed for Britons in the USA.

British Expatriates: (⌨ www.britishexpat.com and www.ukworldwide.com). These websites keep British expatriates in touch with UK events and developments.

Trade Partners: (⌨ www.tradepartners.gov.uk). A government-sponsored website whose principal aim is to provide trade and investment information on just about every country in the world. Even if you aren't planning to do business abroad, the general information is comprehensive and up to date.

Worldwise Directory: (⌨ www.suzylamplugh.org/worldwise). Run by the Suzy Lamplugh charity for personal safety, providing a useful directory of countries with practical information and special emphasis on safety, particularly for women.

Australian & New Zealand Websites

Australians Abroad: (⌨ www.australiansabroad.com). Information for Australians concerning relocating plus a forum to exchange information and advice.

Kiwi Club: (🖥 www.kiwiclub.org). Information and support for New Zealanders in Austria, Switzerland, Singapore and North America.

Southern Cross Group: (🖥 www.southern-cross-group.org). A website for Australians and New Zealanders providing information and the exchange of tips.

Websites for Women

Career Women: (🖥 www.womenconnect.com). Contains career opportunities for women abroad plus a wealth of other useful information.

Women Abroad: (🖥 www.womanabroad.com). Offers the chance to subscribe to a monthly magazine of the same name and access to advice on careers, expatriate skills and the family abroad.

Spouse Abroad: (🖥 www.expatspouse.com). Designed with the expatriate spouse in mind with particular emphasis on careers and working abroad. You need to register and subscribe.

Expatriate Mothers: (🖥 http://expatmoms.tripod.com). Provides help and advice on how to survive as a mother on relocation.

Third Culture Kids: (🖥 www.tckworld.com). Designed for expatriate children.

Travel Information & Warnings

The websites listed below provide daily updated information about the political situation and natural disasters around the world, plus general travel and health advice and embassy addresses.

Australian Department of Foreign Affairs and Trade (🖥 www.dfat.gov.au/consular/advice/advices_mnu.html).

British Foreign and Commonwealth Office (🖥 www.fco.gov.uk/ travel).

Canadian Department of Foreign Affairs (🖥 http://voyage.dfait-maeci.gc.ca/menu-e.asp). Also publishes a useful series of free booklets for Canadians moving abroad.

Gov Spot (🖥 www.govspot.com/ask/travel.htm). US Government website.

New Zealand Ministry of Foreign Affairs and Trade (🖥 www.mft.govt.nz/ travel/report.html).

SaveWealth Travel (🖥 www.save wealth.com/travel/warnings).

The Travel Doctor (🖥 www.tmvc.com.au/info10.html). Contains a country by country vaccination guide.

Travelfinder (🖥 www.travelfinder.com/twarn/travel_warnings.html).

US Department of State (🖥 http://travel.state.gov/travel_warnings.html and http://travel.state.gov/warnings_list.html). Also contains warnings about drugs (http://travel.state.gov/drug_warning.html) and a list of useful travel publications (http://travel.state.gov/travel_pubs.html).

World Health Organization (🖥 www.who.int).

APPENDIX D: WEIGHTS & MEASURES

Although most countries officially use the metric system of measurement, nationals of a few countries (including the Americans and British) who are more familiar with the imperial system of measurement will find the tables on the following pages useful. Some comparisons shown are only approximate, but are close enough for most everyday uses. In addition to the variety of measurement systems used, clothes sizes often vary considerably with the manufacturer (as we all know only too well). Try all clothes on before buying and don't be afraid to return something if, when you try it on at home, you decide it doesn't fit (most shops will exchange goods or give a refund).

Women's Clothes

Continental	34	36	38	40	42	44	46	48	50	52
UK	8	10	12	14	16	18	20	22	24	26
USA	6	8	10	12	14	16	18	20	22	24

Pullovers

Pullovers	Women's						Men's					
Continental	40	42	44	46	48	50	44	46	48	50	52	54
UK	34	36	38	40	42	44	34	36	38	40	42	44
USA	34	36	38	40	42	44	sm	medium		large		xl

Note: sm = small, xl = extra large

Men's Shirts

Continental	36	37	38	39	40	41	42	43	44	46
UK/USA	14	14	15	15	16	16	17	17	18	-

Men's Underwear

Continental	5	6	7	8	9	10
UK	34	36	38	40	42	44
USA	small	medium		large	extra large	

Children's Clothes

Continental	92	104	116	128	140	152
UK	16/18	20/22	24/26	28/30	32/34	36/38
USA	2	4	6	8	10	12

Children's Shoes

Continental	18	19	20	21	22	23	24	25	26	27	28	29	30	31	32
UK/USA	2	3	4	4	5	6	7	7	8	9	10	11	11	12	13

Continental	33	34	35	36	37	38
UK/USA	1	2	2	3	4	5

Shoes (Women's and Men's)

Continental	35	35	36	37	37	38	39	39	40	40	41	42	42	43	44	44
UK	2	3	3	4	4	5	5	6	6	7	7	8	8	9	9	10
USA	4	4	5	5	6	6	7	7	8	8	9	9	10	10	11	11

Weight

Avoirdupois	Metric	Metric	Avoirdupois
1 oz	28.35 g	1 g	0.035 oz
1 pound*	454 g	100 g	3.5 oz
1 cwt	50.8 kg	250 g	9 oz
1 ton	1,016 kg	500 g	18 oz
1 tonne	2,205 pounds	1 kg	2.2 pounds

* A metric 'pound' is 500g, g = gramme, kg = kilogramme

Length

British/US	Metric	Metric	British/US
1 inch	2.54 cm	1 cm	0.39 inch
1 foot	30.48 cm	1 m	3 feet 3.25 inches
1 yard	91.44 cm	1 km	0.62 mile
1 mile	1.6 km	8 km	5 miles

Note: cm = centimetre, m = metre, km = kilometre

Capacity

Imperial	Metric	Metric	Imperial
1 pint (USA)	0.47 litre	1 litre	1.76 UK pints
1 pint (UK)	0.57 litre	1 litre	0.26 US gallons
1 gallon (USA)	3.78 litre	1 litre	0.22 UK gallon
1 gallon (UK)	4.54 litre	1 litre	35.21 fluid oz

Square Measure

British/US	Metric	Metric	British/US
1 square inch	0.45 sq. cm	1 sq. cm	0.15 sq. inches
1 square foot	0.09 sq. m	1 sq. m	10.76 sq. feet
1 square yard	0.84 sq. m	1 sq. m	1. 2 sq. yards
1 acre	0.4 hectares	1 hectare	2.47 acres
1 square mile	259 hectares	1 sq. km	0.39 sq. mile

Temperature

° Celsius	° Fahrenheit	
0	32	freezing point of water
5	41	
10	50	
15	59	
20	68	
25	77	
30	86	
35	95	
40	104	

Note: The boiling point of water is 100°C / 212°F.

Oven Temperature

Gas	Electric	
	°F	°C
-	225–250	110–120
1	275	140
2	300	150
3	325	160
4	350	180
5	375	190
6	400	200
7	425	220
8	450	230
9	475	240

For a quick conversion, the Celsius temperature is approximately half the Fahrenheit temperature.

Temperature Conversion

Celsius to Fahrenheit: multiply by 9, divide by 5 and add 32.
Fahrenheit to Celsius: subtract 32, multiply by 5 and divide by 9.

Body Temperature

Normal body temperature (if you're alive and well) is 98.4° Fahrenheit, which equals 37° Celsius.

APPENDIX E: SERVICE DIRECTORY

The The following companies offer services to those planning to live and work abroad. Please mention *Buying a Home Abroad* when contacting companies.

Agents (Property)

KBM Consultancy, No. 4 Carpenters Buildings, The Avenue, Cirencester, Gloucester GL7 1EJ, UK (☎ 01285-656700, ▤ 01285-657090, ✉ karen@kbm-europe.co.uk). Contact: Karen Mulcahy. Family-run business specialising in helping families to find their holiday home from home in Spain.

Propertunities Ltd,13–17 Newbury Street, Wantage, Oxon, OX12 8BU, UK (☎ 01235-772345, ▤ 01235-770018, ✉ villas@propertunities.co.uk). Contact: Maureen Knight (Sales Administrator). Costa Blanca, Costa Calida. Homes in unspoilt locations. Widest selection. Inspection tours. After-sales service.

The Property Mart, C/ Maestro Torralba 9, Urb. La Zenia, Orihuela Costa, Spain (☎ 0966-730005, ▤ 0966-730391, ✉ info@property-mart.com, 🖳 www.property. mart.com). Contact: Ivor or Judith (Property Consultants). New and resale properties. Personal and friendly service. Visit our website.

Insurance

Costamedconsulting, C/Maestro Torralba 13, Urb. La Zenia, Orihuela Costa, Spain (☎ 0966-730006, ▤ 0966-730391). Contact: Janice M. Wretman (Consultant). Conveyancing, wills, inheritance documents, home/health insurance, fiscal representation and notary translations.

Interglobal Insurance Services, Lumbry Park, Selbourne Road, Alton, Hampshire GU34 3HF, UK (☎ 01420-566170, ▤ 01420-566120, ✉ global@inter-grout.co.uk). Contact: Nicole Grace (Client Services Manager). International private medical insurance plans for singles, couples and families. **See advertisement inside back cover.**

Legal Services

John Howell & Co., 17 Maiden Lane, Covent Garden, London WC2E 7NA, UK (☎ 020-7420 0400, ▤ 020-7836 3626, ✉ info@europelaw.com, 🖳 www.europelaw. com). Contact: John Howell. Fully insured, specialist English solicitors with 14 years' experience and 19 associate offices in Spain.

Publications

Focus on France and **World of Property**, Outbound Publishing, 1 Commercial Road, Eastbourne, East Sussex BN21 3XQ, UK (☎ 01323-412001, ▤ 01323-649249, ✉ outbounduk@aol.com). Quarterly property magazines.

Woman Abroad, Postmark Publishing, 1 Portsmouth Road, Guildford, Surrey GU2 4YB, UK (☎ 01483-577284, ✉ subscriptions@womanabroad.com, 💻 www. womanabroad.com). The magazine written especially for women living or working abroad.

INDEX

BUYING A HOME IN SPAIN

Buying a Home in Spain is essential reading for anyone planning to purchase property in Spain and is designed to guide you through the jungle and make it a pleasant and enjoyable experience. Most importantly, it is packed with vital information to help you avoid the sort of disasters that can turn your dream home into a nightmare! Topics covered include:

- Avoiding problems
- Choosing the region
- Finding the right home & location
- Estate agents
- Finance, mortgages & taxes
- Home security
- Utilities, heating & air-conditioning
- Moving house & settling in
- Renting & letting
- Permits & visas
- Travelling & communications
- Health & insurance
- Renting a car & driving
- Retirement & starting a business
- And much, much more!

Buying a Home in Spain is the most comprehensive and up-to-date source of information available about buying property in Spain. Whether you want a detached house, townhouse or apartment, a holiday or a permanent home, this book will help make your dreams come true.

Buy this book and save yourself time, trouble and money!

Order your copies today by phone, fax, mail or e-mail from: Survival Books, PO Box 146, Wetherby, West Yorks. LS23 6XZ, United Kingdom (☎/▤ +44 (0)1937-843523, ✉ orders@survivalbooks.net, ▦ www.survivalbooks.net).

ORDER FORM – ALIEN'S / BUYING A HOME SERIES

Qty.	Title	Price (incl. p&p)*			Total
		UK	Europe	World	
	The Alien's Guide to America	Autumn 2002			
	The Alien's Guide to Britain	£5.95	£6.95	£8.45	
	The Alien's Guide to France	£5.95	£6.95	£8.45	
	Buying a Home Abroad	£13.45	£14.95	£16.95	
	Buying a Home in Britain	£11.45	£12.95	£14.95	
	Buying a Home in Florida	£11.45	£12.95	£14.95	
	Buying a Home in France	£13.45	£14.95	£16.95	
	Buying a Home in Greece & Cyprus	£13.45	£14.95	£16.95	
	Buying a Home in Ireland	£11.45	£12.95	£14.95	
	Buying a Home in Italy	£11.45	£12.95	£14.95	
	Buying a Home in Portugal	£11.45	£12.95	£14.95	
	Buying a Home in South Africa	£13.45	£14.95	£16.95	
	Buying a Home in Spain	£11.45	£12.95	£14.95	
	Rioja and its Wines	£11.45	£12.95	£14.95	
	The Wines of Spain	£15.95	£18.45	£21.95	
				Total	

Order your copies today by phone, fax, mail or e-mail from: Survival Books, PO Box 146, Wetherby, West Yorks. LS23 6XZ, UUK (☎/▤ +44 (0)1937-843523, ✉ orders@survivalbooks.net, 💻 www.survivalbooks.net). If you aren't entirely satisfied, simply return them to us within 14 days for a full and unconditional refund.

Cheque enclosed/please charge my Delta/Mastercard/Switch/Visa* card

Card No. _ _ _ _   _ _ _ _   _ _ _ _   _ _ _ _

Expiry date_____   **Issue number (Switch only)** _____

Signature _____   **Tel. No.** ☎ _____

NAME _____

ADDRESS _____

_____

_____

* Delete as applicable (price includes postage – airmail for Europe/world).

LIVING AND WORKING ABROAD

Living and Working Abroad is essential reading for anyone planning to spend some time abroad including holiday-home owners, retirees, visitors, business people, migrants, students and even extraterrestrials! It's packed with over 450 pages of important and useful information designed to help you **avoid costly mistakes and save both time and money.** Topics covered include how to:

- Find a job with a good salary & conditions
- Obtain a residence permit
- Avoid and overcome problems
- Find your dream home
- Get the best education for your family
- Make the best use of public transport
- Endure motoring abroad
- Obtain the best health treatment
- Stretch your money further
- Make the most of your leisure time
- Enjoy the sporting life abroad
- Find the best shopping bargains
- Insure yourself against most eventualities
- Use post office and telephone services
- Do numerous other things not listed above

Living and Working Abroad is the most comprehensive and up-to-date source of practical information available about everyday life abroad. It isn't, however, a boring text book, but an interesting and entertaining guide written in a highly readable style.

Buy this book and discover what it's *really* like to live and work abroad.

Order your copies today by phone, fax, mail or e-mail from: Survival Books, PO Box 146, Wetherby, West Yorks. LS23 6XZ, United Kingdom (☎/🖨 +44 (0)1937-843523, ✉ orders@ survivalbooks.net, 🖳 www.survivalbooks.net).

ORDER FORM – LIVING & WORKING SERIES

Qty.	Title	Price (incl. p&p)*			Total
		UK	Europe	World	
	Living & Working Abroad	£14.95	£16.95	£20.45	
	Living & Working in America	£14.95	£16.95	£20.45	
	Living & Working in Australia	£14.95	£16.95	£20.45	
	Living & Working in Britain	£14.95	£16.95	£20.45	
	Living & Working in Canada	£14.95	£16.95	£20.45	
	Living & Working in France	£14.95	£16.95	£20.45	
	Living & Working in Germany	£14.95	£16.95	£20.45	
	Living & Working in Holland, Belgium & Luxembourg	£14.95	£16.95	£20.45	
	Living & Working in Ireland	£14.95	£16.95	£20.45	
	Living & Working in Italy	£14.95	£16.95	£20.45	
	Living & Working in London	£11.45	£12.95	£14.95	
	Living & Working in New Zealand	£14.95	£16.95	£20.45	
	Living & Working in Spain	£14.95	£16.95	£20.45	
	Living & Working in Switzerland	£14.95	£16.95	£20.45	
				Total	

Order your copies today by phone, fax, mail or e-mail from: Survival Books, PO Box 146, Wetherby, West Yorks. LS23 6XZ, UK (☎/▤ +44 (0)1937-843523, ✉ orders@survivalbooks.net, 💻 www.survivalbooks.net). If you aren't entirely satisfied, simply return them to us within 14 days for a full and unconditional refund.

Cheque enclosed/please charge my Delta/Mastercard/Switch/Visa* card

Card No. _ _ _ _   _ _ _ _   _ _ _ _   _ _ _ _

Expiry date_____   **Issue number (Switch only)** _____

Signature _____   Tel. No. _____

NAME _____

ADDRESS _____

_____

_____

* Delete as applicable (price includes postage – airmail for Europe/world).